UNDERSTANDING THE NATIONAL HEALTH SERVICE REFORMS

STATE OF HEALTH SERIES

Edited by Chris Ham, Director of Health Services Management Centre, University of Birmingham

UNDERSTANDING THE NATIONAL HEALTH SERVICE REFORMS

The Creation of Incentives?

Peter A. West

Open University Press
Buckingham · Philadelphia

Open University Press
Celtic Court
22 Ballmoor
Buckingham
MK18 1XW

and
1900 Frost Road, Suite 101
Bristol, PA 19007, USA

First published 1997

Copyright © Peter A. West 1997

11484357

Learning Resources Centre

A catalogue record of this book is available from the British Library

ISBN 0 335 19243 2 (pb)   0 335 19244 0 (hb)

Library of Congress Cataloging-in-Publication Data

West, Peter A.
   Understanding the National Health Service reforms: the creation of
   incentives? / Peter A. West.
      p.   cm. — (State of health series)
   Includes bibliographical references and index.
   ISBN 0-335-19244-0 (hb)   ISBN 0-335-19243-2 (pbk)
   1. National Health Service (Great Britain) 2. Health care reform —
Great Britain. I. Title. II. Series.
RA395. G6W43 1997
362. 1'0941–dc21   97-3914
                                                               CIP

Copy-editing and typesetting by The Running Head Limited, London and
   Cambridge
Printed in Great Britain by St Edmundsbury Press Ltd, Bury St Edmunds,
   Suffolk

To my parents

CONTENTS

SERIES EDITOR'S INTRODUCTION

Health services in many developed countries have come under critical scrutiny in recent years. In part this is because of increasing expenditure, much of it funded from public sources, and the pressure this has on governments seeking to control public spending. Also important has been the perception that resources allocated to health services are not always deployed in an optimal fashion. Thus at a time when the scope for increasing expenditure is extremely limited, there is a need to search for ways of using existing budgets more efficiently. A further concern has been the desire to ensure access to health care of various groups on an equitable basis. In some countries this has been linked to a wish to enhance patient choice and make service providers more responsive to patients as 'consumers'.

Underlying these specific concerns are a number of more fundamental developments which have a significant bearing on the performance of health services. Three are worth highlighting. First, there are demographic changes, including the ageing population and the decline in the proportion of the population of working age. These changes will both increase the demand for health care and at the same time limit the ability of health services to respond to this demand.

Second, advances in medical science will also give rise to new demands within the health services. These advances cover a range of possibilities, including innovations in surgery, drug therapy, screening and diagnosis. The pace of innovation is likely to quicken as the end of the century approaches, with significant implications for the funding and provision of services.

Third, public expectations of health services are rising as those who use services demand higher standards of care. In part, this is stimulated by developments within the health service, including the availability of new technology. More fundamentally, it stems from the emergence of a more educated and informed population, in which people are accustomed to being treated as consumers rather than patients.

Against this background, policymakers in a number of countries are reviewing the future of health services. Those countries which have traditionally relied on a market in health care are making greater use of regulation and planning. Equally, those countries which have traditionally relied on regulation and planning are moving towards a more competitive approach. In no country is there complete satisfaction with existing methods of financing and delivery, and everywhere there is a search for new policy instruments.

The aim of this series is to contribute to debate about the future of health services through an analysis of major issues in health policy. These issues have been chosen because they are both of current interest and of enduring importance. The series is intended to be accessible to students and informed lay readers as well as to specialists working in the field. The aim is to go beyond a textbook approach to health policy analysis and to encourage authors to move debate about their issue forward. In this sense, each book presents a summary of current research and thinking, and an exploration of future policy directions.

Professor Chris Ham
Director of Health Services Management Centre
University of Birmingham

1

THE POLICY CONTEXT

INTRODUCTION

In this chapter, we examine the policy background that led up to the major changes in the NHS in the 1990s, introduced by *Working for Patients* (Department of Health 1989), referred to throughout this book as 'the NHS Reforms'. In particular, we examine the policies developed in the period of Conservative government from 1979, towards the public sector and public expenditure in general and the NHS in particular, before looking at the policy climate that led up to the 1989–90 NHS reform programme.

Although the Reforms, usually described as the 'creation of an internal market', are the focus of this book, several other NHS management reforms took place under the Thatcher government. (In addition, in the late 1980s and early 1990s a number of major reforms were made to the GP contract and to the funding and organization of social services. Neither of these areas are pursued in detail in this book, though the reader should note that for care of the elderly, the changes came close to the establishment of an internal market, with local authorities as purchasers encouraged to divest themselves of their provider units. Key differences include the much greater role of client payments for social care and the diversity of providers. The latter point of course reflects the small cost of establishing an elderly care home relative to the costs of setting up a major hospital.)

There is a sense that if reform of the NHS was needed in 1988–9, then the earlier rounds of management reforms, mostly under the same Conservative administration, must have failed in some way. Alternatively, it may be that areas of the public sector, particularly those that attract frequent press and opposition comment, are bound to come under the ministerial spotlight from time to time. That is, when a government stays in office for a long time, it will occasionally have to return to a problem area. Whatever the primary justification, there is no doubt that the NHS received its share of attention from Thatcher governments, even before 1989. The 1990s Reforms are therefore most appropriately seen as part of a continuum of reform of the public sector and the health service across the Thatcher years (Butler 1994a).

ECONOMIC AND SOCIAL POLICY 1979–90

The Thatcher government was very much in favour of market mechanisms as a method of allocating resources. As far as possible, it tried to reduce the size and cost of the public sector, given its belief in two key principles: the private sector as the engine of economic growth and consumer sovereignty as the primary basis for resource allocation. In its economic policy, it endorsed the economic philosophy of monetarism, closely associated with the American economist, Milton Friedman. The monetarist approach holds that control of the overall supply of money (including all methods of purchasing such as credit) is essential for control of inflation. Other economic measures are seen as ineffective – they are thought not to work or to work too slowly or unpredictably to be helpful.

While monetary control is the main weapon for controlling the macroeconomy (overall national income, exchange rates and employment), competition is the main weapon for controlling the microeconomy (the markets for individual goods and services). Monetarist and market economists argue that competition will generate constant pressure for efficiency by keeping prices and wages down to the level that the customer is prepared to pay. Given the disadvantages of large monopolies, a public sector monopoly was doubly a target for change under Mrs Thatcher because the public sector was uncontrolled and insatiable (Thatcher 1990: 6, 124). Through the taxes to fund it, the public sector was seen as taking money from the pockets of sovereign consumers and preventing the market working in major areas of the economy, including social services but also transport and energy. The Thatcher government set out to reduce the size of the public sector by tight control on public spending and selling off major state assets. The government argued that the state had no place in the market for a wide range of services. These services included public utilities such as telephones, gas, water and electricity, as well as manufacturing such as British Steel, British Aerospace and what eventually became Rover Cars. The essential thrust of this policy was that public sector monopolies were necessarily inefficient because they did not face the discipline of the marketplace and/or relied too heavily on government subsidies. Even though a number of the utilities were effectively 'natural monopolies' – industries where a single operator would have lower costs than competing operators, because of the high fixed cost of a national network infrastructure (gas, electricity, water, telephones) – they were sold to private sector shareholders. Elements of competition were introduced by encouraging new operators (for example Mercury as a supplier of telephone services) or splitting the public monopoly (for example National Power and Powergen as competing electricity generators). Where competition could not be relied on entirely, as in the utility industries, regulation was introduced. (Oftel, Ofgas and Ofwat have become familiar names as a result of their role in regulation.)

The utilities and nationalized industries noted above were run by quangos rather than by government departments. As such, it was easier for government to detach itself from them than from major public services like health and education. For these services, and for social security (the other main spending department of government), privatization of the whole service was not a ready option. Since consumers receive education and health care free at the time of use – a policy too sensitive to permit a changeover to substantial, new, direct charges – there was, and remains, no private customer income to attract a private operator to supply direct to consumers, except where consumers opt into the private sector. (Defence raises a different set of issues which are not pursued here.) Only policies such as vouchers, partial consumer payment or some other form of public purchasing from competing providers could begin to create a market in health care and state education. While these have been tried to a degree in education, through voucher experiments for example, education is quite distinct from health. The resources required for an individual are seen as relatively predictable in education, and assumed to be largely constant across most children in each age group. Innovations based on making the individual the purchaser of their own care do not offer such ready and equitable solutions to the uncertainties of health care needs and demands.

Mrs Thatcher makes clear at several points in her memoirs that the NHS was by no means the least well regarded part of her government's public sector. For example, it is seen as a 'touchstone of commitment to the welfare state' (Thatcher 1990: 570) and as offering 'high quality of care . . . at a reasonably modest unit cost' (p. 606). While acknowledging that, given a clean slate, she would prefer 'a bigger private sector, both at the level of general practitioners and in the provision of hospitals' the NHS is seen by Thatcher as an organization with sufficient public support and affection to mean that '[a]ny reforms must not undermine public confidence' (p. 607).

In its election campaigns and during government, the Thatcher administration therefore consistently rejected suggestions that it was planning to privatize education and health by introducing major user charges. Indeed, the political sensitivities over charging for health care led the Conservatives to assert, often at elections, that 'the NHS is safe in our hands'. Similarly, the principle of free school education was never seriously challenged by mainstream Conservative politicians. Policy therefore concentrated for much of the 1980s on making these free services of higher quality and lower cost within a clear commitment to go on with free provision at the time of use.

The relatively high cost of health and social security in the UK, compared to other areas of public spending, means that they are almost bound to attract attention from any party in government. This is likely even though the NHS has kept spending on health in the UK (as a proportion of national income) well below that in other developed countries. Tighter financial control through the introduction of cash limits was Labour policy in 1977. Prior to this, supplementary estimates were used to uprate spending plans in the light of inflation. But under cash limits, the Treasury estimated inflation, and the gap between expected and actual inflation was given to management to solve. Clearly according to such a policy the expected rate is increasingly likely to become the actual rate because of its influence on the expectations of public sector workers and suppliers, so the policy is less draconian than might at first appear. But the introduction of cash limits remains an effective method of rationing the resources going on public services in the face of rising consumer expectations and pressures such as population ageing. Capping total spending is necessarily at variance with any specified entitlement for individual users (an issue we return to in Chapter 6 on the future of the NHS) and so enforces elements of rationing at some point in the chain of resources from the Treasury to the local consumer. It is probably the vague, unspecific contract between the British people and the Secretary of State for Health that allows such rationing with so much acquiescence from the public. You cannot readily ask for what you do not know you could have.

CREATING A MARKET – CONTRACTING OUT

Attempts were also made to control costs in public services by privatizing elements of the service which were not ethically sensitive (DHSS 1983a). While selling hospitals or letting contracts for patient care to the highest bidder would raise the spectre of US market-led medicine, commercializing rubbish collection, hospital meals or catering raised fewer difficulties at that time and was seen as a logical Tory challenge to the monopoly power of public sector unions. By 1987, savings were estimated at £73 million per year with about 20 per cent savings on individual competitive contracts, even though by this time the private sector had only won a third of contracts (for domestic services) or less. In practice, the greater efficiency of competing providers was often achieved partly through reductions in the pay and conditions of staff rather than through pure efficiency changes. For example, the state of the labour market made it possible to withdraw elements of the previous Whitley Council pay awards for health service workers. Contractors were found to offer rates close to Whitley, but without bonuses or overtime and with little sick pay. Part-time working also reduced national insurance costs and removed pension rights from support staff (National Audit Office 1987).

These measures were not enough for the Thatcher government during the 1980s. Expenditure on health care and education continued to be major 'burdens' on the taxpayer and prevented further reductions in the rate of income tax, a vital policy objective. A particular concern, frequently quoted by ministers, was the variable performance of education and health services. For the same cost, different parts of the system appeared to achieve significantly different results or activity. Uniform levels of efficiency therefore offered the prospects of additional services for no extra cost.

If privatization was not an option in the achievement of better performance in health and education, policy needed to find other ways of achieving uniformly high efficiency. But in both education and health, governments in the past had often found it difficult to influence what happens on the 'shop floor'. Independent professionals with a good deal of community support and respect are difficult people to influence from a distant Whitehall. Teachers might argue that, in the 1990s, the government took much more control by a systematic undermining of the prestige and independence of the teaching profession, including the introduction of the national curriculum. This has not happened in medicine, probably because health care is a much more personal business. Patients want trust and confidence in those providing their health care and are likely to believe that they were treated well, in most cases, partly because they do not know what they should get. As a result, health professionals in the UK remain high in public esteem and government control is weaker than in other parts of the public sector.

In addition, local government involvement in education (and local political and non-political membership of health authorities) has frequently tempered the local impact of a central policy. For example, in spite of continuous pressure to contract out support services, a number of district health authorities did not contract out significant services during the 1980s, refusing to comply with government guidance (National Audit Office 1987).

In education and health, the government was also restrained by the general popularity of free public services. Nigel Lawson describes the NHS as 'the closest thing the English have to a religion, with those who practise in [the NHS] regarding themselves as a priesthood' (Lawson 1992: 613). In 1982, the Chancellor, Geoffrey Howe, used a paper from the Central Policy Review Staff (the Whitehall think-tank) to introduce the discussion of lower teacher/pupil staff ratios and compulsory private health insurance for some of the population. These were two suggested responses to the burden of public spending on a slow-growing economy. The result is described by Lawson as 'the nearest thing to a Cabinet riot in the history of the Thatcher administration' (p. 303). Leaks to *The Economist* sparked off discussion of a major dismantling of the welfare state and potentially set back fundamental reform of the NHS for some years.

Governments throughout the history of the NHS have typically tried to implement their policies predominantly by changing the management and control of the service, not the core principles of entitlement and free provision. (Where charges already existed, however, the Thatcher government was prepared to raise them appreciably; prescription charges for example have risen by over 300 per cent since 1979.) Some of the attempts to change management in the 1970s and 1980s are summarized in the next section.

HEALTH SERVICE MANAGEMENT POLICY

We begin our review of cycles of reform in 1974. Prior to that date, the administrative structure of the NHS was predominantly as it was when set up in 1948. The NHS was reformed in 1974 by an incoming Labour government that largely carried out a pre-election

Conservative plan. This established new regional and local bodies which were based on populations rather than sets of facilities, as the old hospital management committees had been. It also transferred community services such as district nurses and ambulances from local government to health service control.

In England, between 1974 and 1982, the hospital and community health services were run by these regional, area and district health bodies. Family practitioner and related services were administered separately, outside the region/area/district structure in England and Wales, but jointly in Scotland and Northern Ireland. This reflected the separate funding vote for primary care in Parliament and the independent contractor status of primary care providers, agreed when the NHS was founded in 1948. (The discussion here and elsewhere in the book concentrates mainly on services in England. More integrated models of service management, across primary, community and hospital care, operated in Scotland and Northern Ireland before the 1990s Reforms. Subsequent authority mergers in England have produced similar bodies, though only Northern Ireland has social services purchased by the same body as health care.)

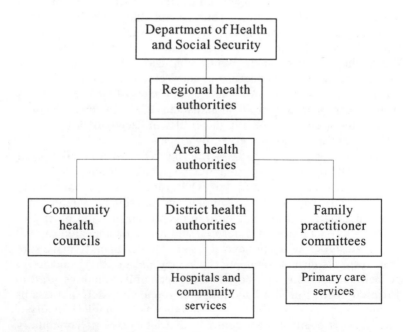

Figure 1.1 NHS (England) 1974–82

The three-tier structure (region, area, district) was planned by the outgoing Conservative administration in 1974 but implemented by Labour. In itself this is interesting because it shows the role of the Labour Party as the friend of the NHS. A Conservative plan, already under way, was implemented to avoid yet more instability in the NHS. The 14 English regional health authorities (RHAs) were created in 1974 with a population of around 3.5 million each. They were made responsible for strategic planning of local hospital and community services and the special services that are required in only one or two centres for a population of this size. Area health authorities, with a population of around a million people, were mainly involved in service coordination across a group of hospitals and districts. Districts were managed by consensus between professionals, without a formal health authority of local community representatives. (In some parts of the country, usually due to geography, area health authorities had only a single subordinate district and the AHA managers were the effective district managers.) To provide a local consumer voice, community health councils were set up at district level, with members drawn from the local community but with no management powers. They have continued in place under the subsequent managerial changes and the 1990s Reforms, but typically they lack the resources necessary to make them very effective. They usually have only one or two full-time staff and are not widely known by the public. More generally, they suffer from the public confusion about who runs the health service. Perhaps because of local elections and council tax, local authorities are well known. Health bodies of all kinds are less well known and many people think that the NHS is run by local councils. Without elections or a high profile, the accountability of the NHS to the public must be very limited.

The justification for the 1974 reforms was that a population of around 250,000 (a district) was about the right size to support a major hospital (district general hospital – DGH) and a range of community services, but that effective planning and coordination required a larger population of about 1 million people. In this and other elements of NHS reforms, the hospital and its needs appeared to play the greatest role. While policymakers are often at pains to make sure that hospitals do not dominate the policy debate, they tend to do so because of their high cost and higher public relations profile. Hospital doctors need a wide range of supporting staff and equipment to work effectively, if at all, and they will complain loudly if they are not available. By contrast, district nurses or community psychiatric teams can eke out a service by spreading their limited human resources more and more thinly. Thus much of the planning for district health services has been geared towards the optimum size for a comprehensive hospital.

The creation of the district general hospital in 1964 effectively led to more and more concentration of services into a single, monolithic provider serving a district, the predominant model or ambition of almost the entire NHS. Concentration was driven by professional demands that access to the fullest range of services was required to support accident and emergency departments and to make the most effective use of junior medical staff. The latter factor has become even more important in the recent past and has driven NHS managers to close down many small and single specialty hospitals because of their limited scope for medical and other professional training and the difficulty of providing effective medical cover and supervision. As we will see in later chapters, this process of concentration and the reliance of hospitals on small numbers of junior medical staff has had profound effects on the ability of the 1990s Reforms to create a meaningful market (see Chapters 3 and 5).

However, not long after the 1974 reorganization, there was widespread concern inside the NHS and among politicians that three tiers of decision-making — district, area and region — was too many. Decisions were slowed down by the need to get three groups to endorse a plan of action, as well as the Department of Health and Social Security and the Treasury in the case of major investment decisions. There was some criticism that area health authorities covered too large a population and too wide a geographical area. Local politicians were probably more comfortable with the smaller districts as they were more likely to fit closely with constituencies and allow MPs in particular to use their influence more effectively. While the three tiers survived, the debate continued and was resolved in a further round of reorganization, described below.

In the mid-1970s, the oil crisis increased pressure on public spending, leading to a period of restraint that provoked industrial action in the NHS and, in response, the setting up of a Royal Commission on the NHS, by the then Labour government. The long gestation period of the Commission's work, however, meant that the basic organization of health services remained unchanged for the rest of the 1970s. The Commission ultimately reported to an incoming Conservative government in 1979. While some commentators have noted that there is much to recommend in its proposals for gradual improvement rather than restructuring on a grand scale (for example Edwards 1993), no clear policy changes followed from its report other than those responding to its criticism of bureaucracy and the levels of administration in the health service.

THE NEW BROOM – THATCHER TAKES CONTROL

The Thatcher government set about its first reform of the NHS with the speed and determination which were to become its hallmark. Its first reactions and proposals were published in *Patients First* in 1979, the relevant structures were set out in 1980 and the whole thing was to be in place by 1982 (see Levitt *et al.* 1995 for a detailed history of these and other recent changes in the administration and management of the NHS). In this round of reform, the government reduced the administration of hospital and community services. (Family practitioner services were relatively unscathed, arguably because increased managerial muscle for them would threaten the independent status of GPs, a fiercely guarded principle established when the NHS was founded.)

The government's difficulty in slimming down the structure was that while there was considerable pressure to plan many health services for relatively large populations, associated with continuing falls in the number of hospital beds due to changes in treatment, there was bound to be a role for local operational management. In other words, while the area was potentially the right level to *plan* the health service, it was not the right level to *manage* it. In the political infighting, areas lost the battle of policy and public relations and were eliminated in this reorganization (DHSS 1980). However, the post-Reforms NHS map in the mid-1990s started to look more and more like the area map of 1974, with many current, recently merged districts covering very similar patches and populations to the old areas. Arguably, the wrong tier was abolished in 1982 for planning, particularly once the planning and delivery of health care had been separated, as they were in the 1990s. That is, planning and provision were unified at the district level in 1982 when planning might be done better at a higher level (the current purchasing bodies) and management of provision at a lower level (the current Trusts). In other words, Conservative policy on NHS management did a U-turn in the late 1980s.

In 1982, district health authorities became the new bodies responsible for local hospital and community health service planning and delivery. They had up to 19 members, including four or more from

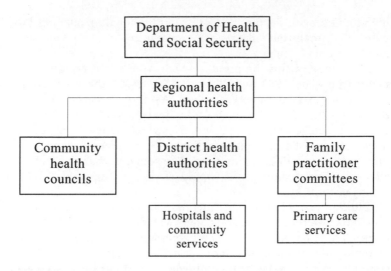

Figure 1.2 NHS (England) 1982–90

local authorities, seven generalist members and representatives of medical schools, consultants, GPs and nurses. Although set up to provide a local voice when planning was at area level, community health councils continued to work at the same level as DHAs, giving two public bodies working at one level. This continues to be a source of some confusion on roles and responsibilities.

DHAs continued the previous pattern of consensus management by a triumvirate of district administrator, district medical officer and district nursing officer, supported by finance, personnel and works specialists. But the government was not satisfied that this was delivering the kind of efficient management that it sought. It therefore appointed Sir Roy Griffiths, then head of Sainsbury's supermarket chain, to examine NHS management (DHSS 1983b). (Mrs Thatcher's memoirs make only the most cursory of references to his report, noting that the idea for NHS reform had been in her mind since talking to DHSS officials in 1979 and that the Griffiths Report was just one step on the road.)

Griffiths was apparently soon frustrated with the lack of clear management responsibility in the NHS. When things went wrong, there was, in his view, a lack of clear accountability, because of the consensus approach. However, while in favour of clearer general management, he also emphasized the importance of involving doctors in management. The widespread development of clinical directorates, with doctors and other professionals managing large parts of hospitals (but rather less of community services) is an important legacy of Griffiths.

Under the Griffiths proposals, which were again rapidly implemented between 1983 and 1984 (DHSS 1984), the NHS became much more diverse than ever before. As part of the devolution of responsibility to local managers, individual units were given the freedom to organize management in ways which suited local requirements. Administrators applying for posts as general managers of their current or a different unit could be found exchanging notes on structures and deciding who would sit at the 'top table' of unit management.

A further feature of the Griffiths reorganization was the introduction of fixed-term contracts. Managers who failed to deliver what was required were unlikely to have their contracts renewed, an easier way of removing someone than terminating a permanent public sector contract. This has led to a situation where many health service managers appear to expect a relatively short stay in each post, certainly less than (say) five years. But two or three years is a short time to change the culture of a major institution, especially when even the most inefficient or obstructive members of the senior professional staff, the doctors, effectively have jobs for life.

Increased managerialism in the NHS in the immediate aftermath of the Griffiths Report, and the associated national advertising of most existing or revised senior administrative and management posts, led to the introduction of a significant number of non-NHS career managers. These were attracted in part by the sheer number of posts, as every senior administrative position was advertised as a short-term contract management job. But salaries remained below the level of comparable private sector posts and so many of those attracted into the NHS were recruited from the ranks of retired armed forces officers and other early retirees. This did not inspire the confidence of staff.

Relatively few of these outsiders are still in the NHS, particularly the former military personnel. Some have now retired permanently on grounds of age but many fell by the wayside because they failed to understand the culture of the NHS. In particular, individuals used to having their orders carried out, and to a high degree of confidentiality of their decisions, found it difficult to deal with doctors and nurses who could not always be relied on to comply with management decisions and might feel free to tell the local press why not. In other words, the chain of general management remained a tight method of control only within the administrative and support elements of the service. Professional staff continued to show considerable autonomy and the procedures for disciplining them remained slow and cumbersome. As a result, the professionals in hospital faced only limited internal control and no outside competitive challenge.

Some managers had a particularly short tenure of office. The first chief executive of the NHS as a whole, Victor Paige, resigned, allegedly over difficulties with ministers on who really made decisions. *The Guardian* in December 1986 published a leaked memo, from a senior level in the NHS, noting pressure from the Parliamentary Accounts Committee for ministers to take responsibility for policy. At the same time, ministerial pressure to carry privatization further was a sign of continuing central control (Small 1989).

It is hard to assess the net results of the 1982–4 changes on the NHS during the rest of the 1980s. Certainly many hospitals and community units appeared to be more visibly managed, with a clearer sense of purpose and direction than in the past. Many doctors became more extensively involved in management through clinical directorates, effectively managing much of their own business within the unit structure. Also, more and more patients were treated each year but this is perhaps the result of long-term trends in medicine, the growing use of day surgery, increased demand and the associated financial pressures to cut beds and discharge patients earlier. However, any government will claim that a positive trend is a result of its own policies, just as they are ready to blame external factors for poor results.

Significantly, the various reorganizations up to this point did little to change the basic incentive structure. Hospitals and other units had no clear incentive to treat more patients, though a few London specialist units had begun to charge for non-local patients. District health authorities faced government pressure to achieve targets for revenue savings and 'cost improvements' – an interesting label from the PR machine. But there was no real competition for health authorities' services and little incentive to depart from general, largely bureaucratic standards of performance. There was also a clear and continuing incentive to argue for more resources from above in the structure, rather than manage them better below. At the same time, the number of patients treated each year tended to keep on rising, due to increased numbers of consultants, trends to shorter patient stays in hospital and the slow spread of technical change such as day case surgery.

RESOURCE MANAGEMENT AND INTERNAL TRADING

Some light is shed on the impact of complex management arrangements during the 1980s by an examination of the Resource Management Initiative, a set of projects designed to begin to create internal incentives for better use of resources. Resource management, which is now widespread (in one form or another) in the NHS, was introduced as a set of pilot studies to improve the use of the available staff and materials by effectively creating an internal market within major hospitals and other health service units. It was presented as a part of the provision of sophisticated management information needed to support sophisticated management, but it was much more about changing the management culture. Large scale changes in computer systems were made, at considerable cost, to record all the internal transactions of the hospital, on the grounds that management lacked the information to manage. Use of (for example) operating theatres or X-ray departments was analysed and charged to the clinical directorate that generated that use for its patients, rather than theatres or radiology being treated as isolated cost centres.

Three particular features are noteworthy from the resource management experiment because they are also features of the post-reform health service. The first is that there is little sign that equivocal findings from the evaluation had any effect on the rollout of similar management and information technology models to the rest of the NHS. Experiments were no longer a basis for learning if *we had got it right* but, rather, a method for ironing out the early problems in something that would be done anyway. Pilots began to disappear in the NHS from this time on, to be replaced by 'pioneers' (see Packwood *et al.* 1991).

The second point to note is that, from an economic standpoint, a great deal of the cost of a hospital is 'lumpy'. That is, a hospital ward, accident department or operating theatre must be set up and staffed with a certain mix of professional staff and equipment before it can function at all. Hospitals also have many small, separate departments with a small number of staff. This staffing cannot change rapidly when activity changes, partly due to simple inflexibility in hiring and firing but also because their services may be needed at short notice. (Economists term this an 'option demand'. Potential users demand the option of using the service, rather than its actual use.)

Given this cost structure, with little change in costs across a wide range of activity levels, the use of average costs for internal or external accounting is suspect. Decisions to change the use of other departments will not incur or save many costs. In other words, across quite a wide range of patient numbers, the staff costs of the hospital may change little. The availability of service is as much a feature as the actual service provided. If every transaction is to be paid for, within a fixed allocation to the hospital as a whole, at an average cost price, then some departments will make windfall gains and losses due to random changes in their work, over which they and others may have no control. For example, a neonatal intensive care department may lose money if not enough sick children come its way and its income falls below its costs. But such a service is in practice providing insurance for all the babies delivered locally and this should be paid for, whether the unit is used or not. Simple internal pricing and costing could distort resource allocation and service provision, for instance by encouraging such units to keep themselves full, whatever the real needs of the babies born locally. More generally, since the main aim was to change incentives, it would have been possible to create incentives which were simple to administer and not necessarily directly linked to the costs of the services.

The third feature of resource management is that creating prices for transactions within organizations runs the risk of creating the appearance of a market when in practice there is no choice. If a medical ward is served by an efficient laboratory but an overstaffed and expensive X-ray department, there is little it can do to shift its purchases between higher and lower cost departments. Many hospital doctors argued that the pricing and charging for internal services was creating a mountain of paper with little effect. Equally, increased activity and cost data probably fuelled the growing debate in hospitals about where resources are used, and why.

Whatever its strengths and weaknesses, the Resource Management Initiative was to set the tone for much of what followed. It had ambitious objectives yet the management changes needed to support them were not fully implemented in the set timetable. It moved rapidly from experiment to policy and, as noted above, was symptomatic of a culture where policy was not likely to change in the light of evaluation. It was also overtaken by yet more changes and so cannot be evaluated free of their influence (Packwood *et al.* 1991). Much of what can be said about the Reforms in the 1990s will echo these views. However, one thing that has undoubtedly changed, and will go on changing, is our ability to capture relevant information. Developments in information technology are making it feasible to collect more and more information automatically on every patient transaction. While the NHS still lags behind many other organizations, its ability to monitor what has happened to its resources is gradually catching up. This will become increasingly important in any drive to introduce tighter monitoring, an issue addressed in Chapter 6.

THE RUN-UP TO *WORKING FOR PATIENTS*

From the mid-1980s onwards, two separate strands of activity, intellectual and political, were drawn together to produce the NHS Reforms as they finally emerged. The intellectual strand was the burgeoning analysis of health care costs and the movement for health sector reform, not only in the USA but also more globally (through, for example, the policies of the World Bank). The political strand consisted of the practical political issues facing any UK government, particularly one keen to see the public sector retrenched. The reform movement was increasingly throwing up ideas that challenged either a simple, private insurance market or a top-down tax-funded system. One lacked cost control, the other consumer responsiveness. 'Managed competition' increasingly became the buzzword for the reformers. But whatever the intellectual movement for reform, politicians face sceptical electors and powerful lobbies. As the experience of the 1992 Clinton administration showed in the USA, even a relatively popular new president cannot get his wife to succeed in health sector reform in such conditions. The strong ties of the UK electorate to the NHS were felt by Mrs Thatcher and had to be weighed up against the potential gains from reform.

The record of the process that led to the Reforms is unusual in that the exercise was largely carried out in secret but subsequently discussed in politicians' memoirs. Both Mrs Thatcher and the Chancellor of the Exchequer, Nigel Lawson, reveal a good deal of the process used to turn health sector reform into an acceptable set of policies. Of course, in examining their version of events, we must beware of seeing politicians through their own eyes rather than from a more objective standpoint.

In the sections that follow, we examine the development of the Reforms from both the intellectual and political angles.

THE ANALYSIS OF REFORM

Health care reform was seen as necessary because, either in its private market or public sector versions, it was seen as offering the wrong incentives to those involved. The lack of incentives was a particular concern of one influential US commentator, Professor Alain Enthoven. Enthoven's diagnosis (Enthoven 1985) of the problems of the NHS focused in particular on the question of incentives. He noted that there were few if any rewards for managers or staff from doing a better job for patients, and there were some perverse incentives to do otherwise, with no payment to hospital departments undertaking more and more work each year, for example. Treatment by one health authority's hospitals of another's patients were rewarded by an adjustment to a remote financial target, perhaps a year or more after the treatment. However, the amount of money moving across to another authority was not based on a negotiated contract and the effective costs of the transferring cases, and gave no incentive to the receiving hospital directly. Instead, it could provide an incentive to shift the caseload to another hospital. Similarly, waiting lists for surgery in the public sector potentially increased the demand for private treatment, weakening surgeons' incentives to treat more NHS patients. Lastly, GPs were also seen as having no incentive to manage or control their referrals to hospital, leading to wide variation between practices.

More generally, in common with other bureaucracies, the NHS was seen by Enthoven as strengthening the case for more resources by constantly emphasizing poor performance (a model that the British Medical Association returned to in 1996 with claims that the NHS was sinking like the *Titanic* under the weight of the Reforms). For example, long waiting lists could be used as an argument for more resources for surgery. Solving the waiting list problem could weaken the case for new surgical facilities. Change in health care means winners and losers, and radical change would need incentives to motivate the winners, in the cause of a better service to patients. However, Enthoven was also careful to avoid a simple association of incentives with money. He proposed that growth and development of the hospital might motivate staff as much as money in their pay packets.

Enthoven's solutions, as we shall see in Chapter 2, are similar in their broad outline to the government's ultimate proposals. He foresaw DHAs with funding based on their local population, providing comprehensive health care for residents. Services to non-residents would be bought and sold on a clear contracted basis. Staff salaries would be locally determined and a range of contracts, including incentive payments, might be introduced for hospital consultant staff. Management would be free to borrow within limits and innovate without central restraint.

However, Enthoven himself saw some weaknesses in the model, particularly the lack of clear incentives for DHA management. He anticipated pressures to favour local suppliers and develop a comprehensive local service, due to consultant demands rather than efficient use of resources. Only a model where the body responsible for procuring care faced competition for members would there be effective incentives for management. As noted earlier, the moves to create unified district general hospitals had effectively created much of the local monopoly of hospital care that concerned Enthoven.

Aside from Enthoven, a number of others have been credited, from time to time, with influencing *Working for Patients* (though not by Mrs Thatcher). Their proposals have many similarities with what emerged and also with thinking in the USA that developed from the spread of health maintenance organizations, in common with Enthoven's contribution. Health maintenance organizations (HMOs) developed in the USA as an alternative to insurance-funded health care (see the further discussion in Chapter 3). They typically provided a comprehensive package of care but controlled access to it by shifting some of their doctors to direct employment by the HMO itself. By integrating doctors, they removed the incentive for doctors to prescribe more of their own services at the insurers' expense. Instead they gave doctors, who sometimes owned the HMOs themselves, incentives to manage patients with fewer treatments, where this was possible.

GP fundholding was developed more or less as it emerged in work by a UK health economist, Alan Maynard (Maynard 1986). Elements of separate purchasers, similar to local HMOs, were put forward by, among others, Goldsmith and Willetts (1988) and Butler and Pirie (1988). Their ideas are considered further in subsequent chapters on individual elements of the Reforms.

THE POLITICS OF REFORM

There is no doubt that, in spite of its new culture, new management, information and budgeting systems and clinical directorates, the government in the late 1980s — in particular Mrs Thatcher — continued to feel that the NHS had not yet got it right. Taken at face value, elections provide fertile ground for policy review as a whole policy platform has to be put to the country. After the Griffiths changes in 1983–4, the 1987 election was, arguably, the obvious time for a further look at health service policy to see if it was achieving the required goals. Mrs Thatcher had at about this time noted the work of Enthoven, suggesting the possible introduction of elements of competition to the NHS. Indeed, Enthoven is seen by many commentators as one of the prime influences on the ministerial review and subsequent NHS reforms (Butler 1994a).

Mrs Thatcher was apparently in no doubt, even in 1987, that the NHS needed a further shake-up. 'The direction of reform I wanted to see was one towards bringing down waiting lists by ensuring that money moved with patients rather than got lost in the bureaucratic maze of the NHS' (Thatcher 1990: 571). In this maze, money was allocated to RHAs according to the size, age and sex of their resident populations, adjusted by mortality statistics for the relative need for health care (an approach known as RAWP after the 1976 report of the Resource Allocation Working Party). Districts were similarly funded and they in turn gave money to their local hospitals and community services. But the last stage of the process, from DHA to service units, was more likely to depend on historic funding than on a clear assessment of what services were needed or provided, and at what cost. As a result, statistics on unit costs show wide variation in the cost of similar services in different parts of the country.

Before the 1987 election, Nigel Lawson's economic policy group had begun looking at proposals for reform. However, at election times, popularity is uppermost in politicians' minds and Nigel Lawson suggests that Mrs Thatcher would not touch the proposals with a bargepole! Given the status of the NHS as a touchstone of Tory (or Labour) commitment to welfare, noted above, and what Lawson describes as 'the many questions still left unanswered' (of a system to make money follow patients), no new proposals for the health service were included in the 1987 Conservative manifesto. Instead, the manifesto concentrated on pushing forward privatization of support services, improving prevention programmes, strengthening management and a further commitment to care in the community (Conservative Party 1987). The NHS was clearly seen as 'not a business but it must be run in a business-like way'.

Through the 1987 election and beyond, Mrs Thatcher was clear that the quality and cost of the NHS, compared to its insurance counterparts elsewhere, protected it from fundamental change. Typically, most European countries with social health insurance spend more of their national income on health care without obviously achieving better health. Thatcher's concern was the 'unjustifiable differences between performance in one area and another' (Thatcher 1990: 606). Aside from an anxiety to avoid upsetting the electorate when the NHS was still a 'fixed point in our policies' (p. 606), a further reason for delay in the NHS reforms may have been personalities. While Norman Fowler was seen by Mrs Thatcher as starting the reform debate going with think-tanks and policy papers in 1986 and 1987, he 'was much better at publicly defending the NHS than he would have been at reforming it' (p. 607). The arrival of John Moore as the new Secretary of State seems to have contributed to a change in the climate of reform.

Disputes over NHS funding in the winter of 1987 appear to have been particularly serious. A series of events, including a funding crisis and a high profile appeal for more resources from the Presidents of the medical Royal Colleges, led to a growing media campaign for additional funding (Hoffenberg *et al.* 1987). A particular series of emotive cases of alleged shortages and cancelled operations, affecting children needing major surgery at a Birmingham hospital, caught the public imagination in late 1987 (Ham *et al.* 1990). These may have fuelled Mrs Thatcher's energy for reform, though she tends to report her intervention in early 1988 as a further step on a logical progression rather than as simply a response to short-term pressures and criticisms.

Other commentators have suggested that the review as an explicit exercise was indeed a response to the pressure from many parts of the NHS simultaneously and a sign, perhaps, that even Mrs Thatcher had to give some ground. Butler (1994b) presents a list of pressures sufficient to daunt almost any politician, including not only the funding argument and the plea from the Royal Colleges but also industrial action by nurses, linked to the government's unwillingness to guarantee that the nurses' pay review recommendations would be fully funded.

After asking the DHSS for information on where the extra money given to health had gone, she received 'a report on all the extra pressures which the NHS was facing' (Thatcher 1990: 608). Mrs Thatcher tells us she remained committed to reform to improve value for money and made the final decision for the review in January 1988. Nigel Lawson claims to have put her back on the path to NHS reform over dinner at this time and, more significantly, determined the future conduct of the review. '[B]ecause of sensitivity, the enquiry would need to be small and entirely internal. The professionals, once they knew it was going on, would not be backward in giving us the benefit of their advice – and, more fruitfully, we could always get the opinions of politically well-disposed practitioners informally' (Lawson 1992: 614). Others believe that the review of the NHS was simply a gut reaction to some tough questioning of Mrs Thatcher on TV about the state of the health service. Either way, the sensitivities surrounding the NHS probably make the start of a new Parliament the only practical time to undertake such a review, according to Lawson. That is, immediately after an election is the time to start doing things that were not in the manifesto, so that the pain will be over by the time of the next election!

Four principles for the reformed NHS are noted in the Thatcher memoirs:

• a high standard of medical care to be available regardless of income;
• users of health services, whether in the private or public sectors, should have the maximum choice (the consumer sovereignty noted earlier);
• changes should be made in a way bringing genuine improvements and not merely a rise in incomes for those working in the health service (an implied criticism of a simple shift to an insurance-based fee for service system);
• responsibility within the service should be exercised at the lowest appropriate level, close to the patient.

Early Treasury interest in higher charges was ditched as it would undermine the wider review. Mrs Thatcher publicly set her face against 'hotel' charges for hospital care in the life of the then current Parliament in January 1988. But later that month, she also said that nothing was ruled out in the review that she had begun.

From an early list of 18 bright ideas designed to bring about the changes required, Mrs Thatcher notes two that were judged worth pursuing: to reform the way the NHS was funded, by replacing general taxation with insurance or tax incentives for private cover; and to reform the structure by which the NHS delivered services for the money it received. The former was dropped early, but tax relief for insurance for the elderly was brought back, supposedly by Mrs Thatcher against the wishes of Kenneth Clarke, by then the Secretary of State for Health. This left reform of the structure as the prime focus (Thatcher 1990: 610). Lawson was reluctant to concede tax relief since growth of private demand would merely push up prices and wages of health care professionals without addressing supply side problems. Eventually he gave in with a concession for elderly subscribers only, introduced with some embarrassment in the 1989 budget (Lawson 1992: 617).

Under the reform umbrella, health maintenance organizations, which would give members a choice of health care provider from a local health fund, were considered and this led naturally to self-governing hospitals which could compete for these patients, without the 'excessively rigid control of the hospital service from the centre' (Thatcher 1990: 611). At this key stage in the debate, two other concerns of Mrs Thatcher are worth noting: that the old system gave no incentives or rewards to hospitals which treated more patients, and that the timetable suggested by civil servants for improved information on NHS costs – six years – was unacceptable. Clearly the Thatcher approach called for a much faster pace of change; overall, the retrospective account of this period reaffirms her enthusiasm for competition between providers as a route to efficiency.

The enthusiasm for reform was tempered by some criticisms but more by concern that it might hold up the pace of change. The Treasury was concerned with short-term expenditure and investment control as a result of independent hospital trusts and the purchaser–provider separation. Mrs Thatcher was concerned that patients still lacked sufficient choice and sovereignty. GP fundholding then came of age as a solution to the lack of choice for the patient. GPs as patient advocates could buy hospital care when needed from competing providers. But, as we will consider further in the analysis of fundholding that follows in Chapter 4, fundholding would also 'make it possible for the first time to put reasonable limits on [GP] spending' (Thatcher 1990: 615). That is, while offering an element of choice of hospital provider by GPs that was close to the patient and professionally qualified to make such choices, fundholding also offered the prospect of controlling previously unchecked expenditure by GPs in the non-cash limited family health sector.

By now, and certainly in her memoirs, Mrs Thatcher felt the final pieces of the Reforms were falling into place. Self-governing hospitals (later changed to Trusts) were to have the freedom to compete for purchaser contracts, and the DHA and GP purchasers would have the freedom to buy from them. What was on offer, through competing providers and separate purchasing DHAs and fundholders, was competition without privatization. *Working for Patients* was born.

2

WORKING FOR PATIENTS

The NHS Reforms were presented to the country in January 1989 (Secretaries of State 1989). The PR machine was in overdrive as the White Paper was explained in major 'road shows' for NHS staff across the country. It was also published in a glossy and readable format. A Department of Health leaflet, also available on tape, took the message to a wider public. While there was some criticism of the PR offensive at the time, it could also be seen as a genuine attempt to get a message across to the vast staff of the NHS, more effectively than in past reorganizations.

In this chapter, the White Paper *Working for Patients* proposals are summarized; the main elements of the Reforms are analysed in the three chapters that follow. To provide a context for the discussion of the Reforms, the next section reviews briefly the incentives that existed in the NHS prior to the White Paper.

INCENTIVES PRIOR TO 1990

In the NHS before 1990, there were few incentives to efficient behaviour in hospitals and community units, though GPs did receive some performance-related payments. Hospitals and community nursing services faced demands and referrals which they had to deal with from the resources allocated to them under a block grant. Treating more patients provided no extra resources, except for the occasional waiting list initiative. Reducing the cost per patient released some resources but these might be taken from an efficient clinical area to meet overspending in another area. As noted in Chapter 1, more sophisticated methods such as the Resource Management Initiative did not fully resolve the problem, much of which derived from the block grant funding of hospitals and community nursing. If extra activity did not lead to extra resources, no amount of internal trading between departments could guarantee to reward all those departments which increased their caseload from within budget.

General practitioners in the UK have always worked as independent contractors, providing services to the NHS while not being salaried employees of it. Their payment depends on a large number of fees and allowances, including some which reward extra work, for example fees for every patient vaccinated or for every cervical smear test carried out. The GP contract was itself being renegotiated at the time of *Working for Patients* and the final contract that emerged changed a number of incentives. For example, payments for vaccination were changed so that GPs were only rewarded for vaccinating the majority of the children on their lists; incentives were increased to obtain complete coverage and payments for vaccinations were denied where targets were not met. Similarly, incentive payments were introduced for running clinics to monitor patients with chronic disease such as hypertension, asthma and diabetes, and for screening the elderly for health problems.

Although GPs had incentives to carry out the screening and health promotion procedures (Department of Health 1987) they did not have any significant incentives to control the demands they made on other services. GPs are often described as the gatekeepers of the NHS. They control access for the public to NHS prescriptions and to hospital, except in emergencies. GPs might commit large amounts of the resource of a hospital through their referrals but faced no incentives to manage patients in other ways, without such direct reliance on the hospital (through home care, for example). Similarly, GPs had freedom to prescribe as much as they wished. While prescribing was increasingly monitored by the PACT system, which was used to pay chemists for prescriptions and which produced GP-based data on every practice and doctor, the data was not used to exert tight control over GPs. It is technically difficult to prove that one particular prescribing pattern was wrong. The only disincentive to high prescribing was the threat of a visit from the family health services authority medical adviser.

This does not mean that all GPs were high prescribers or referred a high proportion of patients to hospital. But the reasons for this lie more in the style of practice of the individual or possibly the degree of support for home care offered where primary care teams developed around group practices. Certainly there was no incentive to be a low referrer or prescriber.

THE WHITE PAPER – *WORKING FOR PATIENTS*

The White Paper had nine chapters introducing a wide range of changes throughout the NHS. Three elements make up the main part of the Reforms, covering the new purchasing role of health authorities, the creation of GP fundholders and of self-governing hospital Trusts. Other elements of interest to economists include the introduction of capital charges and a system to make NHS units pay for their capital developments such as new equipment and buildings, rather than receiving such funding free from the regional authority. Lastly, there were changes which were largely tinkering with the structure and names of different elements which will not be examined in detail in this book, for instance the creation of the NHS Management Executive as an attempt to distance ministers further from the day-to-day running of the NHS – a change that continues to look relatively hollow, given the level of political interference in health service matters.

Each of the three main components of *Working for Patients* is presented here, to show the structural and organization changes introduced by the White Paper itself and the eight initial working papers that accompanied it. The practical effects of the Reforms are then analysed in detail in the three chapters that follow. The NHS created by the Reforms is also set out in Figure 2.1.

It should also be noted that the language of the Reforms was deliberately designed to reduce the sensitivity of a number of changes. For example, 'Trust hospital' is a new term which came to be used instead of 'self-governing hospital' because it is much more ambiguous as a term and has positive connotations. Similarly, health authorities were known as purchasers and are now increasingly known as commissioners, again a term that smacks of something other than simple buying and selling of a sensitive service like public health care. 'Providers' is now the established term for those that sell health care to purchasers, again reducing the use of market language. (If you bought this book, did you buy it from a bookseller or from a book provider? The latter sounds more like a library than a market entity.)

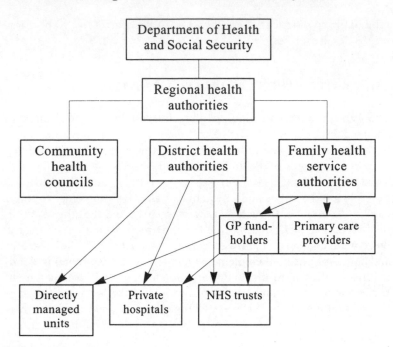

Figure 2.1 NHS (England) 1990

DHA PURCHASERS – A NEW ROLE AND A NEW BUDGET

District health authorities (DHAs) were to become purchasers of health services under the reform proposals. They were to relinquish control of some of their units to Trust status and develop contracts with Trusts, the private sector and their own directly managed units. While a White Paper is necessarily short on detail (the stuff of subsequent papers and legislation), the role of purchasers is particularly vaguely described in *Working for Patients*.

The White Paper also set out details of a modified way of funding health authorities. Prior to 1990, DHAs received funding based on their resident population, adjusted for age, sex and mortality to reflect the potential levels of local ill-health. In addition, if one district's hospitals treated another district's patients, there were transfers of funds between them in the next financial year. This had the effect of taking money away from some DHAs with a growing population and fewer services than their neighbours. Each year, more patients might cross an administrative border to a neighbouring hospital and so the losing DHA could never get hold of a budget big enough to pay for local service developments.

Working for Patients changed this system, altering some of the detailed data on which allocations were calculated and also the adjustment for cross-boundary patient transfers. In future, DHAs were to receive all their budget and not lose some of it to neighbours for services rendered. If they wished, they could let contracts with hospitals outside their boundaries, or they could now expand services in their own local hospitals. This may appear to be a relatively minor issue compared to the introduction of the internal market. But that is far from the case. Potentially, this innocuous change in funding was to have a much greater effect than the creation of the internal market.

The reason why the budget change was so important was that the sums of money transferred across boundaries and the differences in funding targets brought about by the new formula led to major shifts of funding away from inner city health authorities, towards suburbs and dormitory towns with growing populations and fewer services. The effect was particularly marked in London but it has also occurred in other cities. The direct result of the changes in funding was a major reduction in funds for cities, over a number of years. Thus much of the merging of hospitals and the reorganization of services seen in big cities is not the result of creating a market but the result of changing the funds available to those who had to buy in that market.

CONTRACTS FOR CARE

The White Paper provided little guidance on how purchasing would develop. As we will see in Chapter 3, there was relatively little interest in purchasing, compared to fundholding and Trusts, in the first few years after the Reforms. Most of the advice concentrated on the mechanics of purchasing, for example different types of contract for different services, with little about'how a new role might develop. And in spite of its title, the White Paper says noticeably little about how health authorities would address the views of the public on local health services. The Department of Health emphasized in its material for the public that DHA purchasers would take account of patient and GP views in letting contracts (Department of Health 1989a). However, it never specified how this was to be done, and subsequent performance has been highly variable. Butler (1992) has commented that this disappointed both left and right-wing observers, distancing

health services from patients and communities but also failing to provide classic consumer choice. It is also clear that the government
obscured some elements of the implications of purchasing by DHAs.
In particular, its material for the public suggested that there would be
greater choice for patients. In the pre-Reforms NHS a patient could in
principle be referred anywhere in the country. But once contracts
have been let by DHAs, patients could only be referred outside the
contract by the cumbersome process covering extra-contractual
referrals. This never sounded like greater choice for patients.

Potentially, the most patient-focused element of *Working for
Patients* was not in purchasing itself but in the range of quality standards introduced to monitor and control performance in hospitals,
such as waiting time monitoring in contracts. Purchasers would be
expected to show that they were purchasing services from providers
who met these standards. However, the standards themselves could
have been enforced without the introduction of the internal market,
for example by bureaucratic sanctions on those responsible for services such as preventing performance-related pay rises to managers.
Again, the link between the consumer elements of the Reforms and
the introduction of the internal market appeared to be weak.

Working Paper 2 (Department of Health 1989b), supporting the
White Paper, dealt with the contracting process in detail. Block contracts were similar to block funding in the past, with a given sum of
money to be paid for the provision of a service for a broad range of
caseload, rather than for a payment for each case. These contracts
were typically focused on emergency services, where the risk to purchasers from unplanned changes in activity would be greatest, and to
a considerable degree they represented business as usual. Equally,
emergency services meet what economists term an 'option demand',
the possibility that a service will be needed rather than a direct
demand for care itself. It makes a good deal of sense to pay for such a
service by buying capacity, the availability of care, rather than paying
only for each case treated. For example, the costs of an accident
department may be similar for wide ranges of demand, with staff
waiting for patients in quiet periods but not able to take on extra
work. Thus block contracts can be appropriate.

Cost and volume contracts were to be used for buying treatment for
a baseline level of caseload, with extra cases above that level paid for
per case. The price of care for these extra patients could be average
cost or marginal cost – the extra cost of the extra patients with no
allowance for overheads. Cost per case contracts were seen as being
most appropriate for small numbers of patients receiving specialized

treatment. For these groups, the risk to the health authority of paying for each specific patient would be relatively small because the total numbers covered by such contracts would also be small. The guidance is very firm on the importance of pricing being linked to costs with no cross-subsidization of costs between activities. Cross-subsidization is the practice of cutting some prices below costs by using profits on other products to offset the losses. It is a tactic used, for example, to increase the market share of a product which customers might go on buying in the future at the full cost price. It can also occur where a producer has some markets where it enjoys a monopoly and can charge a price above costs to subsidize other products and gain market share. This kind of behaviour was outlawed by the purchasing guidance, which under contracting wanted prices linked to costs to ensure that the internal market worked efficiently. However, the strong monopoly of some emergency services meant that unless there was a good analysis of costs, hospitals could well make surpluses on their block contracts for core services. This could enable a hospital to hang on to non-emergency care contracts by offering a lower price than other hospitals. As we will see in later chapters, there has been considerable variation in prices offered by different hospitals and so potentially cross-subsidization is occurring, whether deliberately or accidentally. The accidental nature may come from the simple fact that hospital managers need a particular income to keep the hospital going. They are likely to have this figure in mind when negotiating with purchasers and may not care much about the amount to be paid in each subsidiary contract so long as the total matches their total costs.

GP FUNDHOLDING

The White Paper refers to fundholding as 'practice budgeting'. The term fundholding came later, in the December 1989 paper on implementation (Department of Health 1989d). Practices with a list size of over 11,000 patients would be eligible to apply for fundholding status and would be given a budget for the purchase of outpatient care, elective (that is, non-emergency) surgery and diagnostic tests. Their budget was also to cover prescribing and practice costs. Underspending could be retained for fundholders, for service improvements, while overspending would be met but rigorously audited.

As well as this special status for GPs who chose fundholding, a further element of budgeting was to be introduced for all other GPs, 'indicative prescribing amounts'. Family health service authorities were required to fix a notional prescribing budget for each GP practice. While GPs would be permitted to exceed the budget without penalty or restriction on their patients, they would be expected to justify their overspend to the FHSA. Such a system was possible because of the major investment in prescribing data collection necessary to organize the payment of pharmacies, through the PACT system. As noted earlier, every prescription is recorded for payment to chemists and so every GP can be monitored on the cost and range of their prescribing.

It was proposed in the White Paper and guidance that funds and budgets would be based on a formula of some kind to ensure equality between fundholders themselves and between them and non-fundholders. But this has proved optimistic for the simple reason that fundholders were volunteers and would always expect to be funded to afford their past levels of activity, at least if they were referring and prescribing above the average rate. As a result, fundholding has always been based on historic activity levels, though moves to a formula have gradually been introduced.

Patients were reassured in Department of Health publicity that there would be no question of them not getting what they needed, though an overspending doctor might have to explain the overspend to another doctor (Department of Health 1989a). But sometimes doctors prescribe too much because patients expect it, according to the Department's material. Indicative prescribing amounts were seen as cutting out waste. And so, in spite of the continued separation in the Parliamentary votes − the allocation of public spending by Parliament − of cash-limited hospital and community services and the unlimited drugs budget, a budget constraint began to be introduced into the previously unrestrained area of primary care.

SELF-GOVERNING TRUSTS

Trusts were seen as a model for large hospitals, at the time of the White Paper. Trust status offered hospitals the prospect of greater freedom and responsibility for their own affairs, with contracting as the mechanism for funding instead of direct operation by a health authority. More detail on the changes implied by Trust status emerged in the subsequent guidance (Department of Health 1989c).

Trusts were to be free to employ whatever staff they wished though, crucially in my view, the rules for employing junior medical staff would continue to operate. (See Chapters 3 and 5 for a detailed discussion of the impact of junior medical staff training on the internal market.) Trusts would also be free to borrow, from the government or the private sector, within an overall external financing limit. (It continues to be almost impossible to find more than a tiny handful of people within the NHS who can explain what an external financing limit really is or how it is calculated!)

To become a Trust, hospitals would need to demonstrate that management had the skills and capacity to run the hospitals and that senior professional staff, particularly consultants, were involved in management. Trust status was not to be used as a way of avoiding closure by a DHA of a hospital no longer seen as having a role. Trusts would also have to continue to provide a core of services for the local population, particularly accident and emergency care, if required by their purchasers, and could not simply leave major service lines (a freedom of most producers in a conventional market and, potentially, a route to the extraction of extra payments for the core services that are seen as essential).

Trusts were to be run by a board of directors appointed by the Secretary of State, with a mixture of executive and non-executive members, led by a part-time chairman. This effectively created a large number of posts of patronage in the NHS, to be filled by direct appointment. Executive directors were to include a chief executive (replacing the general manager) and a medical director (replacing the chairman of the medical advisory committee) together with nursing and finance directors. In practice, nursing directors were not always included though some Trusts appointed nurses to posts in charge of related areas such as the quality of care.

Management of Trusts was nominally to be as open as possible, in the government's proposals. However, the detail implies rather less openness. Trust boards had to hold only one annual public meeting a year, compared to monthly DHA public meetings. Contracts are viewed as commercially sensitive, so less information was likely to be in the public domain. But it is also worth noting that even when health authorities met more frequently and in public, many such meetings were more likely to be attended by their employees and CHC members than by the public at large (see for example Ham 1986).

The implementation of the Trust element of the Reforms differs somewhat from that described above. In particular, Trust status has become the model for all health service providers in the NHS. Once the leading few had obtained the prized badge of Trust status, every unit manager seemed to want it for their unit too, to keep up with the neighbours but also perhaps to get access to the greater freedom to pay managers the going rate for the job! The wide spread of Trust status was also important to the development of purchasing. Unless Trusts developed apace, purchasers would not have the desired flexibility in the internal market. If they continued to manage many units, they would hardly be likely to reduce their contracts with units that they managed; and so growth in the number of Trusts was really essential to the development of the purchaser role. In addition, the number of new Trusts, announced by a proud Minister of Health each year, was increasingly seen as a tangible sign that the Reforms were going ahead – turning what should have been a means to the end of an improved health service into an end in itself, the spread of the Trust model.

Indeed, the pace of Trust expansion was so great that in the final waves, candidates were virtually rushed through, with only three days of an assessor's time paid for in the review of candidates. Imagine trying to assess the quality of an organization of the size of a hospital in three days, and write up your findings! Not surprisingly, the overwhelming majority of units increasingly passed the scrutiny, though a few embarrassing and painful refusals occurred. Typically, a change of the general manager was seen as the way to get Trust status, not a clearly demonstrable change in other parts of the organization and its services.

The rapid pace of growth also affected those who opposed the concept of Trusts. Compared to grant-maintained schools, where a minority have taken on the new status and are seen as a different and perhaps threatening model by schools in local authority control, once every unit was a Trust, there seemed no risk of privatization of the best hospitals in the country, for example. Similarly, once every unit was a Trust, it was hard to see how the Department of Health could exempt them from its guidance and regulations, unless it was to do itself out of a large number of jobs. Trusts for all meant, paradoxically, no change. As will be discussed in the later chapters, the rapid move to Trust status for all fixed most of the health service not in a new model but in an old model with a new label. There simply was not the time to change the culture everywhere and, increasingly, proof of the right culture was not tested. Arguably, the old model survived another bureaucratic change with the core professionals intact.

It should also be noted that, in spite of the PR launch, leaflets and tapes, the whole Trust issue was relatively opaque to the public. Once they were reassured that Trust status did not mean privatization, and once patients could see their local hospital still unchanged, they probably lost what little interest they had in the bureaucracy and management of the NHS. Ask the man on the Clapham omnibus who runs the health service and what Trust status means and he will shrug his shoulders. But ask him where his local hospital is and he will be able to direct you straight there, and probably tell you that while the paintwork has been neglected, the staff are really wonderful!

Before leaving Trusts, we should note the particular position of Community Trusts. While in a few cases an entire local hospital and community service was integrated in a single Trust, this was usually seen as a bad thing, leaving community services open to exploitation by the more powerful hospitals. In most places, a separate Trust was established, based on existing community health units, providing district nursing, health visiting, and community and hospital care of mentally ill people. Each Community Trust was given a local patch and to a considerable degree enjoys a monopoly. As we will discuss further in later chapters, there is some competition over new services – such as when a major mental hospital is closing and a new service is to be established from scratch – but local monopolies remain largely unchallenged, even though it would have been relatively easy to have introduced competing community nursing services. To an economist this is surprising.

Home nursing would be the simplest health service in which to develop a market. Home nursing exists already in the private sector; it would be simple to recruit a small group of nurses to set up a local neighbourhood nursing service. Instead, community services were enshrined in monopolies with a significant management overhead that is often effective but has never been fully tested by market forces. This seems to be another paradox of the Reforms. There was an attempt to set up a market in the field where it would be most difficult for new providers to enter, the hospital sector, and where past policy had led to increasing concentration in fewer comprehensive hospitals, covering a whole district. And at the same time, the service where a market could easily have been created, with almost no investment in facilities, was given local monopoly rights. The explanation has not been documented but I suspect the reason is simply that community services had never given the politicians real problems. They rarely had financial difficulties and their services were usually eked out between competing clients without explicit waiting lists. Compared to the physical tangibility of a single operation, 'home nursing' can be a much more variable commodity and can be rationed in all kind of ways if resources are tight. Community Trusts have recently come under criticism over the way in which care of the mentally ill is provided, but they have the obvious defence that they are only carrying out what has been unchallenged government policy for a long time: the closure of the big mental hospitals and a shift to care in the community. So having never been a problem for ministers, they were spared the full rigour of the market.

WORKING FOR *PATIENTS*?

Extending patient choice was apparently a key concern of Mrs Thatcher's when looking at the NHS. But the reader will find relatively little on this issue in the rest of this book for the simple reason that there was little if anything in *Working for Patients* that touched on patient choice, treatment or the new role for their local health service. The simple choice of where to go and what treatment to have is not defined by the Reforms. There is also relatively little evidence of extensive involvement of the public on wider changes, though we will see in Chapter 3 some examples of how this could take place. The White Paper changed health authorities from bodies which planned health services and delivered them to bodies which assessed needs and bought services to meet them. In neither case was regular and formal consultation with the public built in. There is a three-month consultation period on major shifts of services but typically only after the plans have been crystallized. I have seen little evidence that this has led to a major change of plans except in a few cases where MPs have become embroiled. Similarly, patients were not invited to vote for or against fundholding status for their general practice. Neighbourhoods were not invited to vote on Trust status.

At the level of choice over the future of institutions, the explanation for the lack of patient or public choice probably lies in the lack of a coherent link of most people to their local hospitals. Compared to the daily contact of parents with schools, many people neither have nor want regular contact with their hospitals. They have little idea of how they are managed or run and do not even have regular local elections to remind them that those who run public services are ultimately accountable to them. However, this is less obviously the case for general practice, which is a neighbourhood-based service that patients contact more frequently. It seems surprising that a government committed to choice declined to give patients the choice over fundholding status. Given the criticism of the scheme by the BMA at the outset of the Reforms, the government may well have feared a public backlash and so denied choice to protect us from making (what it saw as) the wrong decision.

At the level of choice over treatment, the move to a contracted environment potentially reduced choice, though pressure to avoid treating non-local patients was growing before the Reforms because of the financial pressures on the health service. We will see particularly in relation to fundholding in Chapter 4 the tension between a greater role for patients in choosing the services they would like and a lesser role, in which decisions are made for them by doctors and purchasers. There are several justifications for a publicly funded and run health service. One of these is the simple fact that patients lack the knowledge to choose effectively. Even when given all the facts and the probabilities attaching to each risk, many patients may feel unable to choose rationally. Indeed, there is more than one standard of rationality in making choices involving uncertain outcomes, based on the expected average outcome or on the maximum gain or maximum loss, for example.

In my view, and that of many others in the health field, there is a clear case for offering patients a choice of treatment, where more than one treatment for a condition exists and there is uncertainty over the best one, or where there is simply a balance between benefits and disadvantages to be struck. Patients should be offered this choice by clinicians. If they are to be consulted on the most fundamental aspects of their care, it seems perverse to deny them choices over which hospital they might prefer for reasons of personal convenience or familiarity, for example. Equally, since many health purchaser contracts reflect past patient flows, past choices may well be endorsed in current contracts. Thus patients may retain a choice linked to past choices as long as the purchasers continue to maintain the same contracts as in the past. Once purchasers begin to move to contracts which prefer one provider, on cost or quality, this choice is taken away. In an ideal world, this might only occur after consultation with recent patients at alternative hospitals but purchasers lack the resources for this kind of in-depth research on every contract. Yet without it, it is hard to see what choice is on offer to patients.

As the Reforms have developed, there has been increased emphasis on primary care led services and locally sensitive purchasing. Potentially, by shifting elements of the planning of contracts and services to a lower level, the scope for public consultation is increased and we may come to see a greater degree of patient influence in decisions. But once the decisions move to the bigger, strategic problems, the general public are likely to find the choices difficult to deal with (see the discussion of citizens' juries in Chapter 4).

VALUE FOR MONEY

Value for money is the final issue considered in this chapter, though we will return to it. The intention of *Working for Patients* was that the creation of an internal market would create better value for money by encouraging competition and increased efficiency. However, when looking at the internal market, it is important to bear in mind that it remains a 'quasi-market' only. Le Grand and Bartlett (1993a) specify the key differences between a market and quasi-market as being that competing suppliers are not pursuing profits in the way that conventional businesses do and demand is often controlled through decisions made on behalf of consumers, rather than directly by them. As a result, the internal market does not work with the same energy and dynamics as might be expected in the soft drinks, car or computer markets. That is, many of the limits on what the internal market might achieve are a consequence of its form, not its functioning.

The further difficulty facing any assessment of value for money in the health service is the sheer complexity of modern medical care. Even simple increases in activity, within a fixed budget, raise questions about whether (for example) additional minor day surgery is clinically appropriate. Furthermore, because departments in hospitals frequently carry out both emergency and elective treatments, there are always difficulties in separating costs adequately for detailed contracting. However, it would also be unfair on those responsible for the Reforms not to note that the introduction of a weak incentive to better performance is better than no incentive at all. Encouraging health authorities to look critically at performance by local providers and their costs is potentially an improvement over the previous regime, where incentives to greater efficiency and value for money were even weaker.

THE CREATION OF INCENTIVES?

In the chapters that follow, we will attempt to answer a number of questions on the post-Reforms NHS:

- Have the Reforms created meaningful incentives for the key stake-holders?
- Are these incentives strong enough to produce the desired effect?
- What other factors are helping or hindering the achievement of the improvements that the Reforms were intended to produce?

The issues will be examined through the research literature, which is thin on empirical detail in many aspects of the Reforms, and from a personal perspective, based on the author's experience in a large number of Trusts and DHAs in the 1990s. The three areas are examined from the standpoint of purchasers and GP fundholders in Chapters 3 and 4, and Trusts in Chapter 5. Chapter 6 then examines what further changes the NHS may require to build upon the gains made and to meet the challenges of the next century.

3

PURCHASING HEALTH AUTHORITIES

INTRODUCTION

The separation of purchasing and providing is a cornerstone of the NHS Reforms. District health authorities (DHAs) are no longer responsible for providing services by direct management of hospital and community health services. Instead, new authorities, which now generally combine the roles of the DHA and family health service authority (FHSA), contract for care with a range of providers. The tension of this contractual relationship, in particular the freedom for the purchaser to take their acute and continuing care contracts elsewhere, is intended to generate market pressures on the costs and efficiency of competing providers.

Following the mergers of many district health authorities with family health service authorities, there are a number of different names for the local health care purchasers, such as commissions and agencies. For convenience, in this chapter we use the term 'health commissions' to refer to current post-Reforms purchasers, carrying out the roles of former DHAs and FHSAs.

In the sections that follow, the roles of the health commissions are examined and compared with other models, notably US health maintenance organizations (HMOs). The chapter then examines the objectives of health commissions and the incentives to achieve them. Practical problems and performance to date are then considered, and an overall assessment of health commissions is set out in the final section. Given the limited evidence, the assessment is heavily influenced by direct personal experience of purchasers, as well as the research available.

CONTRACTING TO MEET NEEDS – A NEW ROLE?

The White Paper charged health commissions with buying the best service they can from Trust or private sector providers, as well as directly managed units (which have all become Trusts). Purchasers were to be able to contract for services both locally and in other areas. But given the claimed significance of this change of role, from joint planner and provider of services, to a purchasing (more often now termed 'commissioning') role, it is surprising how little shape was given to the new model of purchasing (Hunter and Harrison 1993). Most of the early effort after the Reforms went into the establishment of Trusts and the creation of the regulatory framework within which they would operate. Once it became clear that every hospital and community unit had to become a Trust, if only because of the difficulty of proving that units did not meet the criteria, the sheer number of new Trusts created a substantial workload for the NHS Management Executive and RHAs that diverted attention away from purchasing. A substantial number of high profile managers in the NHS also moved rapidly from district (and sometimes regional) general manager posts to become chief executives of major trusts, suggesting that Trusts would be where the action was. This left a vacuum in many purchasers at a time when they were supposedly taking on a new role. Subsequent mergers with their neighbours and between DHAs and FHSAs simply added to the confusion. But although the work of health commissions differs from that of pre-Reforms DHAs, how far does the change represent the creation of new roles?

Arguably, the Reforms added a role to health commissions (that of negotiating contracts with a range of providers), and took away a role (direct management of provider units). But the core functions of health commissions, the assessment of local needs and procurement of services to meet them, were roles of DHAs before the Reforms. They used block grants rather than contracts to fix the funding for providers but there was still a local service plan which providers were funded to meet, however indirect the link between funding and activity. The real impact of the Reforms was probably that it concentrated the minds of health commission staff on this key service planning role and took away the operational management issues that could frequently dominate their agendas. Indeed, there was a real schism visible in some pre-Reforms DHAs between the annual report and the annual public health report. The latter looks rather like an outline needs assessment, with concern for birth and death rates, avoidable mortality and morbidity levels. But the former, instead of building on the public health assessment, often looked more like the annual report of provider Trusts. In spite of the emphasis on planning in the 1974 reorganization of the NHS, a range of studies of planning bodies, reviewed by Harrison *et al.* (1992) show that most health authorities studied were frequently distracted from long-term planning by short-term financial and operational issues at the provider level. It is also worth noting that most senior managers in the NHS got to be district general managers after spells in hospital management. Thus the planning body was run by people who had enjoyed and succeeded in the operational world for a substantial part of their careers. Perhaps for this reason, the level of district management involvement in provider issues was greater than appropriate in many districts.

As employers of local health professionals, pre-Reforms DHAs found it hard to impose a community-wide health perspective (however defined) on the existing pattern of services. Their relationship with key professionals, notably doctors, depended heavily on showing support for the current pattern of services. DHAs were often committed to maintenance of services as part of their own local management empire. Defence of local services was also an appropriate managerial response to financial pressures. The management effort required to save large sums of money through retrenchment of the organization was likely to be greater and greater, over time, as 'easy' savings from compulsory tendering of support services were achieved. Thus DHAs with major teaching hospitals on their patch were typically not successful in reducing expenditure to affordable levels, given their falling population-based funding. In consequence, external mechanisms for change, of the kind introduced by the Tomlinson report on London's hospitals, had to be used to bring about major, strategic change.

In this environment, it was often potentially easier for DHAs to extract more money from the higher tiers of the NHS by claims of underfunding or a need for transitional support. Managers at DHA level defended facilities and services, to a greater or lesser degree, as a part of their *raison d'être*. It was also possible to use apparent failure as a basis for forcing the hand of higher authorities to provide the required support. Enthoven (1985: 14) caricatures this approach, within the US defence department, with the story of the general who reported to the Secretary of State: 'Mr Secretary, I am sorry to have to tell you this, but that million dollars you gave us for shoes were spent on left shoes. Now we need another million for right shoes. We will both be embarrassed if you don't give it to us.'

While this is indeed a caricature, it is one that is recognizable to those who have worked in the NHS, though the basis of the moral blackmail may have been a politically sensitive loss of services rather than a simple mistake. The new role of contracting replaced direct line management and created a need for new skills in market assessment and negotiation. But again these mirror to a degree the old roles of planning across a geographical patch and agreeing resources with the various unit management teams in the district. Of course, the further the new purchasers went towards behaving like actors in a market, the greater the need for novel skills and behaviour. The extent to which they did become marketeers is therefore important to any assessment of their role and is considered below.

Certainly there was little active stimulus from the centre to encourage the development of more market-like behaviour. Instead, the purchasing role was largely neglected until a series of speeches in 1993 (NHSME 1993), four years after *Working for Patients*. These speeches, by a junior health minister and medical physicist (Dr Brian Mawhinney) and by the NHS Chief Executive (Duncan Nichol), set a new agenda for purchasers. The new framework put great emphasis on joint development of strategy with GPs and the public, improvements in data collection and analysis, and disease management that included prevention as well as reactive treatment. New services were to be funded, in part at least, through resources released by setting challenging efficiency targets for current providers. By their very nature, these speeches remained at the level of strategic guidance rather than simple practical activities. The latter have slowly spread through NHS material produced centrally and regionally, also through examples of local good practice and journal articles. Over time, a style of behaviour has developed for trendsetting purchasers – particularly the inclusion of GPs and the public in their planning and purchasing – but there is still considerable diversity in their approaches and at times a gap between what is said and what is done.

The clearest message in the purchaser guidance proposed greater involvement of GPs in local decision-making. This needed particular emphasis because pre-Reforms DHAs often had rather arms-length relationships with GPs, to avoid interfering with the role of the FHSAs. Merger of the two kinds of authority into health commissions will change this but evidence, noted below, suggests that GPs are not yet always in agreement with their local purchasers.

HEALTH COMMISSIONS AS HMOs?

Health commissions can be compared with other models of health care procurement to assess their merits. An obvious comparison is with health maintenance organizations (HMOs) in the United States, since the HMO model was widely touted by a number of commentators during the run-up to the Reforms. HMOs developed in the USA as an alternative to insurance companies. They offer a comprehensive range of services, directly or under contract, to their subscribers. They are sometimes doctor-owned and managed; typically they employ doctors on salaries or profit share, rather than fees per item of service. This system reduces pressure to overtreat patients and provides an incentive to reduce utilization and so generate additional surpluses through the excess of subscriptions over expenditure on patient care. (For a summary of HMOs, see Glennerster *et al.* 1994.)

Comparisons of NHS purchasers with conventional insurance funding are less relevant. Insurers have typically funded whatever patient care was prescribed by doctors and so have typically had a much smaller role, if any, in planning for populations or geographical areas. However, insurers in the USA have begun to look at protocols and guidelines, and other restrictions on clinical freedom, to achieve what is termed 'managed care'. This management is designed to balance the interests of doctor and patient with those of the paying agency. To a degree, this is akin to the management approach of an HMO, since control of utilization can be linked closely to protocols and guidelines for care, reflecting the influence of HMOs on the rest of the market. Insurers must avoid too large a gap developing between HMO enrolment costs for employers/private subscribers and premiums charged by the insurance companies themselves.

Butler and Pirie (1988) proposed competing health management units and Enthoven (1985) notes that in an internal market, health authorities would be like HMOs. Several key differences in the roles and incentives should be noted, however. The main advantages claimed for HMOs are not those that derive directly from competition, which already existed in US health care, but those that derive from increased vertical integration of services and funding. In the pre-HMO fee-for-service model in the USA, patients and physicians could together agree on ever-higher levels of service which were paid for by a third party, an insurer or a state funding agency. Even competing insurance companies faced the same continual pressure on activity and cost per case. HMOs set out to integrate some of the medical decision-makers into the organization that paid for care from consumer subscriptions, using both guidelines and incentives to do so. In this way, they sought to reduce medical pressures for higher (potentially inappropriate) utilization and to lower costs per patient. However, HMOs operate within a competitive environment where consumers (individuals or their employers), can choose between plans offering different combinations of service access, quality, cost and patient charges. In consequence, HMOs must not allow the difference in services provided by themselves and conventional insurers to become too large, in case they come to be seen increasingly as offering a poorer quality of care.

We can compare the integrated care model of the HMO with the NHS, before and after the Reforms. Before the Reforms, care was integrated in the sense that planning bodies funded to take care of whole populations also had direct management control of providers. Hospital doctors were directly employed by the planning body, the DHA, and whatever the degree of management or control that existed in practice, there was an appreciable degree of integration. GPs acted as gatekeepers to hospital, controlling referral to many services, with no financial incentive to refer more patients but some incentives to reduce their work by referring patients to other providers. Typically, although there was (and still is) considerable variation in GP referral, the lack of direct access to specialists reduces hospital utilization overall in the UK, compared to other developed countries. Equally, there remained a lack of integrated care and there was often confusion in the role and treatment of the same patient by hospitals, community services and GPs.

However, the separation of purchasers and providers has done little to increase vertical integration in the NHS, with the exception of GP fundholding. Fundholding has created some integration by giving the purchasing budget to the gatekeepers, linking resource commitments and clinical decisions. Conversely, purchasing by health commissions is now at arm's length from both hospital and primary care providers and so there is potentially less direct integration of health care planning and delivery. This can lead to a lack of a consistent approach, for example where a Trust has both the aspirations to develop a new service and the private or charitable funds to do so, even without DHA approval. While this degree of difference is rare, more generally the creation of Trusts as independent entities certainly pushes them towards policies which increase the role and income of the Trust, rather than the wider public health. There has also been a failure on the part of many purchasers to develop an integrated approach to the care of particular diseases. For example, I have heard one manager quote the increase in the costs of community care generated by a planned slowdown in the rate of surgery for a problem that left patients (if untreated) highly dependent. The internal market and the use of contracts were intended to provide much needed incentives for providers to follow purchasers. But market incentives almost always encourage those selling services to try to increase the demand. It was this incentive that HMOs set out to counter in the USA through greater vertical integration. By comparison, health commissions have also not yet integrated GPs into their purchasing process extensively and consistently across the UK. This is a result of the historic disconnection between GPs and the former DHAs, which prior to recent mergers with family health service authorities were not responsible for GPs. Many GPs also wish to avoid being seen as publicly linked to rationing decisions when health commissions face financial constraints. An HMO model would have brought GPs and hospital doctors, as two of the key providers, more fully into a structure which provided incentives to control demand and to share the objectives of the organization rather than concentrating solely on the services to individual patients. Instead, provider clinicians have been put into a more market-based relationship with health commissions, and only fundholding GPs have really taken on an element of the HMO role.

IF NOT HMOs THEN WHAT?

Health commissions reduced the integration of services and finance and cannot be seen as immediately similar to HMOs. So what are they? The closest models are European sickness funds, many of which have a geographic or occupational base. Under these arrangements, there is less direct payment on a patient-by-patient basis and more use of block contracts and grants. But there is also often greater diversity of providers, with local government, private sector and charitable hospitals offering similar services. In most of Europe, providers were not nationalized in a single act such as that which created the NHS in 1948. The sickness fund often has less of a role, or simply less influence, on the planning of a coherent, integrated service, and patients in Europe have more freedom of access to specialist services. Thus health commissions in the UK are akin to monopoly sickness funds, subject to competition from GP fundholders, with a role in geographic planning and service strategy. This role requires the health commissions to have power over providers. But, arguably, the creation of Trusts potentially shifted considerable power to the providers by giving them a greater degree of independence, with their own chairman and board. Trust chief executives are now more reliant on good references from their chairman and medical director than from their local health commission chief executive. Indeed, fighting with the latter could enhance their status as candidates for the top job at larger Trusts. In practice, health commissions do not have as much market power as might be assumed, for reasons considered later in this chapter. As a result, they have not always had their own way in countering the power of the Trusts.

OBJECTIVES OF HEALTH COMMISSIONS

The overt objectives set for purchasing health authorities were to:

* assess local health needs;
* contract with cost-effective providers for the provision of care to meet needs;
* do so within a fixed cash limit.

Control of total spending is the clearest objective for a health commission, in that there is only one financial bottom line so financial control is the most easily measured objective. It is also an objective that is familiar to health commission staff from their past work in DHAs, since staying within the cash limit has been an objective of the NHS for a long time, pre-dating the 1990 Reforms.

Health commission purchasing plans typically refer to their two non-financial objectives using the terms *needs assessment* and *purchasing for health gain*. The former refers to the detailed assessment of health needs, around which service plans and contracts can be shaped. The latter refers to the improvement in local population health that can be achieved by alternative interventions and is typically linked to targets set under the Health of the Nation initiative. These areas are the core business of public health specialists in health commissions, who have been charged with using general epidemiological evidence and, in many cases, specific local population surveys, to assess health needs and find the areas where health gains – towards Health of the Nation targets – can be achieved. Achievement of health gain requires the quantification of health gain and the development of priorities for expenditure. Both needs assessment and prioritization throw up a number of difficulties, of principle and practice. Before considering these in more detail we examine the incentives facing purchasers as they pursue their objectives.

INCENTIVES TO MEET OBJECTIVES

In developing their purchasing plans, health commissions face a number of incentives, and some disincentives. Although the NHS now uses much of the language of business, or in the words of Brian Abel-Smith, the language of business schools, the main incentives for purchasers remain bureaucratic. They involve fulfilling the expectations of higher levels of the health service at an annual review, focused on simple measures such as financial balance and waiting times for care. Purchasers are bureaucratic monopolies with all local residents as members. While GP fundholding took some people to another purchasing model, for some services (and, now, for all services in a few pioneering locations), the early development of purchasing faced organizational rather than market pressures.

As noted earlier, cash limits provide the simplest basis for assessing health commissions. While the incentive to balance the budget is clear – failure to do so is likely to lead to senior managers being sacked – the assessment of progress towards the other two objectives, needs assessment and health gain through purchasing, is much more difficult. This further weakens the incentive to do better since doing better may not be easy to define or to recognize.

Purchasers almost certainly have another bureaucratic incentive, to keep out of trouble and avoid major political disputes over their purchasing decisions, such as contracts which affect the viability of local hospitals. Since they are a part of the wider public sector, health commissions are always at the mercy of politicians at some level, in spite of the exclusion of political representatives on health commissions. For example, a newly formed county-wide health commission in Hertfordshire was broken up in early 1996, allegedly because local MPs, including a cabinet minister, thought that its purchasing plans threatened the viability of local accident and emergency services in their constituencies. A smaller purchaser, with a local patch, is clearly seen as more likely to protect the local accident department and give the politicians less trouble. Similarly, local MPs in north London set out to protect the casualty department at Edgware Hospital, knowing that the small Conservative majority in Parliament in 1996 gave them much greater influence over health ministers.

Health commissions also need to keep GPs happy with their purchasing as a way of discouraging growth in GP fundholding. Some fundholders only took on the role for negative reasons, that is, to avoid a threat to existing services from health commission decisions and not solely to improve services (Glennerster *et al.* 1994). Fundholding takes resources away from the local health commission, potentially weakening its strategic control over services such as elective surgery. However, at the same time health commissions have been put under bureaucratic pressure to increase fundholding in line with government policy, increasing the transfer of funds out of their budget.

At first sight it is perhaps surprising to find that, in spite of pre-Reform debate about the need to incentivize the NHS, this did not occur for health commissions to any great extent. However, the introduction of a local monopoly purchaser may be only a first step, with scope for more competitive models in the future, if the Reforms are seen as a part of a longer-term agenda. However, the Conservative Party has always denied this, indicating that it simply sought greater efficiency, not a private sector solution. This issue is reconsidered in Chapter 6.

Before examining the problems faced by health commissions in carrying out their role and responding to the incentives above, it is worth noting the disincentives.

DISINCENTIVES FOR PURCHASERS

Health commissions have been encouraged by the Department of Health to assess local needs in detail. But they face a clear disincentive. Detailed health needs assessment is likely to throw up needs which are not currently being met. (See for example Tennant *et al.* (1995) for an illustration of how a detailed look at a single potential procedure, knee replacement, can throw up a large increase in demand.) But the funding of health commissions, by national formula, is not particularly sensitive to local needs for specific procedures or disease programmes. Nor can funding easily respond if different needs assessments are carried out in different areas. The result of a detailed needs assessment may therefore be to put further financial pressure on purchasers' budgets and increase the risk of overspending, in breach of another bureaucratic guideline.

Even if the disincentive to identify unmet needs were changed substantially, the problems of measuring need and choosing treatments to give greater health gain, both in principle and in practice, are so great that improved incentives alone might not achieve a major impact. The problems, initially at the level of principle, then at the task level and finally within the internal market framework, are examined further in the next sections.

COMMISSIONING – PROBLEMS OF PRINCIPLE

High level problems facing health commissions include the definition and measurement of health needs and health gains and the prioritization of needs in purchasing.

Measuring population needs is a highly complex task for several reasons. First, because of the body's complexity, people suffer from a very wide range of health problems. Diagnostic related groups (DRGs), a standard classification of hospital treatments developed in the USA, have over 400 categories, for example. Thus a needs assessment, in diagnostic detail, would be very expensive to carry out on a large and representative local population sample. Furthermore, the threshold for treatment of a given disease may not be well defined or consistently applied in current practice. Therefore a needs assessment should ideally have, as a prerequisite, a clear set of definitions of need, for example covering symptom range and severity. And what of social circumstances? Is the assessment of need, for example a hip replacement, to be independent of income, car ownership and social support?

A further complication is that not all needs will result in a demand for treatment. Thus a needs assessment would ideally include an assessment of willingness to be treated. Equally, as noted earlier, extensive and open needs assessments could also encourage people with identified needs – which they want to be met – to expect treatment when resource constraints might prevent this happening. That is, while needs may drive priority-setting, once the cost of meeting all needs exceeds the budget, priorities may drive needs assessments.

At one level, it is tempting to see needs assessment as primarily a resource problem. Given enough assessors, with enough medical skills, we might measure population needs 'objectively'. But the argument above suggests that once needs had been identified, issues of local or national responsibility for meeting needs would then arise, just as they have in social services. Levitt *et al.* (1995) have noted that detailed needs assessments would also fail to determine priorities between alternative existing and new demands for services. While it is possible to involve GPs and the public in a more complex debate about priorities, it requires considerable sophistication to make the dialogue meaningful. There is an inevitable tendency in public debates for local politicians to demand additional resources for health care rather than face up to the purchasing constraints on the health authority or commission. Thus even within technical, objective needs assessment, prioritization raises problems. But it raises even more problems of its own.

In attempting to set priorities, health commissions face fundamental difficulties, most of which stem from the problem of choosing between different individuals' care, within a national and equity-conscious health care system. Typically, they have verbally sidestepped the problems through a commitment to maximum health gain. This does not begin to solve the problem in practice. Maximum health gain as an objective begs a number of questions, most fundamentally about what health gain is actually achieved by each treatment. Even if we put this aside while research develops, there are also major problems in pursuing greater health gains, however measured, because of the impact on the distribution of health and health care between different individuals and groups. Simple statements of the intention to maximize local health gain miss the point that health gains, once produced, cannot be shared around. Getting more health gain means, except for general environmental measures, getting more health for some at the expense of others.

Purchasing authorities simply cannot ignore the distributional impact of their decisions. Refusing to treat varicose veins, for example, represents a significant change in the contract between the public and the NHS. It also raises questions about the value of a Patient's Charter stipulating maximum waiting times if the package of care available can be changed by purchasers. Without local community support for major rationing decisions, they lack any real legitimacy, and the presence of five local non-executives on the health authority is no real substitute for such local support. Indeed, even with a local majority in favour of excluding varicose vein surgery, individual sufferers could argue that unless the same decision is made everywhere across the UK, it cannot be made in only one part of what claims to be a national health service. Furthermore, varicose vein sufferers who have paid their taxes for many years may feel that they are entitled to use the service for what they suffer from, whatever its relative priority as judged by a purchasing team.

The priority-setting problem is made more difficult by the link between ill-health and other demographic and social characteristics.

Individual communities may be systematically discriminated against by decisions on treatment, for example if sickle cell anaemia (a disease of Afro-Caribbean and Mediterranean races) is seen as offering too low a health gain to be treated. In practice, this may be an extreme example, but any group of disease sufferers constitutes a legitimate constituency and the impact of any purchasing policy on them must be considered.

It is now common for groups of disease sufferers to lobby for their particular treatment needs, while sidestepping the rationing decisions that are needed to free resources. For example, the gay lobby has had a major impact in securing very high levels of expenditure on new and sometimes unevaluated treatments, some of which appear relatively ineffective once the evidence accumulates. Nor is activity restricted to high profile diseases such as HIV/AIDS. As an example at a less intense level, there was growing pressure in early 1996 from sufferers from osteoporosis (thinning of the bones, common in post-menopausal women) for a national screening and preventive treatment programme, while the arguments over effectiveness were still raging in the medical press (see *British Medical Journal*, 3 February 1996). Meanwhile, individual health commissions were attempting to resolve the issue locally in their purchasing plans. But if the NHS is to remain a national service, it seems unsatisfactory for the difficult distributional decisions to be made separately by each set of local purchasers or local clinicians. Of course, after a national debate on health priorities, it might be concluded that these decisions should be handled in this way but there is no clear consensus for this at present. Yet individual authorities are taking decisions about the funding of new and existing treatment technologies with few consistent national guidelines. It is difficult to see any legitimacy in this approach within a national public service. (It should be noted that one of the most high profile cases, that of Child B, where a health commission declined to fund further treatment for leukaemia, was not in essence a case of prioritization. The clinical advice was that the treatment would not work and so the commission took the view that there would be no health gain. Its decision not to fund a research treatment was also compatible with its role as a purchaser of health services, though it perhaps added emphasis to the need to find demonstrable health gain, which is not always possible even for conventional treatments.)

Seeking a local public consensus on purchasing, with local people or their GPs heavily involved, is now seen as a way forward for NHS purchasers. In its most advanced form, an experimental local jury has been used to give a view, as in Cambridge and Huntingdon (IPPR

1996). The jury method involves bringing together a representative sample of the local population and presenting them with the information on which health purchasing decisions are made. The experiment in Cambridge generated a number of interesting results, including support for the principle that a lower quality of care might be given to some patients, below the technical maximum achievable, to enable more treatment of routine cases from the available budget. However, this experiment also highlighted the difficulty of making health care priority decisions. The jury was in favour of a national panel to lead on priority-setting, which to a considerable degree would get local people, whether the public or professionals, off the hook of prioritization.

The traditional role of GPs as gatekeepers to services and the fact that fundholders have been prepared to take on some of the rationing decisions required in a cash-limited NHS make it sensible for health commissions to involve GPs more widely, not least because the public have considerable confidence in them. The public also see their GP often, and the GP could be an ideal means of communicating a range of issues from health commissions to patients. But here again the lack of an integrated HMO model is a problem outside fundholding, as GPs are independent subcontractors who do not necessarily endorse health commission decisions, nor need to be seen to do so.

Consulting members of the public or GPs can also raise its own problems. What if those responding do not share the wider social concern with the distribution of health care and health gain that the NHS espouses? What if GPs feel that smokers should not be treated for heart and lung disease, or a majority of the local public think that gays and drug abusers should not be treated for their HIV infections? While some observers (for example Caines 1996) have argued that we ought to let the public decide, whatever that leads to, I for one would prefer to see the interests of everyone safeguarded to some degree, to prevent the tyranny of the majority.

As long as we have a cash-limited health service, there is no easy way for health commissions to adopt a clear set of purchasing principles explicitly. If they wish to change the pattern of treatment away from that reflected in past treatment decisions (for example to increase cardiac surgery or coronary disease prevention, in the light of a high local death rate from coronary heart disease) they face a difficult decision, choosing which service they should stop purchasing to fund the required expansion. Health authorities have never found such decisions easy to make in the past, and have typically only considered marginal changes in the resources provided to different care programmes (Charlton *et al.* 1981). For the reasons noted above, even simple health gain leaves the health purchaser with decisions about the distribution of health care between winners and losers. Detailed local needs assessments may highlight gaps in provision but where are the necessary resources to come from to meet these gaps and which services will be withdrawn to release the resources?

PRACTICAL PROBLEMS FACING HEALTH COMMISSIONS

Aside from the overarching problems of principle noted above, health commission purchasers have also faced a number of simple, practical problems in developing their role. These include a lack of an integrated approach to care, a shortage or dilution of key skills and considerable bureaucratic disruption from health commission mergers. In the light of these, their performance, which is reviewed below, is perhaps understandable. In addition, whatever their skills, health commissions are operating in an environment that is not a pure market and does not give them the kind of sovereign power that purchasers are supposed to enjoy.

As noted earlier, purchasing in the internal market did not create an integrated approach to care of the kind increasingly likely to be adopted in an HMO. Purchasers are attempting to procure care for a wide range of patients; this care is not provided by an integrated service that matches patients and treatment. An individual patient with a chronic disease may in one year receive services from GPs, hospital consultants, community trusts and social services. Patients may receive this care from many different individual professionals – I have heard a stroke team report that one of their patients saw 65 different carers when receiving treatment and rehabilitation. This care is catered for by a range of different contracts covering acute, community and primary care purchasing teams in most health commissions. Past failures to integrate services, due to traditional, fiercely defended separations between groups employed in the past by primary care, local authorities (such as district nurses and health visitors) and hospitals have confronted purchasers with very difficult purchasing decisions. Most have not begun to resolve these and continue to purchase largely on conventional provider lines rather than dealing with specific problems through an integrated approach.

In any attempt to develop new approaches to longstanding problems, health commissions are heavily constrained by their size.

Purchasers' costs have been scrutinized by the Audit Commission and, in 1995 and 1996, this and related issues of managers' pay prompted frequent calls from politicians to move resources from men in grey suits to staff in white coats. But health commissions have purchasing costs of around 1 to 2 per cent of their expenditure for the purchasing of services. Thus a very small tail is trying to wag a very large dog. It is scarcely surprising that the health commissions lack the skilled workforce, in sufficient numbers, to do so.

Any explicit decisions by health commissions to change the services purchased will be subject to tough scrutiny from the losing providers. Given the resources available to purchasers, they cannot match the skills and knowledge of provider specialists in a field as technical as the delivery of modern health. As a result, they cannot always base their decisions on the kind of detailed analysis that providers might demand. An example of the conflict over specialized services can be found in Vanstraelen and Cottrell (1994). These specialists in child and adolescent psychiatry are highly critical of the knowledge of purchasers about their own special area. More generally, it is striking that there is no real tradition in the NHS of turning poachers into gamekeepers by employing surgeons and physicians in planning and purchasing roles. A few have made the switch to management but very few, if any, can be found in purchasing, which remains the domain of public health physicians. Yet it seems highly likely that any commercial body, purchasing goods and services on major contracts, would employ at least some specialists in their production. In the same way, I know a private health specialist who moved from negotiating rates for an insurer to the obverse job for a chain of private hospitals. Gamekeepers probably do make very good poachers!

While it may be unrealistic to expect local purchasers to develop knowledge equivalent to specialists, there must be a wider concern that the available purchasing expertise is spread thinly across over 100 purchasers, each working on a local solution to similar problems within a nationally funded system. In contrast, specialist, centralized committees advise on the introduction of new drugs to the NHS and, although GPs and hospital doctors may then be free to use and misuse them, a single national standard at least determines their introduction. (This issue is taken up in Chapter 6 on the future of the NHS.)

On top of a history of limited resources and skills for planning service development, pressures to reduce management costs and achieve economies of scale in purchasing have also led to many mergers of health authorities into fewer health commissions, over the period

1994–6. This has created a very unstable environment in which to develop a new approach. The old area populations of a million people are now seen as a more appropriate basis for health commissions. (At the same time, local government has shifted to unitary authority status, creating some local councils with much smaller populations who are now responsible for social services.) In addition, the mergers of DHAs with FHSAs created further uncertainty over roles and responsibilities and absorbed substantial management time. Regional health authorities have themselves been cut down, from 14 to eight: yet another change forcing further disruption on health commissions.

These changes have inevitably disrupted the planning and purchasing processes and, in some cases, the careers of those involved in them. For example, I was involved in an audit of purchasing at a newly formed health commission, which was itself, over time, merging with the local FHSA. One of the two partner health authorities had been a site for the Audit Commission's national pilot review of progress on purchasing, about a year earlier. But this was not known by senior management, many of whom were new to the patch. Clearly, there was little continuity of planning for purchasing as those involved struggled to reconcile data from the two different parts of their area, each of which had previously formed parts of other districts, rather than districts in their own right. Furthermore, with limited skills and resources, a continuing climate of reorganization and the leaching out of funds to GP fundholders, health commissions are operating in a market environment which offers substantially less power and flexibility than *Working for Patients* might suggest.

FREEDOM TO PURCHASE – THE REALITIES OF THE MARKET

In implementing their approach to rationing and purchasing, the health commissions have faced a number of difficulties which derive from the market in which they work rather than the complexity of their tasks. These include issues of choice and market power. Indeed, choice is central to the whole justification of a market as superior to a planning bureaucracy. If there is no choice, there is no market.

Compared to HMOs in many parts of the USA which seek preferred provider contracts for hospital services that they do not provide directly for their registered members, health commission purchasers in most of the NHS, certainly outside the big cities, have only a limited choice of local hospital providers. Community services have been established in Trusts with a local geographic monopoly and so there is little competition there, except for new services tendered beyond the local patch, for example long-term care for previously institutionalized patients. The discussion here concentrates on the extent to which health commissions have a choice of hospital services.

Research suggests that many providers face local competition (Appleby *et al.* 1994; Propper 1994) within a distance that could be acceptable, given that people travel to hospital relatively infrequently. However, health commissions face strong public and political pressure to support their main historic providers. Unlike HMOs and any hospitals contracted to them, NHS purchasers and providers are both part of a public service and are bound to each other by public expectations and past mutual dependence. Consequently purchasers may have little real freedom of action in the market. But a continuing dependency on a few major providers has several effects on purchasing. First, individual service contracts and prices may not be particularly meaningful, within the global sum to be provided for contracted services from a single large provider. That is, Trust hospital negotiators are likely to approach contract negotiations with a figure in mind for the total running costs of the hospital. Reductions in volumes or prices in one area, for example where purchasers believe service standards are too low and contracts should be changed, can be offset by price or volume rises in services where purchasers have less flexibility over volumes. For example, Trusts could argue that more detailed analysis of costs shows that emergency services cost more than previously thought and require additional funding. Expansion of emergency activity has the further advantage that it is difficult for local purchasers to decline to fund it or to take the service elsewhere under contract.

Second, purchasers might resist attempts to obtain funding simply from a reworking of the different contract components. But in doing so, they face another problem for a purchaser/provider relationship. Hospital medicine has, over the last 30 years, been seen more and more as dependent on specialists and subspecialists working in comprehensive, integrated facilities with a wide range of services on one site. As noted earlier, a central thrust of hospital policy in the NHS over this period was the creation of well-integrated, comprehensive district general hospitals, effectively as local monopoly providers of hospital care. Smaller hospitals and those on several sites have all been steered, in many cases pushed, towards a single, local, comprehensive hospital.

A third factor has been the increasing control over junior doctor staffing and the allocation of posts to hospitals. These jobs are approved by the regional postgraduate deans and the medical Royal Colleges. Approval can rest on a range of factors including the case-load, the degree of consultant support, the working hours and experience offered at a hospital. If approval is lost, a hospital is unable to recruit career NHS junior doctors and cannot always rely on recruiting from overseas. It is also harder to recruit consultants where a hospital is not approved for junior staff, since it implies shortcomings in standards and staffing.

The combined effects of these aspects of hospital operation are that attempts by health commissions to change contracts can be challenged by providers as a threat not just to one specialty but to the integrated whole. For example, loss of a Trust's gynaecology contract, due to a purchasing decision based on its cost or quality, could affect the viability of maternity services because of its effects on recruitment and retention of senior and junior medical staff. Loss of maternity provision also threatens the viability of closely linked paediatric services, as there are minimum case numbers recommended for junior medical staff training, as well as a current shortage of paediatric consultants. Loss of paediatrics in turn can threaten a comprehensive accident service where this does not treat children, as well as surgical specialties, notably ear, nose and throat surgery, where there are significant numbers of children as inpatients and day cases.

Of course, it is possible that the level of integration demanded in the past is not as important as medical training policy has generally implied. But as long as junior doctors provide the bulk of medical cover and their training is heavily monitored and accredited, it will be difficult for providers and purchasers to move far from the integrated hospital model. Whatever the real strength of inter-specialty links and knock-on effects, the claim that they are crucial is a serious barrier to change, particularly when local media and politicians are mobilized in support of a threatened Trust's contracts. Indeed, I have known a number of cases where the hands of the health commission were effectively tied because they could not reveal the full facts about the shortcomings of their local providers, and the loss of junior doctor posts, without admitting past acceptance of low standards that would put them, as well as the hospital providers, in the wrong. As a result of these limits on the degree of change in a hospital, the purchasers are substantially weaker.

The size of purchasers relative to providers is also, paradoxically, a potential weakness. Purchasing health authorities typically have contracts with a few Trusts that make up a relatively large share of the income of that Trust. Given the background of planning in the NHS, with one DGH serving one district, there was frequently a one-to-one relationship between purchasing health authorities and their local acute hospital. Geographic monopolies for community Trusts presented a similar pattern for community health care. Thus the contract with a single purchaser could often be 80 to 90 per cent or more of the Trust's income for a given service. When health authorities were merged, this dominance of a single contract remained even where the purchaser came to hold three or four such contracts with Trusts across its patch, rather than just one.

At first sight, a large purchaser might appear to have considerable market power. But in practice, a locally dominant health commission faces a difficulty in changing the contract mix or deciding to withdraw a part of the contracted workload from its main providers, because of, for example, high prices or perceived low quality. Providers are typically reluctant to quote prices without a corresponding volume. Thus a shift of some contract income may simply lead to a reallocation of overheads to continuing service areas. If the purchaser withdraws 100 per cent of the contract for a specialty or service, it could destabilize its provider, by preventing it from meeting its financial targets or affecting the viability of other clinical services. Indeed, providers are likely to claim that even limited changes in caseload may threaten the viability of the service. If the purchaser relies on the provider for a wide range of other local services, as most purchasing health authorities rely on hospital and community Trusts, this is politically sensitive and disruptive to services. But if all the contract is not to be withdrawn, what part of it can remain and how is that part to be retained? Splitting emergency and elective care is just as problematic since loss of one or the other may threaten junior doctor staffing, as noted above, particularly when there is also a lack of any incentive, under the internal market, for Trusts to share key clinical staff in senior supervisory or junior roles.

In addition, if a contract is split between local and non-local providers, it is difficult to determine the allocation of local and non-local contract capacity to GPs and their patients. Unless this can be done conveniently around district boundaries, with some patients using a close provider outside the patch, there may be disputes over which GP practices and patients get the more convenient, or higher quality, service. Indeed, this issue highlights the more general problem that when health commissions buy on behalf of local GPs, they do not allocate quotas for referral to the GPs. In consequence, the

GPs may well refer too many or too few patients in any one year, compared to the contract. Certainly, if GPs are not allocated to specific providers, it is hard to see how a contract split between providers can be made to work. And if GPs are allocated to what they see as an inferior or inaccessible provider, they are likely to complain.

Much of the discussion around this issue has potentially misunderstood the source of market power. A number of observers (for example Akehurst and Ferguson 1993) have argued that big purchasers with substantial market power are needed to face up to big providers with similar local monopoly power. Certainly, Glennerster *et al.* (1994) found that GP fundholders appeared to be able to achieve greater change when they collectively had a large share of the budget for local elective services. But this view can miss the point that market power rests ultimately on freedom to contract with another provider, which Ham has termed the 'contestability' of contracts (Ham 1996). As long as there is some choice of provider, the freedom to change may be more easily exercised by smaller purchasers. For example, as long as there are several highly competitive supermarkets available in a neighbourhood, the individual consumer need not fear their market power too much. By moving purchasing between them, individual small-budget consumers can exercise influence over providers, albeit within a framework for nutrition that may be dictated more by the food industry than by consumer preferences. In contrast, economic theory indicates that where one big purchaser meets one big provider, there is no real market but a negotiated solution under what is termed 'bilateral monopoly'.

The most flexibility and, arguably, the most power to make changes in the NHS internal market for health care rests with the individual GP fundholders. They can move all of their contract for a service without destabilizing their provider as much as a big purchasing authority. They can also ensure that their referral decisions fit the contract closely, avoiding difficulties of the kind which occur when non-fundholding GPs resist a shift of contract by a health commission. And loss of a significant fundholder contract is likely to focus a Trust on the service quality and price without pushing it into a public and highly defensive posture. Using the press to embarrass locally respected GPs is very different, and much more difficult, than doing the same to health commission bureaucrats. There has been some systematic assessment of GP fundholders' prescribing and referral, and the available evidence is discussed in Chapter 4. Here it is sufficient to note the greater flexibility of fundholders. This is due not only to the relative size and freedom of movement of GP fundholders but also because of the ease with which fundholders can put over their purchasing decisions to patients. They can do this one by one and in private, compared to the political difficulties faced by a district purchaser making a public move to a new provider. For example, a fundholder can explain to an individual patient that they will get a better service at a more distant provider (without necessarily mentioning any cost differences). Patients are likely to accept this as a part of the normal referral choice made by GPs. In contrast, a DHA must 'sell' its decision to transfer a contract to the public, the press and to politicians, as well as to the local GPs and providers. GPs are then able to explain to patients that they are forced by the health commission contract to send the patient further away, if they do not like the choice of provider, undermining the health commission's decision in the eyes of patients. Shifting the contract can also look, in the wider public domain, like a failure to sort out the local provider.

In the face of fundamental philosophical problems, limited skills and resources and a lack of market freedom, it is perhaps surprising that health commissions have done anything. But in the great British tradition of struggling (or muddling) through, they have done what could be done, leaving the ideal to an undetermined future. In the next section, we examine the 'warts and all' performance of health commissions.

A PRAGMATIC RESPONSE

In needs assessment, purchasers had available data on the number of patients referred as new outpatients and treated as outpatients and inpatients in each specialty. The referrals provide a proxy indicator of the historic level of need as identified by the local GPs, through their referral behaviour. We know that GPs differ widely in their referral practices, with some referring a much larger proportion of patients than others. But the number of patients treated provides an indicator of the local level of treatable disease, albeit modified by the factors influencing referral by GPs and local consultant decisions, such as the ability of hospital and community care to respond. By rolling forward past activity levels into new contracts, purchasers effectively reproduce the pattern of service demanded in the past by GPs. As data collection has become more complete and more detailed, through minimum contract data sets, it is also increasingly possible to examine the variation in rates of specific procedures and ask questions about the justification of purchasing particular mixes of services. But purchasing based on historic activity data can only gradually change away from past practice. Pressure on management numbers and the low levels of resourcing overall for health authority purchasing means that the pace of change will continue to be gradual rather than rapid. Thus with the exception of one or two areas where change has been readily achievable, contracting by health commissions has produced few radical shifts of services.

Exceptions include the increasing use of day surgery, where purchasers have pushed providers to adopt short-stay techniques at a rapid rate, and the use of initiatives to reduce waiting lists (under bureaucratic pressure) through short-term contracts with providers outside the local health commission area. Also, when replacing a long-stay institution, purchasers have been prepared to look around for a variety of providers and models of service, as noted earlier.

Some health commissions have also attempted to develop a pragmatic local approach to priority-setting by laying down explicitly a schedule of priorities and a list of excluded types of care. But they have little if any formal mandate or consensus from their local populations to do so and face the difficult problems of principle, noted earlier. There is also no higher level contract between the NHS and the British public to support exclusion of any treatment, a fundamental weakness in any attempt to ration care. (It is also worth noting that rationing is typically the label attached to attempts to limit the range of care provided and is seen as a problem for the cash-limited public sector. However, in practice, a contract for private health insurance contains a range of limits and exclusions, all of which could be termed rationing devices. That the term rationing is not applied to the private sector may say more about marketing than about principle.)

In health commission purchasing plans, explicit rationing is still only found in a minority of areas, though there is some evidence that it is growing. For example, in their surveys of health commission plans, Redmayne *et al.* (1992, 1993) and Redmayne (1996) have found some evidence of explicit rationing. By the time of the last of these studies, Redmayne found that 26 of 110 purchasing plans for 1996/7 and 23 of 100 surveyed in 1995/6 contained some explicit exclusions of treatment. While these are relatively close and suggest little recent change, the earliest of the surveys found only 11 purchasing plans explicitly excluding a service. This suggests that exclusions are growing. Equally Redmayne does not indicate how much of a health commission's purchasing might be affected by these restrictions.

Typically the list of restrictions includes a wide range of cosmetic procedures in plastic surgery, a number of procedures to reverse previous elective surgery and one or two exclusions due to accumulating evidence of effectiveness. Reversal of elective sterilization is essentially about people changing their minds. There is some legitimacy in a health commission arguing that this should be paid for by the individual, as there is no direct clinical need for reversal.

For those treatments excluded on evidence rather than priority, the most common is the use of dilation and curettage in women under 40. This has been widely used to treat high levels of menstrual bleeding but there is now a considerable body of evidence suggesting that it does not work very well. For one of the most controversial areas, that of infertility treatment, there has been some confusion in the public debate. One reason for not funding this treatment is that it is simply not very effective, with success rates of 20 per cent or less per cycle of treatment (Anon 1992). But there has been a separate moral debate about whether the health service should be trying to remedy a genetic or acquired problem which does not directly affect the individual's health but only their satisfaction with life as a result of not having a family. Without a clear principle of entitlement, indicating that the NHS will or will not fund such treatments, individual health commissions are in a difficult position.

Similarly, a 1994 survey reported in the *British Medical Journal* (Court 1996) shows how variable explicit restrictions have been within the national service. The results suggested that close to one commission in three was explicitly excluding some services from purchasing plans, though no procedure was being restricted by more than 23 of the sample of 129 commissions in England, Wales and Scotland.

Given all the difficulties of purchasing, it is not surprising that health commissions cannot point to substantial health gains for their local populations. But this is scarcely their fault. Although health gain is a much used expression in the current NHS, there is little direct evidence of health gain across the country, linked to specific local health services. This is because so few treatments have been rigorously assessed. Purchasers also lack the data to identify how much of particular treatments they were purchasing in the early days after the Reforms and what the outcomes have been. A further simple, practical problem is that health gain may take years to be identified from (for example) changes in routinely available mortality data. Even successful health interventions may not lower death rates immediately and those that reduce morbidity are typically not monitored with systematic follow-up. The available data on patient activity was more likely to be based on cases per specialty, with some disaggregation to separate inpatients and day cases. Data on outpatients remains very uneven in quality and completeness. It is, therefore, still uncommon to find a detailed assessment of the need for, and supply of, a specific intervention.

It is worth noting that health commissions have been more radical in changing the pattern of service in a few cases, particularly where they had some freedom of manoeuvre and a clear idea of where resources could be found. In long-term mental illness and elderly care, the prospect of closing a major long-stay institution creates much greater flexibility (though not necessarily enough resources to fund all the new services sought by providers). By 1996, at least one health commission had gone further and issued a tender for the management and, ultimately, the provision of its entire mental health services, posing a real market threat to the current local providers. Others had shifted contracts for services such as elderly care which may be a less integral part of the prevailing acute hospital model.

In a few high profile cases, purchasers have also taken a strong and public view about where a service should be provided, based on the available evidence. One Scottish health board, for example, has taken a decision that all its breast surgery would be handled by a small number of specialists, withdrawing contracts from less specialized consultants and centres. This was a radical and controversial decision and one which has, apparently, not been reproduced widely in other parts of the country. However, similar kinds of monitoring and control of complex services are developing, an approach considered in Chapter 6 as a potential feature of a future NHS.

PERFORMANCE TO DATE

Within the various constraints, noted above, purchasers have struggled to implement the NHS Reforms. So what has been achieved? Health commissions' performance has been examined by both the Audit Commission (1993) and the National Audit Office (1995) to check on the value for money provided.

The Audit Commission found that data was a particular difficulty in the immediate period after the Reforms, because of the poor coding of much hospital data. But it also found purchasers relatively unprepared for their new roles, with many of them continuing to operate with traditional DHA department structures, preventing an integrated approach to packages of care, as noted earlier in this chapter. In my own experience, it often appears that public health departments, the main source of clinical and technical advice to purchasing, have been kept too separate from purchasing, a conclusion also drawn by Hunter and Harrison (1993) from their work with purchasers.

The National Audit Office (NAO) found that the decentralization of much of the process of purchasing had led to considerable variation. There was a lack of a consistent pricing methodology and so purchasing decisions could be based on confusing price signals, with patients moved to nominally cheaper providers when in fact the real cost of the initial provider was lower. There was a lack of consistent data of other kinds on which to base purchasing decisions. Lastly, there was a lack of consistent involvement of GPs, with almost 40 per cent of GPs from 360 practices claiming that the local district purchasers did not consult them. This may be too gloomy a picture, however, and the finding is at variance with those of a study by the National Association of Health Authorities and Trusts. This found that 90 per cent of district purchasers were consulting GPs (NAHAT 1992). (The gap between the two figures may also show that the interpretation of 'consultation' depends on which side of the consultation you survey.) There is, however, some evidence from individual local studies, such as Graffey and Williams (1994), of effective GP involvement in purchasing.

In similar vein, the NAO suggests that provider clinicians should be more heavily involved in contract negotiations so that contract proposals are actually clinically realistic. There is clearly a danger that under current arrangements, purchasers and clinicians will put provider managers between a rock and a hard place, each asking for things the other will not concede but never meeting to resolve their differences. Also it is worth noting that the NAO saw purchaser development as the most important element of the Reforms, ahead of the creation of Trusts, and relatively neglected until 1993.

The evidence on the explicit use of market mechanisms, particularly tenders, is limited. However, the *Health Service Journal*, the trade paper of hospital management, regularly contains advertisements for tenders for specific and relatively self-contained services such as long-stay care, for clients who remain a health service responsibility because they need active health care as well as social care. Where tenders have been tried for acute services, they have sometimes been used as a stalking horse to try to force the necessary changes out of the local established provider. But this relies on other providers being prepared to bid in this kind of market, where the prospects of success may be poor, because the health commission agenda is to be seen to contest the contract with the local provider but not bear the political friction of actually moving it. This is rather hard on the supposed competitors and I have met some provider managers who feel they have done this enough (for example submitting several losing bids for neighbouring provider pathology contracts that were ultimately awarded in-house) and now need a reward in the form of a contract for the effort they have put into contesting others' contracts. For the reasons noted earlier, the integration of acute services may mean that this cannot readily be awarded without major damage to the local provider. (The issue of provider integration is considered further in Chapter 5.)

Some critics of the Reforms have argued that the lack of tangible progress to a more market-based model is largely the result of political restraint (for example Caines 1996) rather than the particular characteristics of the NHS Reforms. Caines was Personnel Director of the NHS in the period around the Reforms and argues that the real responsibility for any lack of progress rests with politicians. Based on his experience in a number of government departments, he claims that little radical change can happen within about two years of a future election because of fear of the electoral damage. Hence instead of encouraging competition and market-based purchasing, the government concentrated on market management and stability in the period after the Reforms. Purchasing hardly changed anything in the first year and set a pattern for only slow and managed change afterwards. Similarly, where there were problems of duplication or excess capacity, market mergers and planned solutions have been encouraged, rather than direct reliance on the force of competition in individual specialties. This avoids potentially costly, and politically embarrassing, bidding wars between major public hospitals.

Combined with the effects of changes in DHA funding, operation of a market could have produced change on a dramatic scale. A working senior purchaser manager, James (1994), commenting from within the health service, notes deficits of £80 million in London hospitals in the post-Reform period, sufficient to eliminate one hospital at least or seriously damage the capacity of several, if not offset by transitional payments from RHAs. He is also critical both of the extent to which Trusts were approved without an adequate check on their financial viability and of the further disruption caused by waves of policy such as the Patient's Charter, the review of long-term care, the Health of the Nation targets and the review of services across

London by Tomlinson. Similarly, Hunter and Harrison (1993) note the pressure on managers from interventions by regional health authorities and the NHS Management Executive, which led to the setting of too many priorities and which had a disabling rather than enabling effect. It is worth noting that, after over five years of the Reforms, central direction of the health service is still very visible. Ostensibly free local purchasers and providers received over 120 Executive letters in 1995, telling them what they should and should not do, and listeners to the *Today* programme are much more likely to hear ministers being grilled on the overall performance of the health service than its management executive.

PURCHASING – A PROVISIONAL VERDICT

This section summarizes the current state of purchasing and represents a personal view, based on involvement directly with many purchasers and a review of much else that has been written by and about them. The verdict is that purchasing is currently not very effective. There are several reasons for this, financial and organizational, technical and political.

Moving to a world of contracts should mean that health commissions are better able to achieve their financial objective. As independent purchasers with a cash limit, health commissions are concerned to write contracts that cannot exceed expenditure limits through extra activity by the providers. Overspending in provider units can occur due to an increase in caseload that provider staff are either unable or unwilling to refuse, the introduction of new drugs and materials, increased reliance on agency staff or simply weak cost control. In the past, overspending was more often found in acute hospitals, where technical and organizational pressures are greater than in community services. Overspends of this kind can still occur but potentially, as purchasers, they are no longer the health commissions' problem.

However, in practice, the public contract with the NHS makes it difficult for purchasers to put pressure on Trusts without hitting patients. For example, health commissions may find it difficult to deny funding for major new drugs or allow a major facility to close due to overspending. Purchasers found it particularly difficult to deal with the rapid increase in emergency admissions in the 1990s across many parts of the country, a pressure which providers can claim is outside their control. (The rise in emergencies may be caused by the lack of integrated care, an issue taken up in Chapter 6.) Refusal to meet costs above contracted amounts could allow providers to tell the media that patients are suffering because of purchaser decisions. As a result, purchasers may be forced to rethink their priorities relatively quickly, to avoid a crisis in provision. Purchasers may not escape the organizational chaos of provider Trusts quite as easily as it might appear.

More generally, the rigid cash limit on purchasers raises a major question for a reorganization of the NHS in which money was supposed to follow patients. If additional activity cannot be paid for at the going price, due to the cash limits on the purchasers, is there any merit in using contracts and prices, simulating a market? If purchasers cannot afford to pay for significant extra activity at all providers, they could offer simple incentives to reward extra activity achieved at little or no marginal cost. For example, purchasers could withdraw 3 to 5 per cent from provider budgets and pay it back in bonuses for meeting agreed activity targets (an idea suggested to me a long time ago by Gordon Best). This could generate incentives without engaging in a complex analysis of individual activities and their costs. Such a system would have offered incentives while accepting that the market was a zero sum game in which no provider could gain more than a small amount.

Purchasers also face serious problems due to the breadth of contracts that they manage and their limited skills and resources. Purchasers are, in my view, simply too underresourced to do properly the job they have been given. Most lack detailed health needs data and are largely using past referral decisions by GPs as the basis for future purchasing. As long as local GPs are getting these decisions right, there is no problem; but if they are not, there is little that purchasing is doing about it. Purchasers would require larger purchasing teams, with more specialist skills matching provider skills, if they were to develop their local purchasing plans on a service by service and disease by disease basis. They would also need a good deal of time to develop these plans, without the organizational disruption of mergers and changes in the population they cover. In a national service, it is not clear why each purchaser should be developing these plans separately anyway, rather than within some detailed guidelines of the kind provided by the national curriculum, particularly in the absence of locally accountable health commissions.

Given national guidelines, the work of purchasers would be mainly administrative, letting contracts for the nationally specified rates, as applied to local population characteristics. But this would highlight potential gaps between funding and national entitlements. Current arrangements leave purchasers papering over these gaps with purchasing intentions that have only limited technical justification, one of several technical problems that purchasers face. It is in practice very difficult to predict levels of disease in populations. A major flu epidemic may lead to the use of an unexpectedly high number of hospital beds, preventing elective surgery. GPs may also see patients with a different pattern of disease from that expected or use their own criteria to decide on referral.

At a more macro level, there are technical difficulties in moving contracts because the NHS has spent the last 30 years developing the role of a comprehensive hospital with all routine specialties represented. Health authorities and new health commissions have taken some politically difficult decisions in the past to close hospitals but most of these decisions have consolidated the big local provider monopoly and not threatened the interests of locally influential consultants. They have also been consistent with government policy to consolidate and save money on fixed site costs by closing some sites. In contrast, shifting clinical service contracts in the internal market can be characterized as seriously damaging to the future of a provider and a threat to all local services. In short, local providers often have a technical monopoly that purchasers can do little to counter. And where providers have good reasons for moving contracts, such as poor quality of clinical care in the past, they run the risk of exposing their past acceptance of low standards if they attempt to justify their decisions in the public domain.

The technical arrangements for purchasing and the lack of consistent links with GPs also contribute to the limited impact of purchasing. Where purchasers get the right level for a contract (for instance a rate that would give local disease sufferers the national average rate of treatment at a nationally consistent threshold) the lack of a clear link to GP decisions makes this of limited value. Imagine an education authority fixing the number of nursery school places but not telling parents the exact criteria for admission. Some parents might send all their children under five, whatever their age, leaving others without a place. Or imagine a police authority, specifying in advance the number of each type of crime it wanted investigated in a year. Who is going to tell the burglars their quota? But in the absence of clear quotas and criteria, what is the value of a local contract for 1,000 hip replacements? If the end result is that GPs refer 1,100 by using their own judgements and providers manage to treat these from the resources available, what was the worth of the contract and the effort that went into it?

Purchasing and contracting have also created a rod for purchasers' own backs by specifying the number of patients to be treated in a year. There is an almost inevitable tension in this, because of the lack of clear criteria to determine when a patient should be treated, reinforced by the lack of close monitoring of thresholds for care by purchasers. Faced with a contract for a given number of cases, beginning in April, there is a clear incentive for providers to maintain at least a regular monthly average of admissions linked to the contract. They might also exceed this rate due to anticipated problems in winter, when emergency medical patients can take beds away from elective surgical patients. More simply, there is a natural tendency to try to get ahead of the contract in case demand falls off in some future month. As a result, there may well be, for example, lowering of the threshold for surgery in the early months of the year, so that the quota of cases is treated before the end of the financial year. Emergency medical admission may be affected in a similar way, particularly at times of low seasonal demand when medical beds are not fully used. But paradoxically, an increase in the following year's contracted amount may simply lead to the same response so that the caseload rises, year on year, with a succession of embarrassing problems for the purchasers as ever-increasing contracts are filled early.

Politically, purchasers also face serious problems of legitimacy. Taking a decision to shift services to a more distant provider will inevitably provoke local resistance. Yet these decisions are taken for a national tax-funded public service by a small group of appointed individuals. While there may be doubts about the turnout for local elections to health commissions, there must be even more doubt about the legitimacy of bodies of appointed individuals running public services. MPs and other local politicians, including those in the party responsible for the current system, seem to have no problems about challenging this legitimacy. There are probably only two ways in which a health commission can carry forward difficult decisions. If it has wide support among local clinicians, both provider Trust and GPs, it can expect a smooth ride on major shifts in purchasing. Alternatively, where ministers have shown that they support radical change, of the kind planned in London and some other big cities, health commissions have been able to claim some higher policy justification and force through change. More important, they have been able to override opposition because they know they will win on appeal to ministers. Where these conditions have not been met, for example in the overhaul of acute services in cities such as Birmingham and Bristol, major plans have been thrown out close to the eleventh hour and purchasers made to look feeble in the face of public and professional opinion.

At one level, the local community is entitled to its voice, though professionals have substantial vested interests, whatever their concern for the public at large. But if the public continues to reject the affordable for the desirable, the most likely outcome is more expensive, short-term confusion, rather than planned transition to a new pattern of services on the ground. Without a much clearer national framework and a clearer contract between the people and the health service, this confusion is not likely to be taken away.

In short, the work of health commissions is probably impossible and certainly very difficult. But they have not been given the resources, the stability or the political support to even begin to grapple fully with the job. Many have made strides on the quality of services, particularly, by pressurizing providers to meet waiting list and other targets. But the kind of market power to achieve greater change, foreseen in much of the debate about the Reforms and much feared by providers in 1990, has not materialized.

In Chapter 6, issues for the future organization of health services are discussed further. Potentially, the most important immediate development in purchasing will be the increased emphasis on GP involvement in locally sensitive purchasing. This will be particularly important under a Labour government, if Labour carry out their threat to abolish fundholding. The policy is also interesting, indeed somewhat paradoxical, because the perceived success of fundholding is one of the reasons for the increased emphasis on primary care led purchasing. The current model, under GP fundholding, is examined in detail in the next chapter.

4

GP FUNDHOLDING

INTRODUCTION

Fundholding was introduced by *Working for Patients* as a major step towards its objectives of decentralizing the decision-making process in the NHS. Certainly it has created a system much closer to one in which money follows patients. Each patient from a fundholder is paid for directly under a contract or single invoice with the provider Trust. Fundholding has also proved popular and, by 1996, fundholding status had been taken up by practices covering half the population of England and Wales (Audit Commission 1996). Since the choice has been left to individual practices, this is a more representative test of opinion than the move to Trust status, which simply became the norm for NHS providers, regardless of staff or patient views. Whether it has also improved value for money or services to patients is less clear, as this chapter shows.

The introduction of GP fundholding was the most radical of the Reforms. While the purchaser–provider split largely focused existing bodies on key elements of their work, fundholding decentralized decision-making enormously. It also created a new set of incentives for GPs, who have always prized their independent contractor status and potentially have the flexibility of a small business. In this chapter, we review the main elements of the scheme and analyse the objectives and incentives of fundholders. This is followed by a survey of potential problems and criticisms and a review of the available evidence on the impact of fundholding. There is a great deal of this evidence, reflecting, to a considerable degree, the ease of focusing on the practice as a unit of observation rather than highly heterogeneous provider Trusts. But as we shall see, the evidence still gives us only a limited idea of GP fundholder behaviour and motivation.

FUNDHOLDING – AN OVERVIEW

Working for Patients introduced the idea that some general practitioners might control the budget for their prescribing and for their patients' use of non-emergency hospital services, and also for practice premises, staff and IT. Almost immediately it found favour with many GPs, and so there was rapid pressure to change the limit on practice size from the announced limit of 11,000 patients to 9,000 when the scheme was introduced and, with further reductions in subsequent waves, to 5,000 patients. Smaller practices, with only 3,000 patients, can also link up to run a purchasing fund or individually opt for 'community fundholding' in which they hold the budget for prescribing and for community services, but not for hospital services. This clearly reduces the risks from a small number of high cost patients, which would put a smaller fund at greater risk, by excluding hospital care, with its potentially very high costs for a single patient. It also reduces the burden of purchasing tasks on small practices, while narrowing the range of their discretion.

Even populations of 11,000 are, however, relatively small for planning and funding health services. Hospitalization is a relatively rare event, even for less urgent and more common procedures, and is subject to considerable random variation. To counter this problem, patients costing more than £5,000 per year were excluded and would not be paid for by fundholders beyond this level. (For details of the scheme see Department of Health (1989) and Glennerster *et al.* (1994).) Potentially, an alternative model (using some kind of insurance or risk pooling across practices, to smooth the risks of annual fluctuations and also individual expensive patients) would have dealt with these uncertainties in a more sophisticated way. But given the speed with which fundholding was designed, it is not surprising to find simple administrative mechanisms used.

To pay for prescribing and services, it was intended that GP fundholders would receive a budget based on their registered practice population and its key health characteristics. However, it has proved very difficult to introduce this formula funding and the budget for hospital and community care is typically set on the basis of past use of services. In prescribing, the availability of the PACT data from the Prescription Pricing Authority has allowed detailed modelling of the relationship between a practice's prescribing costs and the characteristics of its population and area. This has led to the use of standardized prescribing units, which combine elements of capitation funding – calculating the number of prescribing units from the population data, with an element of historic funding – to fix a cost per prescribing unit that reflects local levels of spending.

Fundholding has come to be seen as one of the most successful elements of the Reforms, particularly by ministers but also by many of the fundholders themselves. In the absence of detailed evidence of the impact of any of the 1990 Reforms on public health and the costs of care, popularity may be one of the few dimensions on which success can be judged. Popularity with a section of the medical profession (and not widely forthcoming from NHS Trusts) was particularly valuable to the government, so GP fundholding stands out as the element of the Reforms with substantial professional support.

To a substantial degree, fundholding GPs were in the vanguard of the cultural revolution in health services. They were given the power to press for change locally and challenge the old order of a consultant-dominated, and in places complacent and unresponsive, NHS. But the impact of each fundholding practice is relatively small so there has been little concern that individually they will undermine a service or force a hospital to close (though provider Trusts have an incentive to overplay this effect). In a few places, GPs have formed a large multi-fund, or local fundholders have joined together to negotiate through a consortium. Where they act in concert and do threaten existing services, the government can still defend such decisions as no longer the work of distant health service bureaucrats – the men in suits – but of doctors who know their patients and can best judge the quality of service they receive. The successes claimed for fundholding have also led to a wider recognition of the advantages of much greater GP involvement in local purchasing by DHAs. There has also been a shift in policy towards 'primary care led purchasing' or 'a primary care led NHS' in which the need for services of all kinds is based on local primary care led assessments of health needs and service value.

The downside of fundholding is that it is widely seen as having created a two-tier NHS. Cash on the nail gives Trusts a clear incentive to try to respond to GP fundholder demands and try to attract a higher caseload from them. There have been widespread allegations from Trust clinicians that they have been forced to offer fundholders more preferential terms, such as a shorter waiting list for their patients. The hard evidence is less convincing, as we shall see later in this chapter, but this has not prevented fundholding from being labelled as a threat to the equity principles on which the NHS is founded. The Labour Party is opposed to fundholding because of its supposed inequity but they are also committed to developing the primary care led model of purchasing, offering fundholders and non-fundholders considerable local power over purchasing.

THE OBJECTIVES OF FUNDHOLDING

To assess fundholding, we need to compare what it has achieved with the objectives. It is important in this analysis to separate out the objectives of government from those of the fundholders — including some possible objectives which have not been fully or openly stated.

The government's objectives

The government's objectives almost certainly included not only decentralization of decision-making and improved value for money but also increased control on expenditure in the health service, particularly in primary care. Pressure on expenditure from increased demands on health services inevitably embarrasses a government seeking to reduce taxation. Longer waiting lists and emergencies turned away from full hospitals put public pressure on cash-limited hospital budgets. Growth in drug spending on the unlimited FHSA budget is similarly something to be avoided if spending and taxes are to be cut. Before fundholding, the division of planning and referral decisions between DHAs and GPs made such control difficult to achieve. Whatever the plans made by health authority and provider unit managers to change services, demand is predominantly driven by GP referrals, almost completely for non-emergency cases and for many emergencies. As a result, planning could always be frustrated. By linking GP fundholders directly into expenditure control mechanisms, the government was able to tighten its control on total spending. That is, by conceding decision-making power within the budget, it increased the chances of referral decisions compatible with the budget and, by implication, strengthened the overall force of the government's budget, albeit by voluntary means and not coercion. Many of the objections to fundholding, when first announced, were about the ethics of encouraging doctors to stick within a budget, on the grounds that the government was shifting its arbitrary rationing decisions onto doctors who, it was argued, should not accept the resource constraints imposed. Whatever its ethical impact, the advantages for planning and reducing public expenditure are clear.

General practice was also fertile territory for tighter resource constraints because of the greater independence of GPs (dating back to the inception of the NHS) and the wide variation in GP behaviour (Roland *et al*. 1990). GPs are independent contractors working with, but not directly for, the health service. While they earn all or most of their money from the NHS, they have fiercely defended their independent contractor status. As such, they have not been subject to the same formal planning controls as hospital and community services. Tight cash limits in the hospital and community sectors have increased the pressure for managers to reduce the variation in costs between similar services. By comparison, the unconstrained GPs have always varied widely in their prescribing and referral practice.

One demonstration of the importance of GP behaviour is the trend in the mid-1990s to higher levels of emergency admissions, in some but not all parts of the country (NHS Trust Federation 1995). It is likely that a change in GP behaviour, associated with the new GP contract, has been a major factor in the growth in emergency referrals. Certainly, there is no clear evidence of increased disease and mortality on a comparable scale to the growth in emergency referrals in recent years. Patient expectations are also unlikely to have risen rapidly in a short time. In my view, that leaves GP behaviour as an obvious causal factor. Given that GPs had relatively unconstrained access to services before the Reforms, and still have it for emergency services, they were always likely to do what they judged to be best for patients, and possibly for themselves. Since GPs are not trained to a single homogeneous style of practice, and also differ in key personality characteristics such as willingness to resist patient demands on the borderline of technical clinical intervention, we should probably continue to expect wide variation in what GPs do, for as long as the NHS fails to take firmer action to prevent it.

But too much variation is the enemy of efficiency. Economists take the view that increased costs are only acceptable if they bring increased benefits. Some variation is compatible with efficiency, if higher costs produce higher quality, but much variation may be inefficient, with higher costs not producing more or better outcomes. We would get more from our available resources if efficient practice was adopted uniformly and inefficient variation eliminated. Minimizing resources per case, for a given quality standard, is a legitimate goal to make the health service better for patients. Variations in spending committed by GPs do not directly show how much can be released through greater efficiency, because expenditure per patient may be inefficiently low in some cases, with poor quality of care, greater risk of complication or patient dissatisfaction. But it is almost inevitable that in the eyes of critical politicians, lower or lowest cost will be an attractive alternative to the (unknown) efficient cost and quality. Hence the focus on variations in spending as waste, to be cut out wherever possible.

For the government, the attraction of fundholding with a population-based formula was that it could cut out much of the waste from variation in behaviour at a stroke. (To be more precise, it would reduce the rate of growth of expenditure or pressure on services but it could also lead, for example, to purchase of care or drugs of an inefficiently low quality.) Overnight, a large number of GPs would be constrained to common levels of spending on elective hospital and community services and prescribing. This could prevent excessive waiting lists and related problems that were the inevitable result of constraining hospital spending without any matching pressure on GP referral practice. Introduction of a budget for drugs was particularly attractive to government as it would constrain the most rapidly rising area of health spending. The non-cash-limited primary care drugs budget has continued to rise significantly faster than the cash-limited health service during the 1980s, increasing 67 per cent between 1980 and 1993, compared to a rise of only 34 per cent in hospital spending (Office of Health Economics 1995). Indicative and fundholding drugs budgets provide a basis for control. Of course, it was in the government's interests to stress the benefits of local decision-making and a better, more responsive service than to highlight the elements of control in the new regime. In practice, equalization at a stroke, through formula funding, has proved impossible to implement due to the difficulty of fixing the formula. But acceptance of budgets at least means that there are constraints at work, even if they are imperfect constraints.

It follows from this analysis that one objective of fundholding was to impose more standardized expenditure control on primary care as the source of prescribing and hospital and community referrals. The actual budget-setting process, compared to this ideal, highlights a number of the practical problems of introducing fundholding and is discussed later in this chapter.

We should also note, before moving on to the objectives of the fundholders themselves, that fundholding has become only one plank in a wider strategy to shift more services, and more control of service development, to primary care. This policy has continued and increased in emphasis since the Reforms and is now a cornerstone of government thinking on the NHS. While a shift to primary care is seen as offering better local access and more user-friendly services, it probably also reflects concern that hospitals are expensive, high technology machines which, in the USA in particular, have run away with the budget. Primary and community care are seen as potentially cheaper alternatives to be encouraged. For all the rhetoric on the better service offered in a primary care setting, the reality is therefore that cost, as well as service, objectives lie behind the policy. Again, this does not invalidate the policy but makes the debate more difficult as some objectives remain less overt and less open to debate than others.

GPs' objectives

There was no major government initiative to evaluate fundholding following the Reforms. However, a number of initiatives developed, some based on one-off data collection and others using routine data sets such as the PACT data on practice prescribing. In an early major study in England, Glennerster *et al.* (1994) sampled 17 first wave practices and a similar group of second wave entrants. This research is distinct in considering in detail the stated objectives of GPs before fundholding and going some way towards linking objectives and outcomes. Many of the other studies have concentrated on monitoring prescribing and referral data and give us less information on individual practices and their objectives.

The overwhelming verdict in Glennerster and colleagues' study is that GP fundholders were primarily interested in improving their service to patients. This includes improvements in waiting times and the attitudes of hospitals and consultants, protection of referral rights in the face of restrictions due to health commission contracts, and increased scope for local service developments. These GPs were also keen to develop some of their own services. The main focus was on physiotherapy and counselling, services which have typically not been readily accessible in the NHS but are likely to be popular with patients. There was less enthusiasm in the early days for on-site consultant clinics or minor surgery, but the Glennerster *et al.* study shows that these developed in later waves.

My own first-hand experience of a later wave fundholder illustrates the kind of objectives found by Glennerster and colleagues. First, the practice had been deeply worried when their local health commission's contract for orthopaedic surgery was completed early in the previous financial year, effectively meaning that no new referrals would be treated for several months. In the absence of a clear quota system, allocating the contract volume across practices, they were at risk of having patients who, because of the time of year they presented, could be denied treatment for an unacceptably long time. (Equally, the speed of completion of the health commission's contract could mean that patients on the waiting list at the start of the financial year would be treated much more quickly than in the past – a benefit often overlooked.) This particular practice also valued the chance to use a local community hospital for some of their less complex clinic referrals, and the GPs were concerned that financial constraints on the health commission would lead to this service being taken away. Inevitably, the services at the community hospital were less sophisticated than those at the major hospitals and included some, like physiotherapy, that could easily be transferred to primary care. In consequence, these services were always likely to be of more interest to the prospective fundholders because they offered some real flexibility, compared to the referral of major cases to the main local DGH.

Glennerster *et al.* found that in addition to the concerns noted above, some simple freedoms, such as the power to use the staffing element of the budget as they wished, were highly valued by GPs. GPs had often been in dispute with FHSAs in the past, for example over the interpretation of the rules for the subsidy to approved staff joining the practice team. Here was a chance for fundholders to escape such bureaucratic tangles, albeit at the cost of shouldering the administrative burden of fundholding.

The Glennerster *et al.* study also highlights the attractions of obtaining additional funding for information technology as a 'golden hello' – a financial welcome or gift in kind such as a new practice computer system – to those entering fundholding. Fundholding also offered GPs a chance to do something novel in what can be a repetitive professional life in general practice. Some critics of the scheme have described it as a potentially expensive way of increasing the job satisfaction of mid-career GPs, 'an answer to the mid-life crisis, perhaps, but is this a firm enough basis for a major change in health policy?' (Coulter 1995a: 120). This may be a rather harsh verdict when so many of the practices taking on fundholding appeared to be dynamic and successful, rather than depressed and drifting through a mid-life crisis. The two fundholding practices I know best were both clearly 'going places' before fundholding arrived, with new premises and well-motivated GPs.

On the face of it, fundholding offered GPs the chance to release some health service funds to invest in premises they owned and, in the initial period after its inception, the chance to make money from minor surgery. But in spite of the potential personal financial gains on offer from these two uses of expenditure, there is relatively little discussion of money for the practices themselves in the research studies. One of Glennerster and colleagues' respondents talks of the sharks who will get the scheme a bad name but there is no admission of gain as a motive, perhaps because it was not so for most GPs. There were also some inevitable difficulties for GPs in pursuing the objective of financial gain for the practice through fundholding, particularly before the budget-setting process was clear, since it could have been a lot of work for no money at the end of the financial year. But there are also ethical problems with admitting that financial gain was an end in itself, so we should perhaps not be entirely surprised that it receives so little mention. It should also be noted that since fundholders were volunteers, they had some scope to negotiate a budget that would give them as much flexibility, and scope for saving, as possible. They may also have benefited from the levels of funding in the early years, given the pressure for the NHS to show that fundholding was a success by signing up a large number of GPs.

INCENTIVES FOR FUNDHOLDERS

Fundholding created clear incentives for GPs to manage their use of hospital and community services and prescribed drugs in ways that had previously offered no benefit to them. GP fundholders can now substitute lower cost care, or more accessible or higher quality care at the same cost, for a currently used service. Fundholders have clear incentives to purchase care from within their budgets, using lower cost providers or reducing referral and treatment rates where they can, so as to leave a residual surplus which can be used to develop other services. Although fundholders cannot keep the savings directly they can invest in practice premises, potentially enhancing an asset which they own. They also have an incentive to develop new services as a way of increasing patient satisfaction and patient health if these offer other benefits, such as a lower demand for GP time or hospital referral. New services could also have an impact on the growth of the practice, though there is still no real advertising or market culture in general practice.

It is important to note here that fundholding could be providing incentives that work against the interests of patients. Using more distant but cheaper providers than the traditional local hospital imposes travel and time costs on patients but not on GPs. Use of a possibly lower quality provider at lower cost is now worth considering. There are limits to a GP's ability to assess quality of care: what the GP sees may appear to be as good a quality of care, and also lower on cost, when in fact the quality of care is worse for the patient. To judge service quality, GPs must largely rely on the comments and post-discharge health state of their patients. This may provide only a limited perspective on the service quality of the treatment and the long run clinical outcome. Equally, since fundholders have no experience of a provider to which they have not previously referred, they may lack the confidence to send patients there, whatever the actual quality of care on offer.

CHOICES FOR FUNDHOLDERS

From an economist's view, the importance of these incentives is that they stimulated some thought about what to do and how to treat. Economists particularly oppose the idea that there is only one way of responding to a problem, unless the alternatives have been systematically assessed. Consideration of both costs and benefits is essential to achieving efficiency. Choices may coalesce on a single preferred solution but this should be tested, from time to time, by offering choices at different costs. Thus the main interest for economists lies in the strength of incentives to stimulate changes (or potential changes) in behaviour, as well as the costs and benefits of such behaviour. The substitution of practice-based care for hospital care and of one drug for another are key areas of behaviour where the overall efficiency of the system may be capable of being increased – that is, where additional benefits can be achieved from within the given budget.

For community services, fundholders were restrained from radical freedom of action by the creation of local monopolies of community services. While a few have found distant community Trusts to employ (nominally) their attached staff, most have accepted the local monopoly provider of community health services. Nonetheless, fundholders have negotiated service changes (Audit Commission 1996), for example changes in the skill mix of the nurses attached to their practice, in spite of having to negotiate with a local monopoly. This may say something about the effective power of different professionals rather than the market environment itself.

Therapy services, notably physiotherapy and counselling, have been a popular choice for fundholders seeking to improve their practice-based care. Such services are relatively easy to relocate, perhaps

with some change in equipment or technique, but give the fundholders much more secure access for their patients than a hospital-based
service with a waiting list. So for this type of care, GP fundholders
face a meaningful choice based on a set of prices or costs and a decision about which services to use.

Turning to hospital services, fundholders face potentially different
choices for different elements of the service. For outpatient services
such as diagnosis and treatment, the incentives and scope for change
may be more limited or less satisfactory. An outpatient referral for an
assessment and diagnosis takes place when a GP feels the need for
more specialized skills, beyond those available in the practice. Where
the referral is for a diagnostic test, it may be easy for fundholders to
find a lower cost alternative provider, for example using a private sector laboratory for pathology or taking on some testing in their practices. But for X-ray and more sophisticated imaging, any choice of
another provider will probably require patients to travel further. This
may not be particularly burdensome for many patients with access to
a car and who make an outpatient journey relatively rarely. But a
longer trip imposes some costs on patients, which GP fundholders do
not have to meet – an example of how the costs and benefits to fundholders and patients do not coincide.

Fundholding creates an incentive to reduce referrals for diagnostic
tests and specialist assessment, where possible, and to increase local
practice management of patients. This may be appropriate, at least
where referrals were made to get patients with unresolved problems
off the GPs' hands – a criticism sometimes made by hospital consultants – or to refine a provisional diagnosis. But where a specialist
assessment was indeed required, it can only be provided by someone
with the necessary technical skills. As an alternative to a hospital
referral, this can be done within the practice by bringing consultants
to patients or extending GPs' roles into the skilled areas of consultants. Practices may wish to spend the savings from fundholding to
allow this, for example sending a practice partner on a course in der-
matology or using local consultant-led clinics to train GPs further.
There are also local initiatives around the NHS to improve specialist
skills among GPs and provide GP-led local clinics, such as in cardio-
logy. But these kinds of developments are not widespread and so it
may not be appropriate for fundholders to increase their threshold for
referral to hospital. There is simply a lack of a substitute for a specialist opinion in many cases, though a choice of specialist is possible.

Once a referral is made, there are several outcomes, some of which
again introduce scope for action by fundholders. Return to the GP,

with a specialist opinion and management plan, imposes no further hospital costs but may affect the costs of prescribing. If GPs feel obliged to follow hospital prescribing regimes, then an element of their chronic disease prescribing may be out of their hands. If a repeat visit to outpatients is requested, fundholders may have more scope for action. Repeat visits to outpatients are often the result of poor patient management and a lack of willingness of a hospital centre to let go of its patients. A big outpatient clinic in which junior staff see patients for a few minutes is no real basis for effective disease management. By requiring a consultant review of a case, fundholders may be able to reduce the future use of outpatients with little impact on the quality of care, assuming that they are provided with appropriate guidelines for management and re-referral. In short, preventing some repeat visits could be a relatively uncontentious source of savings for the fund, and fundholders have an incentive to pursue them. Consultants may also be glad to see relatively ineffective repeat visits reduced but their employing Trusts have an incentive to keep such visits going if they help to meet a contract and incur low costs per visit.

An outpatient assessment may lead to further costs for the fundholders. A surgical referral may lead to a decision to operate, over which the GP has only limited control. Indeed, where a problem needing surgery is suspected, there is no real scope for the GP to manage the case effectively without a surgical consultant opinion. (Of course, this excludes potential changes in referral due to a reduction in unnecessary and inappropriate referrals *per se*. Evidence on the variation in referral by GPs suggests that these may constitute a significant number and could be reduced by measures such as a practice-wide protocol for consistent referral behaviour.) Continuing to manage patients with a problem that is remediable by surgery, without a specialist surgical opinion, may be a form of care that is unsatisfactory, or possibly unsafe.

Thus while there may be an incentive to shift referrals away from hospital, the practical scope for doing so may be limited. It is interesting to note that attempts in the past to shift minor surgery back to primary care have not been successful, because of the limited ability of GPs to take on significant surgery. For example, Lowy *et al.* (1993) did not find a significant impact on hospital referrals for surgery following the introduction of payments to GPs for undertaking minor surgery in their practices. The effect of paying GPs to do surgery is to lower the threshold at which surgery is done, with GPs doing relatively minor operations that would not normally be referred to hospital, rather than to change the management of more serious cases. In the early days of fundholding a money-making scheme developed around minor surgery. Fundholders were prevented from doing surgery for their own patients and retaining a fee, and so some set up separate companies to carry out their own (or other fundholders') minor surgery, swapping patients between their practices. This gave fundholders direct income from funds and was soon outlawed by the NHS Executive.

It is also worth noting that once a patient is assessed as needing surgery, the subsequent treatment is largely out of the control of GPs. There is no real culture in the UK of inter-consultant transfers of patients between outpatient assessment and surgery (though surgery may be carried out by junior staff following a consultant assessment). Patient transfers occur under waiting list initiatives, but often with another assessment of the patient by the surgeon taking over the case. Thus it is not all that easy for GPs to buy convenient local outpatient opinions for their patients and then look for cheaper surgery elsewhere, unless they are close to a number of competing providers who are happy to offer the outpatient service as a sprat to catch a mackerel. Where the local Trust hospital has more of a monopoly, its surgeons might even refuse to accept contracts which excluded the larger sums for inpatient care. It is also not clear that fundholders have been able to run their own waiting lists (Audit Commission 1996), so once a patient is assessed as needing surgery, the amount of expenditure on their inpatient care (and also its timing) may be out of the fundholders' hands.

The greater difficulty posed by this restriction on patient transfers occurs when GPs attempt to shop around for the best buy from hospitals. An outpatient referral might lead to surgery as an inpatient. The costs of referring to a particular hospital are therefore both inpatient and outpatient costs. This could make it worthwhile to refer to a higher cost outpatient provider if the expected savings from lower cost inpatient or day case care are sufficient to justify it. Alternatively, fundholders might negotiate a package price that includes a specified price for a given mix of outpatient assessment and follow-up, day case and inpatient treatment. This may be seen as a complicated view of the approach that fundholders are likely to adopt. More important, it shows the degree of detail which fundholders would need in order to make the most efficient financial choices for their practice. The difficulty of doing so may be what is limiting the rate of change of referrals.

However, fundholders might well use their freedom to refer elsewhere to negotiate beneficial changes, particularly in the rate of day surgery carried out on patients and the length of patient stay. In some specialties, notably ophthalmology, there has been a strong trend to minimum use of hospital beds, since a patient after eye surgery can be looked after at home, given satisfactory pain control, if they can see with the other eye. But in spite of this, some hospital providers have continued to keep patients in hospital for several days, at a cost to the NHS and potentially against some patient preferences. Fundholders can influence this by asking for a higher rate of day surgery and a lower cost per case. Similarly, the pace of introduction of keyhole surgery has been very variable across the NHS. While fundholders would risk lowering the quality of care if they encouraged untrained surgeons to take up their scopes for operating, they should again be able to use their market power to increase the rate of uptake of these methods safely, where they are shown to increase patient satisfaction and reduce the side effects of surgical pain and recovery time.

Fundholding also provides incentives to give cheaper drugs, irrespective of any side effects on patients or simple patient preference. Here GPs are well placed to monitor the effects because the patient is likely to return to them with any significant problems. By comparison with hospital referrals for specialist opinions and subsequent surgery, the scope for substitution in drug provision looks much greater. There is a bewildering array of drugs available in the NHS and many practices have only recently come to grips with the choice through the introduction of practice formularies. These can vary from simple lists to a guided approach to prescribing. Drugs also have a limited patent life, after which they can be copied by generic manufacturers and sold at prices which undercut the branded product. There is therefore a clear option to shift to a generic version, with only limited possible effects on patients due to the quality of production or the packaging of the therapeutic element within the product. Different drug regimes may also offer different benefits, for example a more expensive cure compared to long-term maintenance therapy. Finally, there is the simple substitution of a cheaper but inferior product.

The use of drugs in the NHS is to a degree affected by the confusion of government policy towards drug costs and towards the pharmaceutical industry as a major employer and exporter. For example, if the government believes that generic drugs should be widely used when a drug is out of patent life, it need only dictate this policy to pharmacists to have it carried out. Instead, fundholding and the indicative drugs budget scheme have introduced complicated means to the same end. Similarly, the Department of Health was carrying out trials, in the mid-1990s, of a system known as PRODIGY which steers GPs towards a final prescription, using a computer. The choice can clearly be steered in particular directions, towards one brand or another, so what need then for budgetary incentives?

Since drug spending was not constrained before the NHS Reforms, it was always likely to be the area of greatest change. There was certainly no reason why a practice would want to spend more on drugs *per se* after fundholding since it could prescribe all it chose without cost before the Reforms. (But there may be scope for using drugs as an alternative to hospital referral in a few cases.) In contrast, hospital services were constrained by the cash limit and, in services such as physiotherapy, could well be rationed well below the level GPs would prefer. Thus increased use of these services was always more likely. Indeed, it is possible that for some patients, maintenance on drugs is a response to the lack of immediate surgery to resolve their problem. Without a unified budget for drugs and hospital services, a patient may incur an inefficiently large drugs bill while waiting for surgery. In these circumstances referrals may increase, at the expense of the drugs budget, when fundholding is adopted by a practice.

An increase in referrals is one possible outcome in one of the few sophisticated models of fundholding, developed by Lerner and Claxton (1994). As we shall see in the discussion of the evidence on fundholding, the lack of a clear economic model for what is a clear economic initiative means that data from fundholding practices has not been used effectively to test behavioural hypotheses to any great extent.

TOTAL FUNDHOLDING

Perhaps the most important, and possibly surprising, area where services could shift from existing providers is emergency medicine, a service not covered by conventional fundholding but included in about 60 total fundholding projects subsequent to the Reforms. We do not yet know how these pioneer practices are working, as most started in 1996, but there was a clear indication in the material on their establishment that a policy goal for total fundholding was to shift emergency care away from hospital. On the face of it, this seems unlikely, since hospitals are typically seen as the place for emergency and urgent care. But by no means all hospital care is of this kind. Many emergency admissions to hospital are for chronic problems which deteriorate, or for conditions such as stroke which have a dramatic impact on patient health but do not necessarily have life-threatening implications once the initial episode is over. Domiciliary teams involving GPs and others could potentially treat some of these emergency cases or maintain others to prevent deterioration, if they had the resources to do so, though the evidence on home care as a direct substitute for hospital is limited. (For example, many hospital-at-home patients are terminally ill and so the main outcome is a higher quality of life rather than improved long-term health status.) Until total fundholding was introduced, an emergency admission was the easiest and fastest way for a GP to mobilize resources for a patient, but it may not always be the most appropriate or the most cost-effective way. Once the evidence emerges from total fundholding we will have a clearer idea of how far substitution of this kind has taken place.

INCENTIVES TO 'CREAM SKIM'

'Cream skimming' is an expression widely used in health economics in the USA to denote a particular way of selecting patients for insurance or similar schemes. It involves selecting out high risk patients and denying them entry to the scheme, except perhaps at specific and relatively high premiums. The low risk patients, the cream, are skimmed off, leaving high and unpredictable risks to some other agency. In fundholding, the most expensive hospital patients are those who have substantial inpatient care or expensive drugs and outpatient care for chronic disease management. Fundholders have a clear incentive to try to avoid taking on, and to take off from their practice lists, high cost individual patients or members of identifiable high cost disease groups. Patients costing over £5,000 a year, the cut-off at the start of the scheme, no longer impose costs on their fundholding practice. But when funding is of the order of £40 per practice patient for inpatient services covered by the fund, it does not take many high cost patients to dent the budget substantially. Cream skimming may be less of an issue as long as fundholders are funded wholly or largely on the basis of historic spending. This protects them from the costs of existing high cost patients on their list and limits risk to patients developing new diseases. However, it may change the willingness of fundholders to accept transferring patients with high cost diseases.

Glennerster *et al.* (1994) have shed some interesting light on this, though their findings are not conclusive. After looking at a specific practice in great detail, with a sample of over 1,500 patients, they found that only 69 patients accounted for all the expenditure on inpatient services. They argue that factors such as regression towards the mean and the natural variation in illness in individuals are likely to lead the expenditure on high cost patients in one year to fall to lower levels in subsequent years. Indeed, in the course of some quite sophisticated analysis, Glennerster *et al.* appear to overlook a fairly simple aspect of fundholding and patients' use of services over time – the fact that fundholding for inpatients covers predominantly surgical procedures. Once patients have had their operation, they are not likely to need it again, except for occasional complications, many of which would probably be resolved within a short period of time. It follows that for most surgical inpatients, cream skimming is always likely to be less of a problem. However, for some patients, such as diabetics with problems of circulation requiring amputation or patients with arthritis in both hips, surgery may take place more than once within a few years, at a high cost.

Whatever its importance in surgical inpatient treatment, we should bear cream skimming in mind as a possible type of behaviour for fundholders in the management of chronic diseases which require expensive medication (or hospital medicine, in the case of total fundholding) and in some cases, repeated outpatient visits. As Glennerster *et al.* show, there is a clear incentive to discriminate against groups such as diabetics, the highest cost disease group in their study, or to seek higher funding for them in any formula allocation. Although individually they do not have very high costs – £150 per year for hospital services compared to a practice average of over £55 per year for all patients receiving treatment of any kind – grossing this difference of almost £100 per year up to the practice as a whole suggested that the practice could save at least £30,000 a year by excluding diabetics. This saving is even larger if diabetics are compared with those with no significant illness, though some of these could develop diabetes later, of course. However, whatever the potential financial effects of cream skimming, it is relatively rare and controversial for GPs to suspend patients from their lists, not least because those patients have to find another practice for registration. A GP in the NHS would be likely to face considerable criticism from bodies such as patient interest groups if it became clear that sufferers from chronic disease were facing discrimination. By comparison, other health systems based on insurance probably raise individual premiums routinely as a way of reducing their future liabilities for high cost patients, but the ethics and universalism of the NHS make this far more difficult.

To summarize, in assessing the impact of the incentives created, we need to be clear on the areas where fundholders have a meaningful choice and those where they do not. The more limited the choice, the less we are likely to observe it, regardless of the strength of fundholding. But where a choice exists, we would expect fundholders to take their savings where they can, producing the effects expected from the incentives.

SOME PRACTICAL LIMITATIONS

Because fundholding is new and interesting, it is easy to get carried away with projections of the many things it might achieve. However, there are a number of practical limitations on fundholding which can weaken the incentives above. These include the budget-setting process, the handling of savings and the nature of general practice as a business.

Setting the budget

The budget-setting process has received a good deal of attention from researchers because it is central to the whole operation of the scheme. When fundholding was first announced, the intention was that fundholding would work within capitation-based budgets derived from practice populations. Here, at a stroke, consistency of spending in general practice would be largely achieved. However, as subsequent budgets showed, this would have forced a considerable degree of restraint on some practices, who would have been unlikely to accept it. Government faced a trade-off between growing the scheme and insisting on financial restraints through capitation funding. They settled for funding based largely on past activity and prescribing but with plans to shift towards various benchmarks over time. This could be important in creating a honeymoon period for any high prescribing and high referring fundholders, before financial restraints hit them. One possible outcome is that they reduce their high spending by identifying obvious savings. Another is that they do not become involved in overspending or difficult budget negotiations. To date, the available evidence does not shed much light on this issue.

More generally, the fact that fundholders are volunteers whom the Tory government was keen to keep on board meant that there was always a tendency for budgets to be higher rather than lower. Fundholders could simply walk away from the scheme if the budget was seen as too tight. In other words, the voluntary nature of the scheme probably builds in some excess funding.

Annual budget setting is also difficult because of the likely annual variation in the incidence of illness in relatively small populations. To help think about this, think first of a single family. They may go many years without any significant health service treatments but from time to time one of the family may have a major treatment, costing many times the spending in the years without serious illness. Expenditure on this family by the NHS will thus be very small most of the time but with occasional large peaks. Moving up to the scale of a street or a neighbourhood, we would expect to find one or two people having a major treatment each year and several people with long-term illness, so that there is less year-on-year variation. To test the impact of this annual variation on fundholding, Crump *et al.* (1991) simulated the effects of annual variations in GP referrals on the local health authority population and on practices of a given size. They projected costs and identified the costs of referrals for a large number of hypothetical years. This gave them a large number of estimates of total cost. For the population as a whole, the variations in referrals between practices tended to even themselves out. For a DHA, 90 per cent of the projected randomly occurring total costs per year were within less than 6 per cent of the mean cost, showing considerable stability of demands across a large population. For an individual practice, with a list size of 9,000 patients, this range increased to over 27 per cent and the variation only fell to 15 per cent when list size was increased to 24,000 patients. That is, by chance, the patterns of ill-health and treatment costs of a single practice could vary substantially from one year to another. We should therefore expect to find substantial variations in GP referral patterns, whatever the incentive effects of fundholding itself.

On top of the impact of annual variation was the problem of poor data quality. Hospitals were hard put to provide even recent data on fundholder activity. Budgets were consequently based on negotiations around practice and hospital data on how many referrals had been made in the period immediately before fundholding started, with no sophisticated adjustments for the changing annual demands of illness in the practice population. Dixon (1994) reports that fundholder estimates of referral and treatment activity could be as much as 30 per cent higher than the hospital estimates for the same period, because of weaknesses in data capture in hospitals. But this could be the result of the voluntary nature of fundholding. As noted earlier, since fundholders were volunteers, those offered too low a budget would not join. This in turn means that health commissions have an incentive to create that 'golden hello'.

Basing budgets on past referral volumes and spending on drugs avoids penalizing fundholders who are high spenders as a result of high levels of local need. But it also has the effect of rewarding, through possible savings, the new fundholding practices who were less efficient in the past. Furthermore, the linking of activity and local prices can reduce the force of the budgetary incentives to change behaviour, because we have an administrative system rather than a market. In many areas, Trusts do not charge the same prices to GP fundholders and health commission purchasers. When Trusts raise their prices to fundholders, fundholders who receive a budget based on last year's activity and this year's prices will gain income. If the fundholders keep their contracts with the Trusts, the Trusts gain additional income effortlessly. They gain this income out of the budget of the health commission, which has to support referrals by non-fund-holders (see Dixon 1994). Equally, if fundholders shift referrals away from the higher priced Trusts, they save on the price rise, even though they have been funded to meet it – an unfair outcome in the view of some critics of fundholding. These are the potential effects of trying to be fair to fundholders when the total spend available to the NHS, per head of population, is relatively arbitrary. If fundholders were funded under a population-based formula, these difficulties would be avoided. But they would be replaced by a clear demonstration to GPs of the arbitrariness of health care funding, which could have undermined the fundholding scheme rapidly. Dixon *et al.* (1994) quote a number of formulae developed as alternatives to simple budgets based on utilization and prices. These predict budgets for fundholders that are between 6 per cent and 12 per cent below the average funding that they received.

The lack of good pricing data, and indeed of a clear definition of the cost of a single procedure, both raise problems for fundholding and the achievement of greater efficiency in the NHS. Dixon (1994) found for a single procedure that prices could vary by over 400 per cent! That is, one procedure may cost up to five times more at one hospital than another. In addition, some hospitals are much less sophisticated in their pricing than others. This could give fund-holders the chance to buy their expensive operations from a provider charging an average cost that did not reflect complexity. They could then buy their less complex surgery from providers who offer a specific lower price for such procedures. (Like many other possible effects of fundholding noted earlier, this is based on some sophisticated analysis which fundholders may not have the time to carry out in practice. The available evidence, considered later, suggests that fundholders have not introduced as much change as might have been predicted.)

Formula funding

The Department of Health has attempted to move further to consistency in budget setting by introducing a formula of some kind, as originally envisaged. However, to avoid the kind of confrontation that this might produce with the group who have been most supportive of the Reforms, the formula approach has been developed only slowly. The Department of Health initially introduced elements of a budget as 'benchmarks' against which regions could assess their own current funding for fundholders. The development of guidelines has also been limited by the lack of good data on outpatient activity, though this problem is disappearing over time. Thus the first guidelines, introduced in a Department of Health Executive letter (EL(92)83), concentrated on inpatient care. In the absence of a clear link between hospital use for fundholding procedures and local factors other than age and sex, it proposed using an age-sex weighting of practice populations, together with estimated national prices of procedures, to determine the fund for hospital inpatient treatment. Given the concerns with price data, however, the use of local prices for setting funds was considered, with the national price estimates serving as a 'reasonableness test' for local prices.

In developing prescribing budgets, the Department of Health made use of standardized prescribing units, which reflect a wider range of population data. But again, to protect fundholders from large changes in their budgets and to temper the effects of a formula, regional expenditure was to be used as a base for actual budgets. Thus on all fronts the move to capitation funding is proceeding slowly and cautiously, to avoid undue pressure on individual practice funds that could cause political friction or embarrassing resignations from fundholding.

It is also worth considering the possible effects of measures to reduce the impact of random fluctuations in disease on a formula-based budget. A formula, as noted earlier, could leave fundholders short of money in years of above average illness and gaining windfall profits in years of lower than projected demand. This problem could be smoothed out if fundholders entered longer-term contracts with local providers, based on the average level of demand, with some range above and below for random changes. Every year, some adjustments might be made and payments exchanged where the random changes were well outside the expected range or consistently led to demand above the projected norm, using a moving average. This would avoid any incentive to increase referrals all the time. However, if the contracts did become longer, then the scope for recontracting would be reduced. A fundholder could hardly expect to renege on a contract after a couple of high demand years, for example, without some compensation to providers. But this would begin to undermine the very flexibility on which fundholding is based. An intermediate solution would be to insure against an agreed range of high cost but rare procedures, where the gains from insurance would be greatest. Alternatively, fundholders could pool resources with other practices to cover particular high cost groups of patients, which would also reduce any incentive to cream skim. But if we keep on widening the group which shares the risk, we could end up with a population-based cost-sharing system in which the individual GP can refer without any concern for the cost of care – in short, the NHS without fundholding. It follows that the core of fundholding is at variance with any widespread cost-sharing approach. If fundholding is to work, GP fundholders have to bear the cost of care on their budgets.

Inequality in funding

Before moving on from the budget-setting process, one last issue should be noted. The devolution of responsibility for fundholding, to 100 different health commissions, has inevitably introduced substantial variation in the methods used. This again raises questions about the justification for local variation within a national health service. Dixon *et al.* (1994) calculated the budgets for fundholders and the implicit budgets with which health commissions buy services for non-fundholders. After adjusting for differences between average costs per case effectively paid by health commissions and prices offered to fundholders, they conclude that non-fundholders appear to have resources equivalent to as little as 59 per cent of those of fundholders for inpatient and day case care and 36 per cent of the resources of fundholders for outpatient care. While these are the worst cases, and depend on some potentially unreliable data, even the best often did not reach the same level as fundholders' resources. The National Audit Office (1994) in its study of fundholding found wide variations in funding per head of population in fundholding practices, within and between regions. For example, in two regions in 1992–3, the NAO found budgets per head of practice population of between £90 and £145 to £160. Similarly, the Audit Commission (1996) showed that savings varied between regions, with some RHAs clearly steering health commissions to much higher levels of funding than others in their regional formulae. But there is still no sign of a tight formula for fundholders and we are left with the feeling that, for all the concern with inequality of funding, no one is prepared to take on the fundholders at a time when fundholding is one of the elements of the Reforms which has significant support and the volunteers within it must be kept happy.

Aside from the budgets themselves, fundholding has been criticized as introducing a two-tier service because Trusts are likely to respond faster to a fundholder with cash to pay for an extra patient. We will examine the evidence for this later. But it should be noted here that, under local rules for budget setting, it is less a two-tier service than a multi-tier service, with considerable scope for inequality. As a result of years of neglecting the wide variation in the spending incurred or effectively committed by general practitioners, the variation is too wide to be readily pulled back to a standard. Even if we had a clear idea of what the standard should be, past spending will always be used as an alternative indicator of local needs in any challenge to a formula approach.

Managing the savings

The handling of any savings on the budget can obviously affect the incentives and observed behaviour of fundholders. GP fundholders making substantial savings cannot continue to expect a budget in excess of expenditure for ever. Detailed guidance from one region notes that some underspending may be retained where it is due to lower than expected rates of activity. Retention protects the fundholders against the possibility that a random reduction in rates of intervention may be followed by a random increase in local disease incidence and required activity. However, the guidance in question also notes that if lower than expected activity persists for two years, the budget will be reviewed, suggesting a limited grasp of natural variation, perhaps, but a pragmatic view of health service funding.

Nationally, fundholders are allowed to carry forward any amount of savings for up to four years. Spending on new staff is allowed, but only to the extent covered by savings, not beyond. Savings can be spent on conventional hospital and community services not covered by the budget – the essence of fundholding – and also on equipment or material for patient care or health education. Lastly, savings can be spent on improving the premises.

In practice, it is likely that large savings will attract criticism from health commissions and lead to a budget review. In the absence of a clear national formula for deciding the allocation to each fund, based on the population it serves, the budget is necessarily linked to past activity and its costs. Repeated large savings may indicate that the past level of activity is a poor predictor of future activity, for whatever reason, and funding agencies have an obvious incentive to review such budgets and claw back any excess for reallocation. As a result, fundholders have an incentive to pace their savings and limit the amount of savings in any one year. For example, a practice which believes it is able to cut its expenditure on drugs by £100,000 may risk criticism and/or clawback of some of the savings if it achieved such a reduction in a single year. By spreading the savings over several years, the practice is more likely to be able to retain and redeploy the savings made. Thus fundholding practices have an incentive both to moderate the savings made in any one year and to attempt to spread them over several years. Coupled with pressure to maintain a steady state in the early years of fundholding, this means that we should not expect to see too many dramatic changes in a short period as a result of fundholding.

THE IMPACT OF FUNDHOLDING

The impact of fundholding on prescribing and on referral to hospital has been studied by a number of research groups and by the Audit Commission. The evidence, reviewed below, covers the changes in the key budget items which fundholders purchase. However, it typically lacks a detailed assessment of the economic pressures on fundholding. That is, it provides evidence of the change in volumes without evidence of the changes in budgets and prices. As a result, it fails to indicate how far the economic incentives that could be created by fundholding have, in practice, been created, thereby generating a predictable response from GPs.

More fundamentally, although some elements of the research are based on a relatively clear economic model, many are not. Indeed, some researchers have rejected an economic model as inadequate. Coulter (1995b: 235) comments that 'economic theories often do not fit the real world of clinical practice, since the vagaries of doctors' and patients' behaviour cannot be explained by reference to anything as straightforward as profit maximisation or supplier-induced demand.' This hardly does justice to the sophistication of modern health economics but, that aside, it leaves researchers in a difficult position. Fundholding is unambiguously an economic experiment. If we do not have a theory of how fundholders might behave, we have only data on what happened. Without a testable theory of why it happened, we may be left with a 'so what' conclusion. In practice, the health service researchers in the field do indeed use economic theories to underpin their work. For example, they typically assume that fundholders are attempting to make savings but much of the data collection excludes the financial information that would test this hypothesis properly.

Linked to this absence of a good economic model, much of the research lacks good economic data. Almost all the published research provides details of referral activity and prescribing, with no data on the budgets set for the fundholders covered, changes in those budgets over time or changes in key prices, such as hospital and major drug prices. Nor did any of the major research studies make a systematic attempt to follow up whether, when a change in practice occurred, it was driven by service or financial considerations. Instead, in the main, we have a long list of data from which limited economic conclusions can be drawn.

Prescribing

Fundholders, given a budget based on past spending on drugs, have a clear incentive to review their prescribing to see what funds they can release. There are often a number of alternative drugs on the market for a given disease, and prescribing offers the clearest scope for substitution, albeit with possible effects on patient care. However, as noted earlier, where practices identify savings they have an incentive to pace these over time to avoid generating too large a surplus in a single year. A staged approach is also compatible with a review of different therapeutic areas, one at a time, by the practice. Where possible, fundholders may also be able to introduce policies to shift some patients to the use of over-the-counter medication, again releasing some of the prescribing budget. But the biggest users of medication, the elderly and those with chronic diseases, are exempt from prescription charges and so will always prefer a prescription to paying over the counter.

The research evidence on fundholding has been brought together by Coulter (1995b) and Dixon and Glennerster (1995); a major study, noted earlier, emerged in 1996 from the Audit Commission. Coulter, Dixon and Glennerster provide comprehensive reviews of the impact of fundholding at the level of individual practice referral and prescribing; they also note studies of prescribing which suggest that fundholders have responded to the incentive to restrain prescribing costs. Steps taken include the introduction of formularies and a transfer of prescribing to generic items. The Audit Commission (1996) notes that two-thirds of fundholders had formularies when surveyed, but two-fifths had formularies before entering the scheme. That is, only 26 per cent developed a formulary after becoming fundholders, a limited gain from fundholding. More strikingly, one-third of fundholders have not developed a formulary, a finding that highlights the difficulties of relying on local incentives and devolved responsibility to achieve a policy aim of less costly and more consistent prescribing.

Coulter (1995b) notes that savings may plateau after a few more years, though, as noted above, more sophisticated behaviour by GPs could lead them to store up some savings for future release. This is an inevitable consequence of the ways in which savings are realized. Once a formulary has been introduced, further reductions in cost depend on individual changes in prescribing rather than across-the-board savings. As some drugs come off patent and, in some cases, move to over-the-counter availability, there may be further scope for savings, from time to time, as generic substitution and patient-purchased medication become possible across a wider range of treatments. Also, there may be further scope for reviewing use of prescriptions as well as the drugs used when opportunities for simple savings run out. However, the Audit Commission found that, if anything, the fundholders were making their savings in the early years rather than staging them over time. Early years' savings were not repeated in later years by fundholders.

It should be noted that the restraint on expenditure on drugs that was associated with fundholding did not reduce total spending on prescribing readily. Rather, it reduced the rate of increase of practice expenditure on drugs. Bradlow and Coulter (1993) found that fundholders increased their expenditure on drugs appreciably less than non-fundholders, whose spending rose by 18.7 per cent in the six months after the NHS Reforms. The smallest rise was in dispensing practices. These practices, in rural areas, provide the drug to the patient directly, without a visit to a pharmacy. As such, they make profits from the supply of drugs. It is not clear how much money is involved but it may be as much as 40 per cent on top of the GPs' basic income. Such GPs have an incentive to use drugs which offer them a higher margin, typically branded drugs, rather than unbranded generic drugs. This in turn means that they may have greater scope to reduce their drug expenditure, but potentially at the expense of their practice profits from dispensing – another example of the need for greater economic sophistication in modelling fundholder behaviour.

Maxwell *et al.* (1993), working in Scotland, also standardized their data for the amount of drugs given to the patients of fundholders and non-fundholders. This supported the finding that fundholders were tending to restrain their prescribing, from a higher initial level, more than non-fundholders. However, this study also found that the non-fundholders were reducing the number of daily doses prescribed per patient per year, suggesting that even non-fundholders faced some pressure or influence making them reduce elements of prescribing, as intended under indicative prescribing.

More convincing evidence comes from later research, by Wilson *et al.* (1995). Using much larger regional samples, the changes in fundholding practices (100 in total spread over three annual waves) are shown across net ingredient costs and items prescribed per thousand prescribing units (effectively weighted populations), net cost per item and the extent of generic prescribing. Overall, the costs of fundholders were more contained than non-fundholders. However, scope for further reductions in prescribing costs remained, with first wave fundholders still prescribing generics for 13 per cent less of prescriptions than the third wavers. (This is compatible with the idea that these practices, which entered fundholding early and with less use of generics, are staging their savings by shifting to generics gradually.)

But the key weakness, to an economist, is that none of the studies tells us how the budget for prescribing or the price of any major drug components changed over time. It would be reassuring, for an economist at least, to find that generic substitution was concentrated on areas where the savings would be greater. Similarly, since overall both fundholders and non-fundholders have been increasing their spending on drugs, it would be helpful to see if the budgetary pressures on the fundholders were substantially tighter over time than the indicative budgets imposed on the non-fundholders. Drug expenditure over the period 1991–2 to 1993–4 showed annual growth rates falling for non-fundholders from 15 per cent to 11 per cent and for fundholders from 12 per cent to 8 per cent. It follows that if fundholders' drug budgets are driven primarily by average or non-fundholder spending, fundholders already below average prescribing levels are likely to continue to enjoy savings over time, while if they are driven by their own historic spending they are likely to settle down to a lower level of growth with fewer future savings.

Before leaving the issue of prescribing by GPs of all kinds, the confusion in government policy over many years should again be noted. The government has a central agreement with the pharmaceutical industry to control the profits made in the UK, primarily from sales to and through the NHS. If the government wishes to reduce the costs of drugs, it could do so by using its monopoly power to lower profits and prices or impose generic substitution by community pharmacists, eliminating the excess cost of branded drugs out of patent in a single blow. But instead the government has left much of the control of the drugs bill in the hands of GPs through fundholding and indicative budgets. This may be because it does not wish to be seen to be squeezing the drugs industry too hard, though the companies are sufficiently sophisticated to see how policy affects them. Alternatively, it may reflect a reluctance by government to be seen to influence individual prescriptions. If another Thalidomide scandal emerges in the future, where a prescribed drug caused serious malformations before its side effects were known by doctors, the government would probably prefer that the use of the drug was the result of individual prescriptions rather than government fiat.

Hospital referrals

There have been quite a few studies of referral and fundholding. These studies face a difficulty in using simple data, for example the number of referrals to hospital, as an indicator. Fundholders making savings from one element of their budget may lower the threshold for referral to hospital that is used for another disease group. Alternatively, they may avoid dramatic changes in referral if they believe these will affect future years' budgets.

None of the research studies has dealt fully, if at all, with the limitations on total referrals as an indicator or the further problems caused by year-on-year variation in the illness of patients due to chance. As noted earlier in the discussion of budget-setting, general practice populations are of a size where we should expect year-on-year variations in population ill-health, due to chance. While prescribing is a common event in general practice, hospital referral is less common and elective admission still less common. It is therefore not surprising that the rates in practices monitored since fundholding show fluctuations and not a steady trend over time. However, given these fluctuations, it would be helpful to see longer-term trend data on these practices, to see if the beginnings of a downward trend is maintained. Howie *et al.* (1995) draw particular attention to the annual fluctuations in activity and conclude that, while longer-term data may be of some help, the development of an acceptable capitation formula to cope with variation will be difficult.

Coulter (1995b) concludes from the work of her group that there was little difference in referral between fundholding and non-fundholding practices, and the Audit Commission found little change in referral contracts. However, the data in these studies has several drawbacks. First, the data for fundholding is inevitably compiled from a relatively short period of time, with a very small number of annual budget rounds on which all the resource decisions depend. The data shows considerable fluctuations over time. Of ten fundholders examined by Surender *et al.* (1995) (the Coulter research group), five had their highest rate of referral in the third year, three in the second year and two in the first year. Second, the research tells us nothing about the other changes in outpatient activity, except to note generally that fundholders made savings from reduced follow-up consultations, more day surgery, lower prices and use of cheaper providers. But these are precisely effects predicted by models of fundholding and suggest a clear impact. Certainly, without data on the prices and budgets for hospital services, it is not possible to share the conclusion that budgetary pressure was not affecting referral behaviour (Coulter 1995b). If fundholders with an expressed interest in improving patient care could increase referrals *and* save money, then there is no reason to expect them to allow further savings to dominate over service improvements. But money is simply not mentioned!

Howie *et al.* (1995) show, from detailed studies of a small group of fundholding practices, that referral behaviour did appear to change. They were able to research this issue for individual marker conditions and compare what happened in the year after fundholding with what happened before. For some conditions, for example diabetes, the proportions attending outpatient clinics had fallen from 32 per cent to less than 18 per cent, almost half. Some observers were inclined to dismiss this result as the study had no non-fundholding control group and results may have been due to hospital-led changes in diabetes management. Of course, as Dixon and Glennerster (1995) point out, we do not know if reducing outpatient contacts improves or damages patient health. Interestingly, Howie *et al.* also found reductions in inpatient and day case surgery rates, even though a rise in day surgery might have been expected as a substitute for inpatient care.

Before moving on to other aspects of referral, it is perhaps worth noting one possible explanation for the differences between the results of Coulter in England and Howie in Scotland. It is well known that the NHS in Scotland enjoys higher levels of funding than England, on the standard indicators. It is therefore possible that Scotland has worked with much lower thresholds for referral and treatment than England. Thus while Scottish fundholders could make relatively easy savings without compromising care, English fundholders might have found this more difficult. Again, we really need more information on the budgets and prices faced by the two, as well as their thresholds for referral, before we can make even this tentative conclusion.

Shopping around

A further aspect of referral by fundholders is their choice of provider. Given the freedom to purchase from a range of providers, we might expect to find fundholders shifting referrals to providers offering lower prices, higher day case proportions and/or higher quality of care. Although it may be difficult to get completely frank answers from fundholders where money is concerned, there is evidence that they rate quality of patient care as more important than price in making their referral decisions. Whynes and Reed (1994) found that confidence in the consultant, patient convenience and communication were rated more highly than price. Equally, the GPs' value of the technical quality of care differed from their valuation of service elements so that the quality of hospital facilities was rated less important than the price. More generally, the available evidence from a number of studies suggests that fundholders were relatively conservative and did not shift large numbers of referrals between providers. This is compatible with their views that they would support local hospitals and had gone into fundholding as much to protect their local service as to shake it up or escape its clutches. In this context, it is important to recall that prior to the Reforms, GPs had the freedom to refer further afield if they chose, so local referral in part indicates satisfaction with the local service before 1990. A further factor may be that by using their power to threaten to shift referrals if they chose, the fundholders were able to bring about the improvements that they wanted from local providers. We examine this issue below.

Quality of care

Fundholders were clear that quality of care was an issue for them on entering the scheme. They have no direct financial incentive to raise quality; they do, though, have a clear professional goal and the rewards that go with achieving it. Potentially, a further incentive is the chance to take more control over service provision. Consultants in hospital have that name because, originally, they were consulted by GPs and gained their income from referrals, rather like barristers taking work referred by solicitors. But once they joined a salaried service, they were better placed to dictate what they would and would not do for GPs. I once attended a meeting, after the NHS Reforms, where the local maternity service was to be discussed. Although one or two local GPs had contributed to the plans, the main message was one-way, with the consultants dictating the service that they proposed to give the GPs. The model of consultation looked a long way from locally sensitive or primary care led models.

Fundholders now believe that they have been successful in improving quality, though much of the available evidence relies on fundholder opinions. Fundholders reported to the NAO that they had been very successful in improving waiting times, with two-thirds getting faster admissions for their patients and slightly more getting faster outpatient appointments. A smaller proportion reported improvements in communications, with around half the NAO's respondents reporting faster responses on letters, diagnostic tests and reduced follow-up of patients. Similarly, the Audit Commission (1996) report has a whole appendix of examples where the care of specific diseases has been clarified through greater use of written guidelines and improved communication between hospitals and GPs. To the layman, brought up to believe that the NHS has always offered a more integrated service than US and European health systems, some of these improvements seem modest, for example common registers of patients suffering from a given disease, written guidelines for referral or simply an improvement in the courtesy with which patients are treated. Perhaps it is a comment on the workings of the NHS that these modest improvements could only happen with major reform rather than cooperation and collaboration locally.

Two issues make it hard to judge the effects of fundholding in isolation from the rest of the Reforms. The first concerns the impact of the Reforms on providers. They were under pressure to compete for referrals and contracts from any purchaser and so may have made a number of improvements to retain their market share, even with no fundholder pressure. The second difficulty is that, as with other elements of the Reforms, we are not looking at a static picture but snapshots of a changing NHS. Thus we might find that all GPs have gained a service improvement and fail to appreciate that this may have been brought about by fundholding but extended to all GPs. This is a likely outcome, given the criticism of fundholding as creating a two-tier service. For example, I know of a pathology service which introduced taxi collection of specimens to encourage GP fundholders to stay with them and to fight off private sector pathology laboratories. But, mindful of the 'two-tier' criticism, the NHS pathology service made sure that non-fundholding GPs received the same improved collection service.

Savings and service developments

Fundholders have a clear incentive to try to make savings for practice or service developments, and they have certainly made savings. The National Audit Office (1994) study of fundholding found that fundholders saved £31.8 million, of which they retained £28.3 million for the development of local initiatives and facilities. This represents only about 3.5 per cent of their budgets and so does not indicate massive savings or enrichment of GPs through development of practice premises, for example. The Audit Commission similarly found savings of about 3.1 per cent, mainly achieved out of the budget for hospital services, which accounts for almost half of the fundholders' budgets. (While greater proportional savings from the drugs budget were anticipated earlier in this chapter, savings on hospital services may be used to switch services to primary care, not to reduce them.) Although this appears a modest saving, the Audit Commission found that it translated into about £83,000 per practice. This kind of money would pay for four or more additional (non-medical) staff in a practice with perhaps only four or five GP partners, so it is sufficient to make a difference at the practice level, but only if this level of saving can be sustained year on year. Given the feedback from past savings to future budget, it may not be, so employing staff may not be sensible unless they are on temporary contracts. Hence there may be a bias towards spending on bricks and mortar. Several years of savings at £80,000 would fund a building project in the practice, for example, and even one year's savings could achieve significant improvements in the basic fabric of the premises. It is therefore not surprising that 60 per cent of the savings from fundholding have been spent on premises.

A few practices made much greater savings and attracted critical headlines. The NAO report shows that in 1992–3, 21 per cent of fundholders made savings of over £100,000 in one year and 73 per cent of funds came in below budget. (This frequency of savings appears on the high side, given the variation in annual sickness incidence, discussed earlier, and may reflect generous funding, a prerequisite to keeping the volunteer army of fundholders happy.) Interestingly, the proportion of funds underspending by more than £100,000 did not fall as fundholding developed. In half of the RHA areas, more practices reached this savings level in 1992–3 than in 1991–2, suggesting that the budgetary screw was not being tightened over time in a consistent way.

The extent of savings led the NHS Executive to look at the different causes of savings and ask regions to recover savings which were not directly creditable to the fundholders, for example where their budget was based on incorrect price or volume information. Other kinds of savings have been pursued in some regions and a significant sum handed back, either in a straight payback or for service improvements in local providers. Savings were also used to purchase equipment, not only for the practices but also for local hospitals, to enable them to increase their rate of day surgery (NAO 1994), for example.

Apart from premises, fundholders were keen to use savings to develop services such as physiotherapy and counselling, often on the premises, and a significant minority of fundholders have negotiated non-standard packages of community health services. It is not clear how far these substitute for other services and expenditure on drugs in contributing to improved patient outcomes, though counselling may substitute directly for demands on GP time. One study of three practices (Hackett *et al.* 1993) has found that on-site physiotherapy was associated with lower spending on drugs for musculo-skeletal problems.

It is interesting to contrast the views of two of the leading observers of fundholding on this issue. Coulter (1995b) notes that it is debatable whether local practice physiotherapy, counselling or visiting consultant clinics are cost-effective. Glennerster *et al.* (1994)

argue that a balance is needed between medical need and consumer demand if the NHS is to survive in a consumerist world. That is, it may be important for the NHS to provide services which people like and not just those which have a scientifically demonstrated impact on health. This is one example of a wider public debate about health and other social services, as well as education. Such services are no longer seen as only providing an expert-led service but also must respond to consumer demands for service, comfort and perceived (rather than proven) benefit. If we go down this road, I believe that we are potentially moving to services which have the flexibility to respond differentially to service demands from different consumers. If the technical fix is no longer exactly the same for all with the same need, and if the service elements can vary, there will be more scope for topping-up payments to fund more services for those that demand them and can afford them. We return to this issue in discussing the future of the NHS in Chapter 6.

Transaction costs

The last element of the evidence from fundholding covers the transactions costs of fundholders. Fundholding has put NHS purchasing power in the hands of a large number of small players. Each of these has to contract with a range of providers and, unless in a consortium of fundholders, duplicate the efforts of other local fundholders covering the same ground in their contracting. The evidence on the costs of these additional financial transactions is sketchy but there must be costs to fundholders themselves and to those providing budgets for fundholding and providers.

Fundholding practices receive a management fee, initially set at £30,000 per practice per year, and this has been increased several times since the Reforms. However, this is clearly only a part of the costs of the scheme. In Scotland, the lead fundholders studied by Howie *et al.* (1995) reported working about half an hour a day extra on non-patient activities, amounting to over 100 hours per year, a small but significant additional cost. Dixon and Glennerster (1995) quote estimates as high as £81,600 per practice per year. The Audit Commission (1996) found costs of around 4 per cent of fund, implying even higher costs per year, but 1.5 per cent of this cost was for information technology. Equally, since drug spending was already heavily monitored through the PACT system, the implication is that the real cost of managing the hospital and community health elements of the fund may exceed 4 per cent. For a practice of 10,000 patients, the fund for hospital services may be around £700,000 to £750,000 (Dixon *et al.* 1994). These are the main services for which transaction costs will be incurred and would otherwise fall under a health commission contract. A cost of £80,000 represents 10 per cent of the costs of the fund. Even with some adjustments for community service transactions, which are typically limited to one provider and relatively uncomplicated contracts, and for some of the additional costs of drugs budget management, the costs of purchasing by fund-holders look high compared to health commissions.

Equally, as was argued in Chapter 3, the resources of health commissions may well be inadequate for the tasks they face. (The Audit Commission notes that only half of fundholding practices had an annual visit from their health commission, suggesting that whatever the current administrative costs of the scheme, they are not always leading to good management of fundholding by health commissions. Again, the lack of resources of health commissions may be leading to too low a level of management involvement.) While fundholding may be a more expensive model of purchasing, it may not be *too* expensive. It may, for example, deliver higher quality purchasing and services in return for higher costs. The real test is what it delivers for these transaction costs. The evidence reviewed above shows that much of the gain lies in rather soft areas of service improvement that would be hard to value and compare with the costs.

THE VERDICT ON FUNDHOLDING

Before drawing our verdict, another parallel with education is useful here as a backdrop to the discussion. Higher education could be funded through budgets given to secondary schools. Teachers who know their 'clients' well could purchase, choosing between spending more on the brightest and the neediest (those needing more remedial teaching before they can embark on higher education). Would the public and individual parents be happy with the discretion and power that would lie with the teachers? Or would we prefer so important a service as education, with its impact on a wide range of life chances, to be funded by (for instance) the current system of mandatory local authority grants for those attending approved courses? The risks of inequity, anomaly and bias look quite large in this example if we decentralize too much. (I am grateful to Jon Sussex for this analogy.)

Given the evidence reviewed earlier, what are the merits or drawbacks of fundholding? Is it really the cornerstone of the Reforms, a much needed injection of local, flexible, consumer-sensitive decision-making or a major, and costly, source of inequality in an NHS committed to equality? To comment on these questions, but not necessarily to answer them definitively, we can assess fundholding against the standard economic dimensions of efficiency and equity. Of course, this begs further questions about effectiveness that are not pursued in detail here. That is, fundholding could be leading to more efficient purchase of ineffective medical care!

Much of what was planned and has happened through fundholding was not focused directly on improving either the technical efficiency of the health service (resources used per case), the allocative efficiency (resources used for one type of case of a given social value, relative to those used for another type with a different social value) or equity (the extent to which patients are treated similarly across the NHS). In consequence, the data collection was also not fully focused on these issues and does not fully answer any of the questions posed on fundholding. We can look at both the efficiency and equity standards in turn.

At face value, fundholders have a direct incentive to obtain services at a lower – rather than a higher – price for a given quality. However, this incentive is weakened if fundholding budgets are protected against higher costs of local providers by the method of budget setting. Under these circumstances, fundholders may be more clearly focused on getting better quality from local providers, for the going price, whatever that price may be. If the quality improvements which fundholders claim are genuine (such as shorter waiting times and better communications) and were achieved at a constant price, then it is reasonable to infer that efficiency has increased. But where prices to fundholders have increased, and there is little direct research on how such prices have moved, they may be achieving these gains at a price which may not be efficient. Similarly, where practices have reduced referrals, and managed cases in some other way, this may save costs but we lack the data on outcomes to know if the quality of care provided has been changed. The same is true of the switch to less costly drugs but not to generics, where no real difference in care may take place.

Before becoming too negative on this aspect of fundholding, we should note that a situation in which GPs refer for services that are free of charge encourages them to refer beyond the point at which the gains of a referral outweigh the costs. Thus whatever the weaknesses of fundholding, it at least introduced some possible price sensitivity.

There are no clear financial incentives to technical efficiency in the non-fundholding regime.

Turning to allocative efficiency, while we know that fundholders have switched some resources to services which patients value, for example counselling and physiotherapy, we cannot say with any certainty that the care of these patients constitutes a better outcome than the care of the patients from whom the savings were effectively made. In the absence of any clear technical data on the social value of health care, particularly in areas of care where the long-term health benefit is uncertain, we can only conclude that fundholders think that they have achieved a better outcome, otherwise they would not shift resources to new practice services. (Of course, in some case, the savings used to pay for these additional care activities may have been generated by windfall savings when the incidence of illness fell. The reduction in care to pay for new services is then a reduction somewhere in another potentially overspending fundholding practice or in the health commissions' contracted care. In this case, the value to the fundholders of extra services may be very marginal, for they do not have to balance it against a reduction of some other service.) Here again, we must also remember that health commissions have great difficulty setting priorities and establishing the criteria needed to achieve allocative efficiency. So fundholding may be no worse than the alternative.

Overall, the efficiency of fundholders' purchases of services cannot be readily compared with those of health commissions. As a result, the equity of fundholding has attracted most attention. The main claim is that, because of the way they have been funded and the way they spend their money, fundholders get better services for their patients than non-fundholders. Both Dixon and Glennerster (1995) and Coulter (1995b), in surveying the evidence, conclude that inequality may well be occurring, but the Audit Commission (1996) found no consistent inequity because so many fundholders were not actively managing the waiting list. Certainly providers have an incentive to try to attract fundholders for the extra cash and may be able to rely on a local monopoly of the health commission contracts. But many providers do not appear to try very hard to get this extra business and to risk creating more inequity. As a result, even if fundholders and non-fundholders have effective access to the same resources, fundholders may get a better deal.

At least one aspect of inequality may be explained by the combination of provider and fundholder incentives and the annual funding round in the NHS. Providers have an incentive to treat their health authority elective surgical contract caseload as fast as possible in the financial year, to avoid the risk that winter medical problems may disrupt progress, and to ensure that they do not undershoot their contract. Providers also may have no incentive to make sure that the pace of surgery is even and the contract does not run out before the financial year end, in March each year. With more day and short-stay surgery, the efficiency gained by providers may well lead to contracts with health commissions being filled before the end of the financial year. This can leave providers with spare capacity towards the end of the financial year, precisely when a prudent fundholder begins to spend reserves on additional cases. What could be more natural than that those with money and patients get together with those with space and time to treat them? But before we cry foul, we should not overlook the faster treatment of the health commissions' patients earlier in the year. Potentially, some fundholder patients wait longer than we know, but not on any official list that can be scrutinized. They wait instead for the time when the money to pay for their care is definitely available and the end of the financial year is approaching! Then the fundholders can safely push for rapid treatment for their patients.

More generally, we again need to beware of motes and beams. In spite of its stated aims, the NHS has never been equitable, nationally, regionally, locally, personally. Treatment has been a lottery with wide differences in the detection of particular health problems even in the same practice and wide differences in the resources available per head, with Scotland and Northern Ireland particularly appearing to benefit beyond their differential need. It may be that as long as inequality (at least within countries) is not systematic, it is easier to accept. That is, a lottery is preferable to having predictable winners in fundholding practices.

Clearly, if fundholders are systematically given access to more resources than non-fundholders then there are indeed predictable winners. But the research evidence does not show this is the case and the NAO verdict in late 1994 is probably still correct, that none of the regions visited in the report were able to make direct comparisons of the funds allocated to fundholders and to health commissions on behalf of non-fundholders. The NAO anticipated that as funding moved closer to benchmarks and capitation, this would begin to change. In the same way, if health commissions use local purchasing to begin to establish clear quotas for services to particular patches, we will then have a better idea of whether the fundholders' patients really are winning the health care lottery every time. But we should also note that, once fundholding started to prove popular with a significant proportion of GPs, even if only to sidestep the effects of restraints on health commission contracts, it was probably not in the government's interests to fund too much research into whether they really were overfunded.

Fundholding is central to the debate over who has what discretion in the NHS. If GPs are to continue to have substantial discretion in their use of services and drugs for individual patients, there are merits in acknowledging this and building on it, through fundholding and local commissioning schemes in which GPs hold the pen but not the cheque book. If in the name of technical standards or equality of treatment GPs are to lose this discretion, then a more top-down model may be more appropriate, with clearer standards of entitlement and wider use of protocols to determine care (see Chapter 6). But even this would have to depend on GPs to implement it.

We can conclude this discussion by considering some 'ifs' and 'maybes' and see where they lead us. If the budget for a fundholding practice was set in a way that was completely compatible with the resources for non-fundholders, with no sweeteners to keep volunteer fundholders in the scheme, and accurately adjusted for the actual incidence of disease in the appropriate year, would fundholding be an acceptable model? Clearly, this would resolve one of the complaints on equity but would not resolve the issue of a better service in return for cash. However, as soon as fundholders found a lower price at which to contract, either money would have to be clawed back from them or they would start to creep ahead of the non-fundholders. Viewed like this, it is clear that complete equity is simply not compatible with giving fundholders budgets and incentives to use them. If there was no prospect of gain for their patients or themselves, why would they take it on? But once fundholders have made gains through stimulating providers, some of these will spill over to non-fundholders, particularly if providers have to show that they are being even-handed, even when they are not! It follows that inequality may still lead to some service improvements for non-fundholders through a general improvement in provider efficiency.

If all contracts in the NHS were based on the same set of prices, regardless of whether the purchaser was a health commission or a fundholder, would this resolve the dispute over equity? It would in part if linked to a capitation budget rather than one based on historic demand. Fundholders would probably still enjoy some market power in this situation, over quality (for example standards of care and waiting times) rather than price, since the relative ease with which they can redirect patients means that they can contest the local standards of care more easily than health commissions and move patients in ones and twos, without a major political dispute. But we must beware of creating a set of conditions within the market that deliberately sidestep market forces. After all, if we do not want a market, we can get rid of it rather than control it out of existence. Fixed national prices would be inefficient and against the culture of the market. Trusts would still have incentives to reduce costs in order to generate surpluses for service quality improvements that could expand or maintain their market share, but those that failed to do so would not face the same threat to their contracts if prices were purely notional.

If individual fundholders choose to reduce their use of certain expensive drugs, thus imposing some additional side effects on some patients, or if they decide to deny some patients access to a more detailed diagnostic assessment and use the savings to fund services of unproven cost-effectiveness, should we be concerned? This issue is, for me, at the heart of the fundholding debate. The NHS currently fudges many of the decisions about who gets what, a stance that is challenged in Chapter 6. Widespread variation in demands and referrals shows that GPs, whether fundholding or not, play a crucial role in allocating resources between individuals. If we keep the cash-limited system with rationing necessarily taking place somewhere, we face a choice of letting the local fundholding GP decide on whether an individual patient gets a specific treatment or letting a largely unaccountable health commission make some aggregate decisions on behalf of a million people. Health commission decisions even then depend on GPs to maintain them. Given these alternatives, many might begin to view the GP favourably. Health commissions have struggled to make strong decisions on priorities and, where they have, hostile criticism has followed. If a difficult interpersonal decision has to be made, is it better made on technical grounds – varicose vein treatment is less important than hip replacement – or by a doctor who can see and touch the patients competing for hospital care?

I find another analogy with education useful on this issue. We cannot expect a local education authority to specify how many minutes of teacher time, in groups or singly, each pupil will get on each subject. Rather, we allocate a budget to schools and we leave it to the teachers to resolve the microallocation below this point. We also impose a national curriculum and some form of inspection.

In the same way, if we could find the right funding formula we might expect fundholders to resolve the allocation of health care resources between individuals, as well as specifying at a national level whether they could use public money on certain types of care.

For example, fundholders would be subject to the same limited list of prescribable drugs and, if a treatment was truly felt to be ineffective for everyone, it might be excluded from their choices as a pure waste of public money. We could also expect an annual report on how the money was spent, and what judgements were made on the worth of specific treatments. We might also have periodic inspection to make sure that their interpersonal judgements were not systematically biased (for example against the old, the young, the black, the white) and fell within a range that some auditing body found acceptable. We would know that health care funding was equitable, up to a point, and that fundholders might get a little more for their patients, including some services which patients liked for their own sake, and that non-fundholders might get, or press for, some of the same gains. We would also be acknowledging, in the clearest possible way, that GP decisions drive referral and hospital and community health service demands, even without fundholding. As Glennerster *et al.* (1994) suggest, if non-fundholders could also be given a greater say in health commission purchasing too, they might be less inclined to look critically at fundholding.

But, if you have been counting, that is a lot of 'ifs'!

5

PROVIDERS

In this chapter we examine a number of characteristics of NHS Trusts which affect their operation in the NHS internal market. Specifically we examine the objectives of Trusts and the freedom of movement given to them under the Reforms, nominally and in practice. This is followed by an analysis of the incentives offered to Trusts to bring about the White Paper's objectives and a review of the resulting behaviour.

The chapter concentrates on NHS provider Trusts. In spite of all the anxiety when the Reforms were announced about a shifting of contracts to the private sector, this has occurred on a very small scale indeed. If anything, the opposite has happened. The sleeping giant that is the NHS has, in many places, developed a more supportive policy on private practice. In Thatcher's Britain, buying health care was a status symbol, and private insurance a widespread perk. In this environment, and where private fees could make a contribution to NHS costs, the sheer size of the NHS gives it a considerable advantage over the private sector. The NHS also employs almost all the consultants on which the private sector relies and in many places has cajoled or persuaded them to undertake more private work on NHS premises. This led BUPA in 1996 to offer preferred provider arrangements for members using its own hospitals rather than the NHS, a perfectly sensible move for an integrated provider and insurer but one which led the NHS to cry foul! In practice, the contribution made to the running costs of a hospital from private practice remains, for the majority of Trusts, relatively small. Trusts usually talk up the income but, in spite of the supposed business outlook of Trusts, most forget to deduct the cost of providing private facilities and confuse income with profit. Outside one or two very specialized hospitals, private practice is only a source of marginal gains for a Trust.

THE OBJECTIVES OF NHS TRUSTS

In order to understand the impact of the new freedoms and incentives faced by NHS Trusts, we need to have a clear idea of their objectives. This is a more subtle issue than it might appear because Trusts remain substantially different from conventional companies, in spite of their place in a sort of market. Trusts are also relatively new bodies and, perhaps because of concern with what might be found, there has been a lack of detailed and systematic research on them. The discussion here draws on a number of studies and also on my direct experience of Trusts in the early years after the Reforms.

Trusts are rather awkward agencies for economics because they do not readily fit the conventional theory of the profit-making firm. This does not mean we cannot study or explain them. Economics has developed more subtle models to analyse the behaviour of organizations that are not pursuing conventional market goals such as profit maximization. Even profit maximization is not that simple. For example, morally indefensible or illegal behaviour which increases short-term profit may damage long-term market share by discouraging customer loyalty. Hence the behaviour of many firms at present is hedged around with the need to be seen to be politically correct in relation to the environment, for example, to maintain long-term customer loyalty.

If the theory of profit maximization does not fit perfectly with the actual behaviour of profit-making companies, it must fit even less well with non-profit organizations. The creation of surpluses which give management a degree of flexibility, including the opportunity to gain status or higher rewards, may still be one of a number of objectives in a non-profit organization. But we can also expect to find that the focus on profits or surpluses is weakened, and a number of other objectives also pursued.

THE CHARACTERISTICS OF TRUSTS

Before looking at some of the theories applied to the ways Trusts, particularly hospitals, work, it is worth considering their unusual characteristics. Health services are not so much a single business, they are more like a collection of small businesses, each concentrating on a particular set of diseases. They may be joined by a series of connections of one specialty with another (discussed later in this section), so that a comprehensive district general hospital is made up of interlinked businesses. But in day-to-day working, hospitals and community Trusts have many services which work in isolation. There is a lack of common interests between surgeons and physicians, speech therapists and district nurses, which constantly frustrates attempts to take the whole 'business' in one direction or another. Senior professionals expect to operate within an environment of clinical freedom where individual clinical decisions, which decide how resources are used, are largely unchallenged. Everyone may agree on a common aim such as the need for newer, better facilities, but who gets to move into them can be a matter for fierce, inter-tribal fighting.

Some diversity of purpose is likely in any large organization, though I once spent a few days training with a group of managers from a major soft drinks firm. Their sole aim appeared to be to outwit their immediate rival – the other world class soft drinks firm – and the unity of purpose was like something from a patriotic war film. But in all commercial organizations there is likely to be both a clear chain of command to resolve competing claims on resources and also a much simpler set of products and product groups. In particular, money talks and areas of the business which can show increased sales and profits are likely to win the fight for more investment. As a result, while there may be separate constituencies with their own parochial objectives, they are each likely to be less powerful *per se* and more reliant on performance to impress senior management. In comparison hospitals (more so than community services) produce many hundreds of different product lines in 30 or 40 different departments providing care, each without a clear financial bottom line before the Reforms and, in many cases, with few really meaningful measures of performance after the Reforms. This diversity of staff and products constantly fragments the staff interests, the work of the supporting departments and the unity of purpose of the organization.

Yet at the same time, it is claimed that each hospital is a highly integrated facility, a complex house of cards in which removal of one or two cards threatens the whole. This integrity seems at variance with the product and staff diversity above. It derives from the specialty linkages which are seen as essential for effective operation of the hospital. In practice, mutual dependence does bring some of the diverse groups closer together or at least make it necessary for each to consider the impact of their decisions on others. The key groupings are maternity and child care, emergency and trauma care, surgery and anaesthetics. As noted in the discussion of purchasing, the claimed integrity of these service areas makes it much more difficult for purchasers to buy flexibly. Rules for junior doctor staffing, which local consultants can often manipulate to get their preferred service, further constrain purchasers and managers. As a result, a whole hospital's future may be closely bound up with the need to recruit several junior staff.

At first sight, we have a paradox here. Hospitals are highly heterogeneous yet integrated, pursuing individual aims yet bound together by a common set of service requirements. How is this possible? There are several answers to this paradox. First, the greatest unity of purpose and integration is usually seen in response to an external threat. Professional standards, the need for a carefully integrated service and the need to staff it with junior doctors are all put forward to justify retention of the fullest range of services. Yet on the ground, in these integrated hospitals, it is possible to find relatively low levels of interdepartment cooperation and cross-referral. Departmental objectives remain diverse, but within the wider objective of sustaining the whole hospital.

The NHS has not really challenged seriously the integration argument. It is possible that we have allowed the NHS to be dominated by only one model of hospital services, the big comprehensive general hospital. Although many patients will benefit from access to a wide range of specialties (for example patients with multiple diseases or injuries), many patients, including those typically treated in private hospitals, do not need more than one specialty for a short hospital stay. But the NHS has not developed hospitals providing this kind of elective care, partly because of the limits placed on doctor training.

Before looking at how economists have tackled the complexities of hospitals, we should note that the issues covered above apply much less frequently to community Trusts. They have much less of a case for integration and there are a number of different models for their services. For example, in many areas the health visiting service is run by the paediatrics department that also runs hospital services. Midwifery may be linked to hospital maternity and not community nurses. Overall, the essence of care in the community is that individuals are treated at home by professionals who visit them. Inevitably, this more isolated way of working reduces the scope for integration of large elements of the service.

ECONOMIC MODELS OF HOSPITALS

Economists have attempted to model hospital behaviour in the face of the diversity of objectives and the frequent lack of direct profit making. Their starting point is usually the theory of the profit-maximizing firm, but Cullis and West (1979) note a number of difficulties in fitting the theory of the firm to hospitals, particularly the lack of dominant decision-makers pursuing profit or other goals. Lee (1971) has suggested that status competition will lead hospitals to compete with others by extending their range of services, creating a prestige advantage over competitors and offering something of interest to doctors and managers. Where investment in new facilities does not have to generate surpluses to meet capital charges, under the pre-Reform NHS regime, this kind of status competition seems highly plausible. But more generally, as McGuire (1985) demonstrates, the main characteristic observed by economists about hospitals is that most of the time they lack such unity of purpose, for the reasons discussed earlier.

Bartlett and Harrison (1993) have examined NHS quasi-markets to identify their impact on the delivery of health and social services. Examining their local NHS market, they note that the published objectives of NHS Trusts are very general and potentially ambiguous. A commitment to the maintenance of the excellence of teaching and research by a Trust, for example, identified by Bartlett and Harrison, gives no idea how the key choices facing a Trust (for example between the pursuit of cost reduction and the development of a responsive service) will be made. Nor is it clear how the quality of the excellent current service is to be measured.

As Bartlett and Harrison note, Trusts are not likely to be profit maximizers. This is not only because they lack the power to carry forward substantial surpluses but also because some types of behaviour (such as 'cream skimming', to ensure within a given contract that only the least expensive cases are treated) are likely to run counter to the NHS ethos and the aspirations of staff. In addition, the NHS is still subject to review by a number of scrutineers, including the Audit Commission, the National Audit Office and the Health Service Ombudsman. In consequence, naked profit- or surplus-maximization is unlikely to be practised, and anything more than a modest surplus may leave a Trust open to criticism.

SO WHAT ARE TRUSTS TRYING TO DO?

Potential objectives for an NHS Trust that do appear compatible with observed behaviour include survival, quality enhancement, maximization of the breadth of services and maximization of caseload. These are examined in turn below.

Survival is an obvious objective for almost any organization. Individuals picked out to run an organization, whether as managers or directors, are likely to have aspirations for themselves and the organization. The Trust chairman and the five non-executive directors are likely to enjoy the status of directorship, with few risks, and will want success and status from the job. Failure is not something that these individuals are likely to find attractive and both managers and directors are likely to see serious losses of staff and services as a failure. Therefore, we can reasonably expect that, at the very least, maintenance of services and market share will be a goal of Trusts and this can be illustrated by a number of case studies.

Nettel (1993), in his interview study of management in a major London teaching hospital, found protection of market share as an objective. In the early months of 1992 this hospital, and its two competitors in the provision of specialist NHS cardiac surgery, appointed new consultant surgeons. The manager reporting this move notes that it is unlikely that the NHS market will need the capacity of three units but each was prepared to engage in a pre-emptive recruitment move to increase its own capacity and attempt to maintain or gain market share.

My own experience of a specialist service in London, one in which a clear plan had emerged from the Tomlinson review of services in London, is that again retention of market share was seen as important, so much so that the clinicians did not want to rely on a planned share of the market but set out to make sure that their share went up, not down during the short-term upheaval. The units earmarked for survival attempted to recruit consultants and attract the caseload from the centre that was to close, to increase their market share and also prevent this share falling to their neighbours. Whatever its advantages or disadvantages to the NHS, this is behaviour that a business economist would recognize as entirely consistent with the behaviour of firms. Indeed, one or two of those involved would fit neatly into the culture of the soft drinks firms!

In several other Trusts, within and outside London, I have found that management is not keen to withdraw from a service because this is seen as some kind of failure, even when the service in question is not large, is not close to the core business of the Trust and has clinicians who would prefer to move away. For example, retention and absorption of a centre for long-term development and care for seriously disabled children by an acute hospital does not make much business sense, particularly in the face of parental opposition. The implication is that one objective of Trusts is to keep the services that they started with, even when this might not be commercially sensible, because of excessive diversification and the cost of management and facilities overheads for relatively small services. By contrast, major firms frequently sell off large areas of their business in order to concentrate on areas which they think they do best. The increased profit seen as achievable by such moves is not realizable by Trusts and so we find a different type of behaviour occurring. Not only do Trusts seek to hold what they have but also to expand their range, a point taken up below.

Beyond maintenance of the current service range, Bartlett and Le Grand (1994) note, among other characteristics, a greater concern with quality of service compared to profit-making organizations. Crude profit-makers have an incentive to cut quality and reduce production costs where this cannot be detected by consumers or agency purchasers. Equally, economic theory shows that quality may not fall when firms want regular business from their customers. Major firms such as Tesco's have deliberately moved upmarket to increase their business, and firms must beware of cutting quality below the level their consumers require, or at least beware of consumers spotting it.

In the NHS, quality reductions are likely to be countered by the professional attitudes and aspirations of staff, who are likely to appeal to higher ethical standards than the good of the Trust in seeking support for the quality of care. The extent of public support for health care professionals makes any criticism from within particularly effective when it is presented in public by so-called 'whistle blowers'. The professions have also been active in preserving the rights of such critics of the system and have expressed a fear that a fragmented and competitive system based on Trusts would threaten both standards and those that criticized them. Equally, domination by the professions of the debate over quality is a way of reinforcing their control over the system and reducing the influence of managers and purchasers. This may be in our interests as consumers but is not necessarily good for the management of the system.

In the discussion on purchasing we have also noted a further aspect of quality, that quality affects patients who do not pay directly for services. Those who pay, the health commissions, do not sit in the queues or lie in the beds and may be poorly placed to judge quality. It follows that, if the professions can be squared, Trusts still have an incentive to cut quality where they think that cost and price matters most to purchasers.

Quality may also be pursued by extending the facilities and breadth of services offered, as Lee (1971) suggested in the USA. Adding new diagnostic or treatment services can be used as a basis for positive public relations and as an opportunity to offer a more comprehensive service to purchasers. In principle, general cost-containment pressures will tend to encourage maximum use of existing facilities before new facilities are developed. However, the NHS and all medical systems face substantial internal pressure to extend services. New consultants are likely to be particularly keen to put into practice the newest techniques that they have recently learned as junior medical staff in the major teaching centres. Routine medicine is very routine indeed, compared to most professional jobs, because there is a high volume of relatively simple work in most consultants' caseloads. Finding new things to do can enrich a job which might otherwise offer a much lower level of job satisfaction.

To a lesser degree, the same observation may be made about managers' behaviour. The chance to work on the acquisition of new equipment, with clinicians keen to use it, makes a pleasant change from the burdens of cost containment. It improves morale and helps to show that management is leading the organization somewhere. There may be scope for positive public relations and fundraising that brings extra kudos to managers. Arguably, the separation of purchasing from providing and the introduction of capital charges, considered below, have provided important counterweights to the demand for new and better equipment from Trusts, and so the pursuit of the new may be more restrained than in the past.

Another potential objective of Trusts, noted earlier, is the total level of patient care provided. Total activity may be an objective of management since increased activity indicates either a growing market share or at least a vigorous organization. Indeed, growth maximization at the expense of profits has sometimes been seen as a highly plausible goal even for commercial firms. Clinicians may be less concerned with the total level of activity, which may mean more work for the same pay, unless there are benefits such as additional staff and the opportunity to divert some resources to preferred activities (such as extra ward facilities, computers, specialized care, research and conference travel). But growth maximization is still an appealing objective in the absence of more subtle indicators such as the gain in health status for patients, because it shows that the organization is in some sense going forward. In contrast, planned or unplanned reductions in activity look like the thin end of the wedge of decline.

Above all, a review of potential Trust objectives highlights the difficulty of identifying, or even of creating, a clear and coherent set of objectives for organizations as complex as Trusts. The picture is not made much clearer when we look at the stated objectives of Trusts, as noted in the earlier example from Bartlett and Le Grand.

Research on management behaviour has found that a key role of management is actually the giving of a sense of purpose and direction. It is management's job to give the impression, at least, that the organization is moving forward and developing. This is very visible in Trust applications and annual reports. The freedom to be more flexible on pay, even to pay lower grade staff more, was emphasized often. So too was the freedom to access capital and improve a tired or flagging estate. Some applicants clearly had ideas above their station, looking forward to the freedom to develop their services, to expand and centralize, with faster local decision-making. These are all consistent with the objectives considered above. So how much freedom do Trusts have to pursue their objectives and what incentives are offered to stimulate them?

CRY FREEDOM

The White Paper proposed that Trusts would have much greater freedom of action. Initially only a proportion of NHS hospitals were to have this special status. In practice, the creation of Trusts rapidly became an end in itself. As noted in earlier chapters, it was difficult to demonstrate a change to a purchasing role for DHAs if they retained substantial numbers of directly managed units. Moving to Trust status was talked up considerably by management across the NHS as it was the route to potential freedoms, though the whole novelty of the Trust concept meant that no one knew what it would achieve. Certainly an early freedom was to pay the chief executive more money, a move which may reflect the different perceptions of a government restraining administrative pay and external Trust chairmen used to somewhat higher salaries in the private sector.

Trusts were to have the freedom to depart from the strict guidelines of bureaucracy and show dynamic and innovative behaviour. They were to have freedom to choose what mix of staff they used to meet their care contracts and to determine how these staff were paid. They were promised access to capital markets in order to borrow for developments, to acquire, own and sell their assets, and to bid for additional capital developments directly to the NHS Management Executive. They would also have the freedom to borrow money to fund new and upgraded buildings. Although limited by professional codes of conduct, the Trusts were also to be allowed to advertise their services to purchasers.

From this list of new freedoms, two stand out as of greatest economic importance: the freedom to obtain capital investment and the freedom to set pay and conditions locally. However, experience to date suggests that both of these freedoms have not in practice operated as widely as those early Trust applications anticipated.

ACCESS TO CAPITAL

Freedom to borrow funds for development was seen as very attractive by Trusts, largely because public expenditure restraint in the UK had limited the funding for new and upgraded buildings by the NHS itself. The health service found a way around this difficulty in the 1980s when the value of land increased rapidly. This greatly increased the value of potential development land on large rural mental hospital and urban long-stay hospital sites that were being closed by the NHS in the transfer of care to the community. Grandiose schemes to replace major London hospitals, for example, were created on the back of the high value of city centre sites. One very large scheme was carried through, at considerable cost, at the Chelsea and Westminster Hospital. Future historians of the NHS may find it hard to understand why the single biggest development in hospitals in the south of England took place in an area already heavily provided with hospitals. In fact, five sites closed as a part of the programme to develop this hospital and the proceeds from these were expected to fund its construction. But when it opened, the brand new hospital immediately threatened the future of a sixth local hospital, the neighbouring Charing Cross Hospital, which was later merged first with the Chelsea and Westminster and then with the Hammersmith, to try to ensure its survival in a new role.

High property values allowed the government to have its cake and eat it, giving scope for increased NHS building and reduced public spending at the same time. However, having built up its expenditure plans on these market values, the plans had to fold when the market fell. Having taken account of the windfall gain in property values, and limited other sources of capital funding, it was not easy for the Department of Health to get additional funding from the Treasury, given the continuing political pressure for tax cuts from within the Tory party. The prospects for redevelopment were therefore very poor in the late 1980s and many hospital redevelopment schemes were cut back.

The chance to borrow money in the capital market seemed to offer NHS Trusts a way out of the cul-de-sac of NHS capital budgets. However, the freedom to do so was hedged around with restrictions and became more complicated over time. The first such complication was that Trusts had to pay for their use of capital, instead of receiving it as a free good from regional health authorities. Even under the old rules, Trusts had to justify the investment in their premises as a viable economic investment. Typically this meant reducing total costs by reducing the number of sites over which services were spread. But even with an option appraisal to prove that the investment was cost-effective, there was the constant feeling of the 'dead hand' of the regional health authority (as seen from the hospital) controlling who got what new facilities. (From the RHA's perspective, this was a part of its strategic planning responsibilities, of course, under which the aspirations of the hospital units had to be contained within the plan and the capital budget. But this also meant that Trusts could not be free if the regional plans were to hold.)

After the Reforms, Trusts had to come to terms with the need to pay for their capital. In the short term, they were protected by a recycling of the money, so that what they were expected to pay in capital charges was equal to what their purchasers had to pay them in contracts. But over time, capital charges have become increasingly real and made it much harder for Trusts to justify longstanding dream schemes, such as a totally new hospital on the edge of the town. If funding to meet capital charges reflects the value of the capital in existing old buildings, for example, neither purchasers nor providers can afford the 6 per cent surplus to be earned on capital or the 10 per cent depreciation provision for a new hospital. As a result, it was no longer always feasible to shed an old site and pay for the investment with the saving in site running costs.

Apart from paying the price in capital charges for the freedom of access to capital, access was also restricted in other ways. Initially, Trusts could only borrow from the private sector if they could show that this was cheaper. The official guidance notes that it is unlikely that the terms for a private loan would be cheaper than a loan from the

Secretary of State. This is because the government of a stable economy such as the UK is seen as the lowest risk for lenders and can therefore borrow without the risk premium that attaches to commercial loans. But on the face of it, this appears to negate the freedom to borrow because the Secretary of State's funds, though cheaper, may not be available from the NHS capital budget. Knowing you have chosen the cheaper option is no consolation if you do not get the investment. Trusts were also forbidden to mortgage their assets, since this could create the risk of a Trust closing and the buildings being sold by a bank which could put the Trust into receivership for non-payment of interest on the loan. 'Hospital closes as bank moves in' is not a headline likely to appeal to politicians claiming that the NHS was safe in their hands!

Trusts have obtained some access to funds, through the annual external funding limit set for them, but it is set for them in negotiation with the regional Trust units, initially a part of a separate regional structure but now merged with the regional offices of the Management Executive that have replaced regional health authorities. This is hardly the freedom from bureaucracy that might have been expected from what appeared to be on offer in the White Paper. Furthermore, since the local purchasers and the regional office typically have their own views about the strategic value of a major development project, the Trusts bidding for Treasury funding frequently find their freedom to make investment decisions challenged. Hence it has not proved easy for Trusts to obtain funds for new developments without considerable support from purchasers at the earliest stages.

Of course, businesses hoping to borrow to finance an investment need to show a convincing business plan and market research to their lenders. The crucial difference is that a typical business is competing to sell to many individuals and proposes to take on the risk of success or failure in its market. Where a firm or a Trust has only one or two major customers, the formal endorsement of the future business plan by purchasers is much more likely to be required. For example, a defence contractor might need to show future contract work with government to justify major investment. But there is a clear tension between allowing purchasers to decide what activity they wish to purchase and allowing them to dictate to semi-autonomous Trusts the facilities in which it will be provided.

If Trusts believe they can recover the additional capital charges of a new facility by site rationalization or other means, should they be allowed the freedom to do so? The short answer may be 'no', if only because the pressure on purchasers to meet the higher costs of a new facility may be too great to resist if the Trust fails to achieve financial stability. Walking away from a brand new building is very difficult for a public service, and freedom for Trusts now may leave purchasers with a funding problem later. So Trusts cannot be free to invest without careful monitoring and support from purchasers. This may be good for the NHS but is clearly at variance with the freedoms offered in the White Paper.

THE PRIVATE FINANCE INITIATIVE – A MAJOR COMPLICATION

The complexities of borrowing and paying for investment have been increased, massively in the view of some critics, by the introduction of the Private Finance Initiative (PFI), on top of the existing rules for investment appraisals and business cases. Under PFI, which goes across all public services, public bodies such as hospitals and universities, but also road building agencies, are encouraged to seek collaboration with the private sector to fund new developments. The aim of collaboration is to develop services which might be wholly or partly operated by the private sector from the new facilities provided. The simplest example is the new car park on a hospital site. A joint deal with a private car park operator, who would build and run the facility, appears to have a lot of commercial appeal. A private operator is likely to be better placed to equip and run a car park than the management of a hospital or university, which is focused on a completely different core business. More significantly, the car park will generate a flow of income from consumers to pay for the capital invested. Similar arguments were also used in early discussion of patient hotels but, not surprisingly in a relatively compact country such as the UK, these have not developed to any significant extent.

As we move closer to the core services of the hospital, the next most suitable area for private investment is private health care within the NHS. A day surgery facility with the capacity to undertake both private and public operations might appeal to an investor. Placing this on a hospital site under a collaborative deal means that additional specialized facilities (for example dedicated theatre equipment, that might not be used to capacity by private patients alone) can be provided. The level of investment needed to create a private ward is also relatively modest, involving mainly redecoration and creation of private rooms, so a number of NHS Trusts have done this for themselves and set out to capture a larger share of the local private sector market, as noted earlier.

But the real justification for the PFI is the impact it has on public sector borrowing. Although the capital investment must be paid for somehow, the ability to shift some costs further into the future, as well as the general hype about the greater efficiency of the private sector, were major payoffs for a government keen to see greater use of markets and lower taxes. To achieve the government's goals, it is not enough for the PFI to fund car parks and private wings, a small part of the potential investment cost of the NHS. The Private Finance Initiative has also increasingly been seen as a method of funding for core facilities. Interest in private funding must be extensively tested before any public funding is provided, even though the initial guidance after the Reforms made clear that private funding was always likely to be more costly. Yet the Conservative government in 1996 continued to insist that ever larger schemes – including whole hospitals, but also the simple upgrading of parts of a hospital – should be tested for private finance interest. There were frequent press releases claiming that major schemes were imminent. The gossip among those who advise on these issues was that few if any deals have really been completed and it may be some time before we see privately funded hospitals, if ever, because the costs of building and operating such schemes could not be brought down to the levels offered by public finance and still leave room for private profits. Similarly, some big construction firms withdrew because of the uncertainty over the rules and the delays in approval.

There are several problems to be resolved if the PFI schemes are to take off. Some are administrative rather than economic. For example, regional offices have had to make up much of the rule book on PFI as schemes have developed, changing the dead hand of region to a stranglehold on progress. Similarly, many of the consortia bidding for major schemes have only come together for these bids. They involve construction and facilities management companies who are still getting to know each other and, at the same time, trying to balance the risk to each party from the financial package.

More difficult to resolve is the issue of the economic payoff for these schemes. Only in a few cases is there a major piece of development land which can be swapped for the new building, rather than being sold on the open market. Other sources of the profit needed to make a project attractive to the private sector are a reduction in construction costs through a change in building methods or specification or a change in running costs through more efficient working in the supporting services provided by the private contractor/consortium. But do these gains really exist, and can they only be achieved through use of private contractors?

In the absence of a well-scrutinized successful scheme it is difficult to know what, if any, economies are possible in construction. In principle, a design and build approach, with a single contractor responsible for construction, without the delays caused by public tendering of each element of the work, could be cheaper. But tendering is only used because it provides scope for testing the competitiveness of any bid for any stage of the work. Since only big firms will be able to afford to put together a bid for major schemes, this may exclude the savings offered by the use of smaller, lower cost contractors at particular stages of the job.

Running costs may be reduced if a facilities management company runs all the supporting services together. (The government has typically excluded medical and other clinical staff from the private component of the future service, to avoid claims that it really has privatized the health service. NHS staff working in a hospital owned, run and managed as a facility by the private sector looks so close to a private hospital that this sensitivity seems a little odd.) Economies in site management are one obvious benefit from a single facilities management contract but the potential number of separate support service managers eliminated does not, on the face of it, offer scope for multimillion pound returns. While it may be possible to run the individual support services more cheaply together than alone, it should also be noted that these services have typically been put out to tender already (and are well known for offering low paid jobs). Thus some of the potential savings from greater private sector efficiency have already been realized, and others (such as from new ways of providing clinical services) have been ruled out to avoid charges of privatization of the NHS.

This is not to say that the PFI cannot work on large schemes; we lack the evidence, though, to show that it can. My guess is that commercial interest stems substantially from the chance for a recession-hit building industry to get a guaranteed building job. If it is necessary to form coalitions with site management companies to do so, then so be it. The site managers will be the ones who have to provide the reduction in running costs, so the construction firms may see their risk from a joint PFI bid as low, compared to the risk for the site management company; though this will depend on the legal framework in each consortium. Access to land, in the right place and at the right price, may also be attractive, but this will always depend on the state of the property market.

Others talking up the PFI are those who have a vested interest as consultants and advisers to the various parties involved. But I doubt if there are the gains to fund the investment if these can only come from the facilities management elements. It can cost £50 to £60 million to build a hospital, and in some cases much more. If the private sector wants to get back a substantial return on this investment (say 15 to 20 per cent per year, to compensate for any risks in future contracts) it must reduce running costs by up to £12 million. That is a very demanding efficiency saving, to be achieved almost at a stroke, since a hospital of this size will probably have a running cost per year of perhaps £40 million. It is the equivalent of laying off 1,200 low paid staff costing £10,000 a year each, perhaps more non-clinical staff than some hospitals employ!

Potentially more serious is the longer-term effect of PFI on public services such as the NHS. In its 1996 report into PFI, the Treasury Committee of the House of Commons (1996) concluded that PFI was increasingly seen by the government as a way of substituting private funds for public funds, not as a way of augmenting public investment. This means that the decision to proceed with a particular scheme could rest more on its profitability to the private investors and developers than its strategic importance to the health service. This distortion of priorities is a major shortcoming of PFI highlighted by the committee.

The profitability of a private investment in public service facilities will depend on costs, profits and the degree of risk involved. Risk is particularly problematic. The Department of Health regards it as essential that the private sector bears some of the risk of the loss of business in the future, due to a change in contracts, because a cast-iron public sector contract with a private operator effectively removes the market forces that are supposed to lead to greater efficiency. (Of course, these can be reintroduced by other bureaucratic means, such as those used to control prices in the privatized utilities.) Critics (for example Kelly 1995) have also drawn attention to a paradox in the PFI approach. The private sector will charge a premium for risk, aiming to recoup its investment costs in a shorter period where a long-term contract is not secure. Hence the transfer of risk becomes the mechanism for *increasing* the cost of borrowing and not merely the route to a more competitive approach. And if things go wrong and the expected rewards are not achieved, it is unlikely that the government would sit back and let a privately funded hospital close. In the end the damage from the political risk of a major closure is much greater than that from the market risk of failing to manage the services to make a profit.

Pending a clear set of demonstration projects, the Private Finance Initiative has had another unsatisfactory impact. It is now a requirement that private interest in any NHS investment is fully tested. In consequence, a large number of investment schemes have to be tested simultaneously for private sector interest. The net effect has been to slow down the process because a variety of tendering rules have to be invented, interpreted and changed by regional offices of the Management Executive. By 1996, most of those involved in PFI had begun to say, in private at least, that there are too many rules and steps to be followed before a private bid can be accepted, or even objectively and conclusively rejected. It would be ironic if the net effect of the PFI was to cut two years off the building process, but only after slowing down the choice of developer by four years!

Overall, there is little evidence that the freedom to access capital has in fact been granted. In a cash-limited public sector, with a number of bureaucratic tiers still expecting to exert at least some influence on the development of new services and facilities, it seems likely that the freedom will remain a token, rather than an actual, increase in flexibility for Trusts, for at least two reasons. First, there is a lack of clarity over who has what discretion in major hospital planning decisions in what purports to be a decentralized system. The political difficulties caused by new (or much expanded) hospitals in Chelsea and Solihull in the 1990s have been an embarrassment to politicians. They are unlikely to give a public health service opportunities to embarrass them further by building more facilities than the NHS can afford to run. Second, and more fundamentally, there is a conflict in the post-Reforms NHS between a national service with a planned network of coordinated services (such as accident and emergency centres, cancer units and maternity units) and market-led investment by individual Trusts to change their future service mix. To date, the centrally planned model has had a low profile compared to Trust freedoms, but in practice the planned distribution of facilities is probably dominating what is built on the ground. Regional managers with a map of the future services – in their heads if not in their hands – have the power to endorse, defer or reject the key decisions made at Trust level, so they continue to call most of the shots.

FREEDOM TO CHANGE PAY AND CONDITIONS

The other important financial freedom offered to NHS Trusts was the flexibility to pay their staff according to their own local scales rather than on national pay scales. This is attractive because labour supply for many skill groups may be strongly influenced by local rather than national labour supply. In addition, some services may be threatened from time to time by a shortage of a particular skill group. The ability to pay more to this group provides an important flexibility that could only otherwise be found by manipulating grading and grade points. Pay flexibility was also important for the government, which clearly hoped that some pay would go down, due to local labour market conditions, reducing the tax cost of the NHS. Local bargaining would also weaken the power of trade unions since each branch could be facing a different offer.

The principle of disaggregating labour relations in the NHS has already been established by moves to contract out support services. This saw the ending of standard terms and conditions of service and the introduction of a diversity of contracts and employers. For the government, the main advantage of local pay is a reduction in costs, since in some parts of the country health service wages provide a higher standard of living than in others, due to lower costs of housing, for example. But the government has found it harder to achieve flexible pay for the key professions in the NHS, who have held on strongly to the central determination of pay through national review bodies, in spite of packages of national and local pay that emerge from some pay reviews. This is because the professions are well organized nationally, with well-established national pay determination, and they command high public support.

Pressure to implement local pay determination for clinical staff was considerable in the first half of 1995. But doctors were ultimately left out, through a political deal which the nursing profession deeply resented. During the 1995 pay dispute, the Royal College of Nursing indicated that it would accept local deals if at least 300 Trusts offered the target rate of 3 per cent without strings. That is, if local deals give a consistent national result, then they are acceptable. (By implication, if they do not – the entire purpose of local pay – then local deals are not acceptable.) The nurses' subsequent decision to withdraw their 'no strike' commitment was sufficient to generate a settlement. The settlement was termed a local deal by the NHS Executive, in that individual Trusts made their own offers. Across the country, the deal was tantamount to a national deal of 3 per cent.

It will be interesting to see if Trusts are able to build on this first local step to develop a more clearly local pay settlement in the future. In 1994–5 Trusts were particularly unhappy about the intervention of the centre, given the promised freedom to negotiate and the perceived willingness of the centre to change the terms of the freedom in order to get a politically acceptable settlement (Chadda 1995). Trusts are also investing a great deal of management time and energy in a topic which can sour relations with staff and which, in the past, could be legitimately said to be outside the control of local managers.

Putting aside recent pay rounds, we should not overlook the characteristics of the UK labour market for health services and its likely impact on local pay. Career doctors work in a substantially national and certainly a regional market. In any given specialty it is accepted that only a limited number of consultant posts will come up in any one year. Qualified senior registrars must be prepared to consider a wide range of locations and may even succeed in getting a job in a far flung part of the country just before one becomes available on their doorstep. There has never been an organized and explicit succession planning process for consultant posts in spite of the amount of organization that goes into some junior staff training schemes. This national labour market may not mean that pay differentials between localities are infeasible. Other professions probably have earnings differentials (such as rural solicitors and accountants, compared to their urban colleagues). But more importantly, since consultants are the prime staff without whom much of the hospital cannot work and junior doctors cannot be recruited, it is likely that Trusts will not wish to be seen to offer less than the going rate for a job which is relatively similar across different parts of the country.

Where shortages develop, Trusts may have to pay more or find ways of accommodating other demands from applicants, for example finding jobs for partners or paying for the family pet to be shipped over from the USA. However, the relative shortages and surpluses of medical personnel are also balanced, to a degree, by the staff planning practised in the NHS. Concern with the high cost of medical training has led the Department of Health to keep a close eye on medical staff numbers in each specialty. As a result, a junior doctor thinking of specializing in a particular area of medicine can probably find out on the grapevine when consultant appointments are likely to become available and how many eligible candidates there are likely to be. This should encourage some junior doctors to leave surplus specialties and enter shortage specialties, as long as they receive sufficient guidance and information on the emerging medical labour market. Some of their freedom of movement has been curtailed, however, by new training grades which may tend to fix doctors within specialties for longer periods. Also the pay differential in favour of surgeons resulting from private practice could leave some surgical specialties oversubscribed relative to medicine, even when the jobs are equally scarce.

For nurses and other professional staff there is more likely to be a local labour market. Career nurses, particularly general nurses, are less specialized in one area of care than consultants, with the ability to move to different specialist areas after undertaking suitable training courses. There is also much greater scope for career advancement locally than is usually the case in medicine. Although there are smaller numbers of jobs in other professional groups, there is likely to be some scope for a local career and therefore a more local than national labour market, at least until the most senior jobs are being sought.

Where there is a surplus of nurses or other professionals locally, a Trust might be able to consider offering a lower local rate for some grades, giving increased scope to pay more for those specialties or services where it is harder to recruit. But in a sense there is a surplus of nurses almost everywhere, in that there are much larger numbers of trained nurses not working in the NHS than working within it. The supply of nurses to the NHS is likely to be heavily influenced by the alternative job opportunities available to them. Nurses have a reasonably high level of general education and in future will be predominantly a graduate profession. They are therefore likely to be seen by employers as having a number of desirable characteristics, including diligence and commitment to the job. Larger employers can also make use of nurses as a part of their on-site health cover. In consequence, a local surplus of nurses need not lead to a lowering of local pay but to migration to other jobs, where these can be found. More generally, nurses may have to be paid in line with local labour markets in which they move and their pay may need to move up rapidly in certain market conditions.

Nationally, a move to local pay has been seen as adversely affecting the interests of nurses and so there is strong resistance from the Royal College of Nursing and other trade unions. Other professional groups have also resisted local attempts to change pay rates, for example by blacklisting certain Trusts which proposed to depart from nationally agreed scales. Compared to the power of an individual Trust, the main health unions and professions look strong, well organized and popular with the public. This may continue to make the struggle for local pay a difficult one.

Trusts might benefit from a different form of flexibility, not on levels of pay but on the work carried out by each staff group. For some professionals allied to medicine, for example speech therapy, there has been a tendency towards shortage, partly due to the limited numbers trained nationally and the attrition rates of these predominantly female professions. In nursing there are certainly large numbers of nurses trained, but more than half of those are not working as nurses. A proportion of these nurses could be integrated back into the workforce through part-time or other working arrangements, and some could be retrained to take on some of the work of the shortage therapy areas. This would probably be resisted by the individual therapy professions but it is difficult to see how a partly trained nurse-therapist, working within well-defined protocols, could be worse than no therapist at all. More generally, shortages of key staff have not led the NHS to break down substantially the demarcation boundaries that prevent one group carrying out the work of another. This kind of re-engineering of the care process has been widely debated but the UK pilot sites have not yet reported.

It is important not to overlook the potential consequences of local pay. Over time, local pay might lower costs by several percentage points. But who would get the benefit of any savings? If purchasers became aware of the cost reduction, as they almost certainly would, then they might claw it back from Trusts in lower contract prices. Similarly, if there were substantial regional pay differentials over time, then regions and the Department of Health might be expected to claw back savings. As a result, the impact of local pay would be neutral on Trusts – indeed it would have to be in the name of equity – and, once a lower local level of pay was achieved, it would be harder to return to national rates in the event of a future shortage of staff in some service areas, because of the extra cost of raising all staff back to the national level. As a result, there would be no real payoff for individual Trusts who negotiated substantially lower rates of pay.

In practice, the move to local pay has waxed and waned, partly due to political circumstances. A number of devices have been used to satisfy government claims that local pay has become a reality and trade union claims that it has not. For example, a mixture of national baselines and local additions has been proposed in pay rounds to give some scope for local negotiations. However, national trade unions have sought the same local top-up everywhere, and so progress on real local pay was still very slow by the time of the 1997 pay review. Clearly, under any two-stage process there are some merits in delaying deals until the going rate minimum is known and then negotiating around that. This kind of sleight of hand may allow the government to claim that it has achieved local pay. But as long as nurses and other health professionals enjoy wide public support, there will be limits to how far politicians wish to take them on, over pay or any other issues.

Furthermore, the government has been reluctant to give Trusts the promised freedom of movement on human resources. Following criticism of the growth in management costs and staffing due to the Reforms, and the substantial cuts in health service management in Wales required by John Redwood when Welsh Secretary, the government intervened throughout the NHS to insist on a 5 per cent reduction in management costs in 1996. By developed country standards, the NHS spends a relatively small percentage of its budget on management and it was always predictable that the creation by the Reforms of more separate entities would be more likely to raise management costs than to reduce them. As long as Trusts have competitive prices – a key goal of the internal market – the government should be indifferent as to whether these are achieved by more managers generating greater efficiency from fewer clinical staff or any other means. Consumers neither know nor care about the management costs of Sainsbury's or Tesco's, as long as the price on the shelves is right. But again this example illustrates the central dilemma of the Reforms. A publicly funded health service that has always had a high profile in political and media circles simply cannot be left to its own devices, in a market or outside one.

TO FREE OR NOT TO FREE?

Compared to the difficulties of achieving the promised freedoms on industrial relations, for example negotiating new pay rates with strong national trade unions, Trusts have much greater freedom to vary the skill mix (the number and grade of the staff) used to treat each type of case, often in ways purchasers cannot identify. This can create surpluses that purchasers are unaware of or may simply lack the resources to monitor. Variation in skill mix therefore offers more scope for local flexibility than pay bargaining. Here again, however, the dilemma appears. Can a nationally funded health service tolerate a wide range of inputs for the same type of case, with a range of quality of care? If not, then enforcement of similar processes (such as similar levels of day case surgery for particular conditions, and similar levels of staffing on wards) again infringes the freedom of Trusts.

Overall, the freedoms to be given to NHS Trusts under the White Paper have not materialized to any substantial degree. This is the direct consequence of the size of the NHS and its importance in public spending, together with the popularity of the professions and the strength of their trade unions. The NHS is simply too large and too costly to be given unfettered access to capital spending by the Treasury and, since hospitals and community services cannot be seen to fail for commercial reasons, the NHS centrally will inevitably bear the risk of borrowing. On pay, the professions continue to be too strong for the government or the Trusts to take on successfully. Trusts are therefore simply not free agents in many important commercial respects. Their greatest freedom of action is predominantly around smaller scale decisions such as taking on additional fundholder contracts or, internally, changing skill mix and staffing for a given caseload.

Given the objectives of Trusts and their limited freedom to pursue them, we now turn to the incentives created by the NHS Reforms and examine the behaviour that they have produced within the internal market.

INCENTIVES FOR PROVIDERS

The intention of *Working for Patients* was to give Trusts many of the incentives of conventional companies while avoiding charges of privatization by keeping assets within the public sector. Trusts, as business entities, have in principle the freedom to influence and change both the range and cost of production; they also have the scope to influence their market share and total contract activity.

Given a contract linking patient care activity and income, Trusts clearly have incentives to reduce the cost of activity, to increase the surplus for internal development (or 'illegal' cross-subsidization), and to increase their caseload at any given price, if the marginal cost of doing so is less than the price realized. Trusts have also typically been set 'cost improvement' targets by purchasers, which derive from the cash limits and inflation forecasts given to the NHS by the Treasury. Although Trusts have limited scope for retaining surpluses and do not have shareholders to satisfy through dividends, there is always likely to be some cost pressure to meet, such as when new drugs and materials are used without an adjustment to the contract price. There is also likely to be a sufficiently long list of bids for new equipment, at any time, to make the use of any spare money relatively easy, but the absence of carry-forward means that accumulation for larger capital items is not so simple.

INCENTIVES TO REDUCE COSTS

Where the price of a service is fixed and the costs not revealed to purchasers, there is scope to create financial gains from cost reductions which either leave quality unchanged or reduce quality in ways the purchasers do not notice. Trusts thus have very clear incentives to reduce costs wherever possible and use the savings to fund new or developing areas of service, or to raise standards for other patients. While this incentive operated before the NHS Reforms, it was weaker in that the management of the hospitals or community units was a part of the DHA management. As a result, any savings generated could be taken away by district level management to fund their priorities, rather than those of the unit. By the same token, units could press for more funding from the district rather than achieving cost reductions. This was particularly likely once savings from support services had been pursued through contracting out. This left hospital management with difficult decisions about how far to press for savings in areas of direct patient care, where staff sensitivity and power were much greater. With Trusts, a clearer link between income and activity should, in principle, focus both management and professional staff on the threat to services from a shift in the DHA contract. Trusts in the internal market clearly have an incentive to be competitive on the price of contracts in order to avoid losing contracted activity from DHAs and GP fundholders.

The incentive to reduce costs is weakened, to a degree, by the need to meet quality of care standards set by purchasers. However, since many aspects of quality of care were unmeasured before the NHS Reforms, there was probably scope for cost reductions in some areas of Trust activity, though management might find it difficult to identify which these were. Similarly, because so little is known about the precise relationship between staff inputs and quality of outcomes, considerable scope probably existed in Trusts to obtain some savings without compromising quality at all, if only because NHS services have not tended to run at a uniform level of efficiency. (See for example the various reports of the Audit Commission on the wide variations across NHS providers in the services that the Commission has examined over a number of years.)

INCENTIVES TO CROSS-SUBSIDIZATION

The NHS Executive has issued a number of guidance documents to try to ensure that Trusts compete on an equal footing and that competition for contracts is based on a comparison of real costs, reflected in contract prices, and not artificially low prices. Early guidance noted that Trusts should not deliberately cross-subsidize services and should only engage in marginal cost pricing when unplanned spare capacity became available during the financial year. That is, in spite of the NHS being asked to behave in a more business-like manner, loss leaders and other pricing initiatives were not allowed, in spite of being a very common feature of business. The situation is complicated by the characteristics of hospital costs. Hospitals have high fixed costs, which include many staff costs, even though staff are usually seen as a part of variable costs, to be hired and fired as demand changes. The high fixed costs of the hospital occur for several reasons. First, in order to be in business as a comprehensive DGH, a hospital must have a full complement of services supporting serious illness. In economic terms, it must be staffed to meet 'option demand' − in this case the option for a seriously ill individual to present at any time, day or night. Second, the complexity of medicine and surgery means that many hospital services can only be provided safely and effectively by a large team. Hiring a consultant cardiac surgeon for a few hours a week is of no use without the supporting operating team and specialist recovery facilities. Cover for sickness and holidays means that doubling up of many staff will also be needed. Thus the minimum critical mass for some services may be close to the maximum capacity needed to meet local demands.

By comparison, community Trusts are much more flexible. Consider, for example, how easy it would be to set up a small home nursing service in competition with a community Trust, compared to the cost and difficulty of setting up a comprehensive general hospital or a cardiac surgery unit in competition with local NHS hospitals. A small scale neighbourhood nursing service could go into business with only one or two staff initially, within a matter of a few weeks.

Returning to hospitals, where the complexity of costing and charging is much greater, we can see how high fixed costs make it difficult to know how much to charge to specific activities. For example, if an X-ray/imaging department is needed with a given capacity to meet the emergency caseload locally, with 24 hour cover, what is the cost of also undertaking elective work? If the marginal cost of extra staff only is charged to elective activity, is this legitimate pricing policy or cross-subsidization? For example, overheads could be shared more equally between emergency and elective activity rather than counting elective activity as the marginal activity.

The energy industry has looked at this problem in some detail because of the high fixed costs of operating national energy networks. In theory, when capacity is fully utilized at times of peak demand, purchasers are expected to pay for the fixed costs of the network. That is, the network is paid for by those whose use decides its overall size. Users at other times are then charged the marginal cost of the energy provided to them. In the same way, a hospital could charge all services needed to support emergencies to its emergency care contracts. Other, elective, services would then be priced at marginal cost. This would not imply any subsidy but merely acceptance of the cost structure of hospitals.

When pricing rules vary, the use of different accounting conventions can lead to considerable variation in the prices to purchasers. Even the apparently simple notion of charging all costs to activities may in practice be complicated and produce a wide range of results. MacKerrell (1993) shows in a simple set of examples how the decision rule used to allocate overheads has a profound impact on the relative prices of different elements of activity. Yet each of the rules used is highly plausible and involves no creative accounting. In a free market, firms decide their prices according to costs and demands and attempt to make a profit, so accounting conventions are less of a concern than the demand for their products. But in the NHS internal market, there is likely to be some public resistance to special offers and spot markets to auction off short-term capacity, even though these measures could improve the overall efficiency of the system. Hence the concern with rules and conventions designed to limit the kind of behaviour that is characteristic of markets, the adjustment of prices around demand and the cost of supply.

Given the three types of contract introduced by the Reforms – block contracts, cost and volume contracts and cost per case – there may be incentives for providers to move costs between different services and contract types in order to maintain income or resist competing threats. For example, a local emergency service may be covered by a block contract. The local provider Trust may have a monopoly of local emergency work because of concern with the health effects of travel to a distant alternative provider. Thus the local hospital Trust has an incentive to load fixed costs onto its core contract for emergency services, ensuring that as far as possible its overheads are covered by income. Marginal costing of elective surgery contracts enables the local provider Trust to use its monopoly of emergency services as a lever in the competitive market for elective services, where fundholding has created a much more competitive market. But is this cross-subsidization? Or is it merely the result of differences in the competitive environment for each service and the resulting allocation of costs between services? Prices for fundholders become even more complicated if fundholder budgets are linked to Trust prices. A price rise in these circumstances may mean more income and no fall in demand, as long as fundholders are fully compensated. This is certainly not typical in conventional markets.

INCENTIVES TO INCREASE ACTIVITY – WHAT PRICE COMPETITION?

As noted above, where a contract is volume sensitive, treating more cases may be another way of generating internal surpluses. In principle, the advantages depend on the marginal cost of activity relative to the contract price. As noted above, hospitals are characterized by high fixed costs, not only for facilities but for dedicated staff groups. Up to the capacity of a clinical team and the facilities, it should therefore be possible to carry out additional activity at marginal cost (for example the extra costs of materials and drugs) and below the average cost. In other words, with no manipulation of costs or cross-subsidization, additional cases (for example from a waiting list initiative by purchasers) genuinely cost less than current cases. This poses some practical problems for the market if the government is determined to maintain a level playing field. That is precisely what markets do not set out to do, typically rewarding success which spreads overheads and reduces average cost still further. Getting bigger often leads to lower costs per unit, as there are more units to contribute to overheads. But this is the path to fewer and bigger hospitals, when the public values highly its access to a convenient local hospital.

Competing for additional waiting list work is the clearest, and least sensitive, way of expanding activity. Indeed, a waiting list initiative is itself something of a criticism of the established providers to a health authority, and so giving a short-term contract to another provider is less controversial than many other moves in the internal market. Increasing income from private practice is potentially more controversial in that critics can argue that, whatever the incentive offered by the additional income, it takes a Trust's focus away from its core objective: the meeting of public health care needs. There has also been criticism from the private sector of the growth in private treatment by Trusts, particularly in relation to the lower level of overheads that NHS Trusts can attribute to elective surgery.

The incentive to compete more widely than waiting list initiatives and the private sector is countered by the impact of competition on the current competitive position of a Trust. This is particularly true for community Trusts, which have been established as geographic monopolies with a clearly defined 'patch'. Competing over the border for established community services such as district nursing and health visiting is only possible by bending the rules. For example, some GP fundholders persuaded distant community Trusts to employ, in name only, attached community nursing staff so that the GPs could challenge the standards and monopoly power of their local community Trust. But even if competition were allowed across borders, it raises the possibility of retaliation. This is more clearly the case in the more open internal market for acute hospital services. In pathology, for example – a service where competition between NHS Trusts, and also with the private sector, is technically very feasible – it is common to find an anticompetitive culture among some staff, countering the entrepreneurship of others. The legitimate argument against competing for others' NHS work is that the NHS is a zero sum game. Income can only be gained at the expense of others, not by increasing the total spend on health care, and so zealous competition could backfire – 'If we compete for their work, they will compete for ours.' As a result, many staff may not be keen to follow management in a competitive strategy. They are likely to see the scope for losing jobs and will not benefit directly from any commercial gains. Compared to conventional private sector workers, they can also cling to the hope that if they stay out of the market, other NHS Trusts might do the same.

Competition has been a particular problem for the NHS Executive, which must show that the market is working to justify the Reforms while at the same time minimizing damage done by market forces because of the risk of political fallout. This led it to produce guidance on how the market should work and what kind of anti-monopoly standards would be used to judge potential mergers (Department of Health 1994). Dawson (1995) has been highly critical of this guidance, on the grounds that private sector models of markets and competition do not fit readily in an NHS where much of the market power lies, in Dawson's view, with purchasers. It is certainly striking that, in a market where most of the mergers appear to have been forced on providers to prevent outright closure of one or other Trust, there is such concern with monopoly power being built up by Trusts. Dawson points out that conventional markets run partly on excess capacity, with competing firms having the facilities and scope to take each other's business if an opportunity arises. Government is proud to point to the introduction of parental choice in schools but rarely mentions that this arose due to a falling birth rate and the creation of spare capacity as a by-product. It seems unlikely that governments would be prepared to invest in spare classrooms and associated facilities so that real parental choice could operate at any time. However, in the health service, since hospital capacity is even more expensive to create and run than schools, the pressure to minimize hospital capacity is probably stronger than the desire to see real competition at work between Trusts.

INCENTIVES TO CHEAT

The allocation of gains from additional contract activity between specialties in an acute hospital Trust may be problematic for hospital managers. Some specialties will always find it easier to increase their activity and derive extra income from purchasers (for example elective surgery services carrying out waiting list initiative contracts for a neighbouring health authority, through weekend working). However, in principle the scope for additional income generation does provide a basis for stimulating increased activity through proportional internal rewards to individual departments. Associated with direct incentives to reduce costs and/or increase activity there may consequently be incentives to change the reporting of costs or activity rather than the reality. For example, classifying day cases as inpatients or outpatients as day cases will increase the income received, under a volume-related contract, without changing real activity. This problem is particularly important where the purchaser receives relatively limited data from the provider on the technical content of each episode of care charged to the contract. Given management cost reductions, purchasers may also lack the staff needed to analyse activity and contracts sufficiently to spot such changes.

More generally the scope for cheating highlights an important difference between the health service and service industries in the market. In a simple sale of goods, the consumer exchanges money for goods and will not pay unless supplied. More complex purchases by organizations or mail order, for example, involve a chain of paperwork from order through delivery note to invoice and receipt. It is easy to prove what was ordered and supplied, unless the paperwork is tampered with. Contrast this with the data given to purchasers. A minimum data set is provided to purchasers but if a devious provider changes a few codes, there is no sign-off of the information to show whether it correctly records the procedure carried out. The Dental Estimates Board follows up a proportion of patients to confirm that what was done was indeed done. But I have encountered no examples of such detailed follow-up by health commissions. While it may be stretching a point to think of providers deliberately changing data, it would be no surprise to find lots of overcounting, for example where a day surgery list of patients is recorded and processed when their operations are cancelled. The history of problems with information in the NHS is scarcely reassuring when thinking about the potential error rate, whether accidental or deliberate.

The economics of 'lemons' (defective secondhand cars) and subsequent developments in the economics literature show that a deliberate rip-off by one party in a transaction is less likely where there is a prospect of continuing trade. But if the provider believes that the main purchaser cannot take a contract away, due to the lack of effective local competition, for political reasons, or because they are incapable of spotting the rip-off, then manipulation of the data to increase income may not be seen as particularly risky.

INCENTIVES TO COHESION

The effects of the Reforms, particularly through the contract negotiations with GP fundholders but also with DHAs, have probably brought many departments and specialties closer together to face the problems of concern to purchasers. Because the income of the department might be adversely affected by withdrawal of a contract due to poor standards of care offered by some of its members, much of the past variation in standards could no longer be tolerated. Uniform standards of care were a particular concern in quality clauses in contracts and so providers have increasingly taken greater interest in their own standards.

This focus on group standards in specialties and service areas also reinforced aspects of clinical management, particularly in hospital. Management reforms since Griffiths in the early 1990s have emphasized the need to bring clinicians into management, not least because of the difficulty of persuading clinicians to accept management decisions taken by non-clinicians. Clinical directorates are now commonplace in the management structures of almost all hospital Trusts, and local management by clinical professionals is also widespread in community Trusts. Contracting under the NHS Reforms potentially reinforces the clinical directorate as the basis for management since purchasers, particularly fundholders, increasingly see the hospital not as a monolithic service provider but as a provider of many different service lines. Increased scrutiny of standards of each line requires a quality assessment by the clinical directorate responsible to ensure that purchaser standards are met or that problems are identified internally, before they threaten the contract.

BEHAVIOUR IN PRACTICE

It would be helpful at this stage in the assessment of provider behaviour to review the practical evidence in relation to goals, freedoms and incentives. Questions we might ask of such research include:

- Have Trusts undertaken aggressive marketing and pricing strategies?
- Have Trusts tended to respond positively to service quality pressures?
- Have Trusts practised cross-subsidization?
- Have Trusts genuinely increased activity under contracting?
- Have large numbers of contracts moved between provider Trusts?

Unfortunately there has been little systematic in-depth research on the behaviour of Trusts to answer these questions, even though much of the framework to do so has been laid down (see for example Shiell 1991). While fundholders have been studied in some detail and over time, Trusts have not. Indeed, even where research has begun on Trusts, it has been overtaken to a degree by the blanket approach ultimately adopted to Trust creation. Early Trusts examined by Le Grand and Bartlett (1993b) were found to be already more efficient than average, with lower operating costs. Research on these alone obviously overlooks the impact of Trust status on less efficient hospitals and community units. Similarly research noted in Chapter 3 showed, at an early stage in the Reforms, that Trusts were in competition, with most hospitals examined having at least one competitor within a reasonable journey for patients. But this research has not been developed to take full account of subsequent market behaviour by the NHS Executive and regional health authorities, much of which appears to have involved careful market management and restraints on competition.

However, some assessment is possible from direct observations of individual Trusts. The behaviour of Trusts, as observed by the author, depends very much on the market environment in which they find themselves.

All the Trusts I have visited since the Reforms appear to have made strides to improve data collection so that performance can be judged more accurately against contract. This has a drawback for purchasers since they may find themselves being asked to pay more for services which have not really grown but have simply been underreported in the past. For example, in a large general hospital visited there was considerable doubt over whether patients in a 16 bed assessment unit attached to the Accident and Emergency department had been recorded as patients when they stayed overnight. Contract volumes and scope for extra contractual patients made it more important to quantify all patient contacts and probably did lead to some increases in measured activity rather than in activity itself.

I have also observed one management group in a hospital take a deliberate decision to reclassify endoscopic procedures carried out in a minor treatment suite as day surgery cases. This would increase the nominal contract income they attracted compared to being recorded as outpatient attendances. While this was the most naked example of fixing the figures, no doubt others have gone on, not least because of the wide range of activities carried out in hospitals and the lack of detailed data quantifying them.

Trusts with a strong local monopoly have typically tried to protect existing services and avoid loss of individual GP contracts since these reduce income at the margin and also send negative messages about price or quality to DHA purchasers and fundholders. Trusts in a more competitive environment have tended to proceed cautiously, making overtures to purchasers to concentrate individual services but being careful to avoid undermining the position of existing small services. For example, a Trust arguing that it should take on more of a surgical service provided by more than one local Trust can argue that there will be economies of scale in medical staffing, with fewer sites to cover, and potential benefits in the quality of care and of junior doctor training. But if the Trust concerned is the smaller partner in some other services, then it runs the risk of having these same arguments played back to it as a reason why it should lose some services.

Competition is likely to be much more aggressive where one factor or another has freed up some of the restraints. An obvious example, noted in Chapter 3, occurs when a long-stay institution is being run down as part of a long-term strategy towards community care. Where a purchaser explicitly offers a tender for a service, Trusts can bid openly without immediate fear of a counterbid for another service which they operate. In these circumstances there is a potential workload – carrying with it funding, staffing and perhaps facilities enhancement – that local Trusts will wish to secure. This kind of competition is now relatively common. However, once new facilities have been established with local Trusts and a continuing group of patients, there may be only limited scope for further rounds of tendering.

As noted earlier, the interdependence of services in hospitals is considered very important by clinicians. Just how important remains largely untested by the development of alternative models other than the small consultant-only private hospital model. The need for many services in an integrated whole will always tend to limit the amount of change in service locations that can be achieved by contracts for individual services. In practice, there are many models around the world of non-emergency hospitals, but the styles of work of consultants and the training of junior medical staff in the UK have so far made such models unattractive within the NHS. My own experience in a large number of planning studies shows that purchasers find it difficult to deal with the strongly deployed arguments of the professionals on service configuration and probably see managed mergers and rationalizations as the only solution. Building new models of the hospital is not something an individual purchaser is likely to take on in the face of professional resistance.

Because of the interdependence of services, competition for individual services has to take place within a wider strategic framework for local hospital services. Where it is clear that a purchaser cannot afford to fund all the local facilities, it is unlikely that they will resolve the issue by letting individual contracts to the Trust tendering the lowest price, regardless of other factors. We are more likely to observe planned mergers of Trusts in which the resolution of site and service distribution issues is turned into an internal operational management issue. Similarly, while the NHS has been developing a disaggregated approach to service planning, a major review of a specific service (cancer treatment) proposed the development of integrated networks of cancer centres as regional hubs with spokes to cancer units at individual hospitals. The solution was put forward by the Expert Advisory Group on Cancer (Department of Health 1995) (chaired by the Chief Medical Officer) to improve upon the low standards of care achieved without an integrated approach. But a planned network would immediately overlay, on local contracting, a raft of restrictions due to the need for co-location of services and equipment. It looks like a return, albeit a sensible return, to central planning.

It is clear that where Trusts really start behaving like market entities, competing aggressively with their neighbours, local purchasers may not be able to control them. I have seen Trusts where key consultant staff have unilaterally moved to a neighbouring hospital, threatening the survival of one of the Trusts without regard to purchaser decisions. Clearly, businesses in monopoly positions can dictate to their customers and those in more open markets can take the risk of changing the service and testing demand. But when Trusts do this, we have issues such as access by the public to its tax-funded services being dictated by a Trust rather than by the responsible health commission. This loss of purchaser control is real, particularly where the losing Trusts cannot readily recruit additional consultants due to national shortages or the damage done to its reputation by the loss of key staff, for example. Of course this could happen before the Reforms. But then the health commission employed the clinical staff and their managers and could in principle dictate the pattern of services. We have seen relatively little overt use of market muscle by Trusts, perhaps because it makes clear just how powerful Trusts could be in the right circumstances. That is, the very power of market behaviour could be so great that a post-Thatcher government cannot allow it to be used.

TRUSTS – MORE THAN A NAME?

Overall there is a serious shortage of research evidence on which to base any assessment of the impact of Trusts and Trust status in the NHS. Once it became clear that all hospitals and community units would become Trusts, the scope for a market in which there would be clear winners and losers was reduced. Trusts clearly need to pursue contracts and maintain or increase activity. But they are now operating within a market environment where Trusts, particularly hospitals, are not really competing aggressively. Political constraints, strong enough to split health authorities to protect Trusts in key constituencies, together with technical constraints on combinations of specialties and junior medical staff to support them, have weakened the market forces faced by Trusts. It may be that in another environment, particularly one with excessive numbers of hospitals and a willingness to see hospitals as businesses grow or fold in response to the market, a great deal more change might have occurred. Certainly this has been the impact of moves to managed care and constrained spending in the USA. But in the UK the political sensitivity of the NHS makes change difficult to achieve. Staff who have seen more than one change of employer (including one I met who has had six changes of employer for the same job in recent years) may be forgiven for seeing Trusts as an interlude of reform with some changes of names and logos but little real impact on services and organizational behaviour, because radical change is too sensitive to be allowed to take place.

However, underlying the current market with its limited ability to bring about change, market forces continue to work, to some degree at least. Ham (1994b) has argued that contestability rather than competitive tendering is the force most likely to bring about further change in the health service, though by its nature the changes may be less visible. As long as a Trust believes there is a chance that a purchaser may withdraw a contract there is an obvious incentive to respond to purchaser pressures to change services. I am sceptical about whether such fear of contract loss is widespread, but where it does exist, the results will not be highly visible changes of provider or crisis due to loss of services. Rather, over time, the kind of service improvements that purchasers seek – shorter waiting, better information, more day surgery – may accumulate. These are the gains that fundholders and fundholder consortiums believe they have made; health commissions are probably achieving many of the same gains. The excesses of the market have been reduced and possibly with them, the pace of change. But positive pressure for change can continue, at least where and when the weapon of contract shifting is a real threat, however rarely it is unsheathed.

All in all, we may have the ingredients for a classic British compromise that will deliver some of the benefits at only part of the cost. Unfortunately we have not measured the gains at provider level clearly enough to prove that the costs of creating markets, Trusts and contracts have been worth the perceived gains in more responsive services and faster treatment.

6

HEALTH CARE FUNDING AND DELIVERY INTO THE NEXT CENTURY

INTRODUCTION

In this chapter we look back at the Reforms and what has been achieved, and look forward to the kinds of further reforms that have been suggested to meet the problems still facing the NHS. In summarizing the impact of the Reforms, some generalizations about overall performance have to be made. It is therefore important not to underrate the difficulty of making such summary judgements. If anything, it has become more difficult because the NHS has become more diverse and adopted a number of commercial-style practices (for example fewer public meetings and more confidential price information) that make the impact of the Reforms harder to assess. Equally, any assessment needs evidence and without positive evidence of change, an unfair summary judgement may be unavoidable. If this is unfair on the Tory government and its health policies in the 1990s, they only have themselves to blame for a failure to pay for the necessary research.

THE OBJECTIVES OF REFORM

The White Paper *Working for Patients* set out to achieve seven nominal objectives:

- 1 to make the NHS more responsive to needs;
- 2 to stimulate a better service;
- 3 to enable hospitals which best meet needs to get the money to do so;
- 4 to reduce waiting times, improve services and cut junior doctors' hours;

5 to help family practitioners improve their services through budget-
holding;
6 to improve the effectiveness of the NHS;
7 to improve value for money.

This list shows signs of hasty drafting! Items 1, 2, 6 and 7 are all versions of the same thing, a better NHS for our money. There is little
that is directly measurable in this group. Even value for money is
problematic, given the different dimensions of value, the technical
and service elements of care and the scope for assessment from the
patient and purchaser perspectives. Nonetheless we can at least try to
assess whether the NHS is indeed better in some sense, an issue
explored in the next section.

Objectives 3, 4 and 5 are more specific and should allow us to say
something about whether they have been achieved. Let us look at
them in turn.

Objective 3 refers to the main impact of the internal market on
providers. Those that are 'better' will attract more caseload and more
contracts. This has happened to only a limited degree for hospitals
because of the difficulty of shifting contracts between providers. As
we have noted elsewhere in this book, hospitals have (or claim to
have) highly integrated or interdependent services, with a critical
mass in each specialty that is needed to support teaching and multi-
disease care. This critical mass cannot easily be reduced without
undermining the hospital as a whole, due to the effects on junior and
senior doctor recruitment. There are also too few hospitals in most of
the country for shifts in contracts not to meet local public and political resistance, so moving contracts is typically not popular, even
when the distance to the next provider is relatively small.

Potentially, the various provider mergers have benefited more efficient providers who have mopped up the caseload from less efficient
ones. There have certainly been many more mergers than major
contract shifts. But it is not easy to see the quality of any hospital service as a single whole, because each department provides, for most
patients, a self-contained service. As a result, some of the losers in
mergers are almost certainly better providers, in some sense, than the
winners. We should also not overlook the fact that most of the merger
activity has been driven by an agenda for planned change and not by
direct market forces.

In community services there have been some shifts of contracts as
a result of the flexibility offered by wider moves away from institutional care. But having seen some of this process at relatively close

hand, there still appears to be elements of Buggin's turn, with a reluctance on the part of purchasers to give too many contracts to one
provider, regardless of the quality of service. This can be sensible
behaviour in a market, avoiding having to face a monopoly supplier,
but it may mean accepting that the most effective providers will not
always get the contracts.

Objective 4 is not one but three, with little to connect them. Shorter
waiting times are a tangible objective. There has been considerable
progress to shorter waits, though we do not know enough about the
criteria used to put people on the waiting list to know if this is really
better care or concealed waiting. Although waiting list and waiting
time reductions were a part of policy before the internal market, the
contracting process probably has increased the pressure that health
commissions can apply to get waiting times down. A separate purchaser of services will tend to apply such pressure more than an integrated planning and providing body. The latter will always have a
greater incentive to accept the reasons for waiting lists rather than
forcing a reduction or embarrassing a provider. In markets, the purchaser is typically not interested in the provider's problems but only
in the service provided.

The second part of Objective 4 is the same old rhetoric about a better service and need not detain us. The third, the reduction of junior
doctors' working hours, is more tangible but probably has little to do
with the work of a market. A market works partly through competing
firms developing a range of price and quality mixes to appeal to different consumers. Firms also constantly try to find different ways of
doing things at lower cost. Skill substitution and the breaking down of
demarcation rules are both part of modern management approaches.
Junior doctor training does not fit this kind of market easily. It is
governed by rules, not all of which are clearly written down, that
restrict the flexibility of hospitals considerably. If you cannot get the
junior staff, you cannot run the service. Substituting other kinds of
staff – for example training nurse anaesthetists, who work in some
other countries – is not allowed. Nor is paying junior staff lots more
money, to recruit and retain them for a much longer working week
and without regular exposure to a range of different types of patient.
Instead of the flexibility of a market solution, we have bureaucratic
rules which may lead to a better quality of service but do not encourage market behaviour. Rather, the whole supply of junior medical
staff – who need a particular mix of training and experience at different stages – lends itself to a planned solution, across whole regions,
for example. Given the importance to the service provided by junior

doctors, this means that the local postgraduate deans, who coordinate junior doctor training, potentially wield more influence on hospital planning than local purchasers. By deciding the allocation of junior medical staff, they can impose a planned solution on the nominal market. (See also the discussion of flexibility in staffing and pay in Trusts in Chapter 5.)

Objective 5 in our list talks of making general practice better by giving GPs budgets. Fundholding may have achieved this, though many of the early entrants were probably already among the better practices. Clearly, some have improved practice premises or services through fundholding and so the objective has been achieved to some degree. Equally, this is only possible where the budget is funding more services than the fundholders wish to purchase from established providers, or providing for a higher cost than is ultimately paid. Thus a better service may come from an element of overfunding of fundholders. Where they can buy in a service at a lower cost than that previously provided, we have improvements in efficiency from which both patients and fundholders might benefit. Equally, if fundholders have simply reduced services for patients to fund practice improvements, the service is scarcely better for the losers. This has probably not occurred on any major scale. Savings are more likely to come from overfunding, random changes in local disease patterns and changes in prescribing policy. Fundholding has probably improved the practices involved but at a cost, in reduced funds for health commissions, that is not well researched. In consequence we do not know whether the overall effects are beneficial.

HAVE THE REFORMS PRODUCED A BETTER NHS?

Let us look at the extent of improvement in a number of stages. Have the Reforms worked? That is, is the NHS really reformed? And if so, has this transition improved the NHS for patients?

Nominally, the Reforms have worked, in the sense that we have an internal market that looks like that proposed in *Working for Patients*. But we certainly do not have a market red in tooth and claw, in which market forces drive change rapidly. This is because politicians have never been sufficiently confident of the better outcomes to push the market approach fully. For reasons discussed below, it may also be because the internal market was set up wrongly from the start.

The climate surrounding the Reforms has probably had an appreciable effect. The culture of British politics changed with the fall of

Thatcher. John Major is presented to us as a more reasonable and caring person who will not force change down the throats of a reluctant people. Similar differences in style have occurred between Secretaries of State for Health, from the pushy Mr Clarke to the conciliatory Mr Dorrell. As a result, as Ham (1994a) points out, the NHS Reforms have proceeded more as an emergent – rather than a consistent – strategy. At different times, under different Secretaries of State, different elements of the Reforms have received more emphasis. Over time, pressure for competition and markets of the kind generated by Mrs Thatcher gave way to concern about standards and the Patient's Charter and a more planned approach to change.

So have the Reforms, implemented in part but without opening up markets to vibrant competition, created a better NHS? To answer this question, we need to say something about what a better NHS would be. Potentially, it could be summarized as a service offering more appropriate care, more quickly, to a higher standard of service, for all patients presenting for treatment. Patients, but perhaps not purchasers, might also add 'more locally' to this list, given the strong public support for local hospitals. Purchasers may more readily see the benefits of larger centralized units with a greater critical mass than the people who will stand to lose their small much-loved hospital.

Is the NHS more responsive to patient needs as a result of the Reforms? We can consider this from both the technical and service sides of the NHS. Certainly medical needs are the main focus of the work of health commissions and they spend considerable time assessing them. But the response to needs depends on a chain of resource and medical decisions. Doctors must assess individual needs and respond with medical decisions that then commit the resources made available through the funding and contracting decisions of health commissions. The NHS has always worked in this way, with two versions of resource allocation to be reconciled with each other and the cash limit. In the past this was achieved by operating with a lack of clarity over what was being funded, so that a wide range of medical decisions on resource allocation were compatible with block grant funding. More detailed needs assessment and contracting began to challenge this process by specifying more clearly for each type of patient what is to be provided. But choices are not left to patients and need not be in the interests of individual patients. For example, a particular patient group may be given a lower priority by health commissions than by clinicians.

It is also difficult to show readily that the NHS is indeed 'more responsive' in its technical treatment of patients. Aside from time spent waiting, on waiting lists and sitting in clinics, there is no easy way of showing this better response without widespread and objective research, on referral, thresholds for treatment and treatment itself. Simpler measures, such as those drawn from patient and staff satisfaction surveys, are always affected by expectations and current headlines as well as genuine satisfaction with the service.

Fundholding arguably has the most scope for improving the response to patients by linking the strands of resourcing and clinical decisions (see Chapter 4). Equally, improvements achieved by fundholding may have come in part from overfunding, routinely or during periods of below average illness, and at the expense of unspecified services purchased by health commissions.

For some of the services covered by health commission contracts, the limit on the number of cases means that Trusts may refuse to treat extra patients towards the end of the financial year even when they have most, or all, the resources to do so. While completion of a year's work in ten months is a more responsive service for those treated, there is no response at all for those refused treatment when the contract has been filled. In the pre-Reforms NHS they may have been treated, with or without a wait, though sometimes only through overspending by the providers.

From a service perspective, my own view, based on limited contact with direct patient care services, is that the Reform process has not really penetrated to the 'factory floor'. NHS professional staff still give the impression that they will provide good technical care and that the patient is there to receive it quietly and gratefully. While some staff do show the kind of customer sensitivity that is typical of the highly competitive airlines, for example, many treat patients as a guaranteed commodity which will never go away. Staff also appear to be reasonably confident that their job will not be lost or that, if it is, they will get another, due to the protection of the key professionals in any retrenchment and the state of the labour market in nursing, medicine and professions allied to medicine. In short, many staff show the classic NHS approach, acting like workers in a monopoly with a guaranteed market and at times showing some frustration with their pay levels and with patient/consumer expectations. This is by no means unreasonable behaviour on their part, however. Staff in the NHS have been themselves 'done to' to a considerable extent, with changes in structures and functions imposed by government and higher tiers of management, though many in the private sector have undergone these changes but still smiled, through gritted teeth perhaps, at their customers.

Ham (1996) has argued that contestability – the scope for use of an alternative supplier – offers some benefits, as long as the provider believes that the potential threat to move a contract is a real threat. This ability to move, it is argued, is as important as actual transfer to the achievement of improved value for money. However, the threat has to be credible. As noted in Chapter 3, purchasers have shopped around very little and so the threat may appear somewhat unlikely to many staff in the NHS.

Block contracts have reinforced the old rather than the new culture, with little feeling that every patient is an additional source of income for the hospital. Clinical staff are often kept at arm's length from the contracting process and so have little opportunity to see the market threats, such as they are. As long as they see no direct impact from competition or contestable contracts, staff may not change their attitudes, particularly when the people they treat are not the paying purchasers.

I remain sceptical about whether most staff really feel that their service is contestable and indeed contested. For example, there has been little if any change in the doctors who actually provide local hospital services following the Reforms. Not all were providing care of a satisfactory quality and cost before the Reforms and many may have improved aspects of their service. But it is a rare event to find doctors or other professional staff laid off because of the Reforms. In late 1996 the first Trust to fail in the market, as opposed to being merged, was faced with closure. But most of the staff were to be taken on by other providers. Only management were due to go, because the Trust was seen to have too high a management cost overhead once it lost the first of its major contracts.

Potentially, the value for money offered by the NHS may have improved, even with no visible change in the service offered to patients. For example, the inefficient use of resources may have been reduced, thus increasing the value for money offered by a constant, rather than improving, level of service. But value for money, another key objective, is an elusive concept in the health service. On the face of it, contracting must have improved value for money by focusing attention on resources and activities together. Often they were very separate in the pre-Reforms NHS. But they are still relatively separate, at least in the sense that price and cost are two different things. Hospitals may allocate overheads in all kinds of ways to produce different prices for a given service. It may be economically efficient for this to occur in certain ways, for example charging overheads to emergency services where purchaser demand is not flexible and where emergency demand requires provision of the full range of services included in overheads. That is, purchasers get charged for the full range of facilities for the caseload that requires them. Other cases can then be charged without these overheads. This may increase the relative surplus from one activity, where the purchasers have little freedom of action, while reducing it in others. More generally, since most Trusts have not studied the economics of utility pricing, the net result is a range of prices for the same services from different providers.

Regular reviews by the Audit Commission also highlight the difficulty of specifying what constitutes good value for money. In coventional markets, judgements of value for money are left to consumers. Consumers happy with price and value for money will buy the product. Once services are procured only on behalf of the real consumers, value for money becomes tied up with the issue of whose values will be decisive, those of purchasers, doctors or consumers. For example, higher rates of day surgery may not be what every patient wants, even though purchasers have pressed heavily for such changes. Pressure to achieve ever-higher rates may prevent surgeons offering their patients a choice of day or inpatient care. Nor is it clear whether the NHS is prepared to offer such a choice.

Potentially, if the NHS was to become better under the Reforms, it needed better management. For example, management of the NHS was supposed to aid the move to greater effectiveness by becoming more businesslike. This has happened to some degree but much of the success of management in the health service stems from the involvement of clinicians. By getting doctors to manage their work, through clinical directorates, managers have avoided having to face professional and technical challenges to their decisions. While clinical directorates may not always take the hard decisions, they at least ensure that decision-making is fully informed. But there is an inevitable tension between running the health service as a business and handing over considerable responsibility to the professionals. Professionals are likely to be more conservative than market-orientated managers and so we might expect market forces to work less vigorously. Accepting the importance of involving clinical staff in management may mean accepting a particular pace of change.

Leaving them out, and allowing them to obstruct change, may lead to much greater inertia.

Managers have been constrained by the politics of the health service and the sensitivity of each group of stakeholders to change. Support for management from politicians has also been rather two-faced. Promises of the management infrastructure to develop the internal market began to look more and more hollow as ministers and MPs attacked the men in grey suits and demanded rapid but arbitrary reductions in management costs. Regional management has been cut and other moves to slim the service have been made through mergers of authorities. Like management in any organization, the fact that the real work is delivered by others makes the impact of the managers hard to quantify and leaves managers as an easy target for politicians looking for cuts.

To summarize, there is no convincing evidence that the Reforms have produced a substantially better NHS. For hospitals in particular this is not surprising. For all the talk of radical reform, the move to Trust status largely ossified the existing institutions and their staff. A Trust was not a bright new tomorrow, a management buy-out with dynamic leadership taking the best of the staff in a new direction. It was a change of name and status for a whole institution that in many other ways remained fundamentally unchanged. A process of gradual change then took place as Trusts attempted all kinds of cultural change programmes, many of which have achieved some success. But the staff themselves were not energized or shaken up by the moves to Trust status, apart from some local rows and skirmishes over what appeared to be, in the early days, opting out of the NHS. It is easy to see much more radical models in which dynamic departments in one hospital could expand to take over the services of others, using hospitals as shells within which a variety of providers worked and not as employers of every member of staff. Such a model is common in the private sector and overseas. It has its own drawbacks but the lack of experiment with it means that we effectively created a new model, the Trust within the internal market, in which most of the direct care was provided by exactly the same people as in the old model. We can hardly be surprised if it takes a long time to stop them doing things in exactly the same way, particularly if purchasers are too weak to force rapid change or threaten major shifts of contract.

In fundholding, with a budget matched closely to local disease patterns and treatment costs, and with no selfish behaviour by GPs, we are more likely to find an NHS that is truly more responsive to patients. Fundholding has stimulated a lot of innovation in a few dynamic practices, even though the general level of change is relatively small. However, there are also drawbacks. For example, too little may still be being spent on some patients if fundholding is both overfunded — thus cutting into health commission budgets — and encouraging GP fundholders to reduce services to fund premises improvements or shift priorities. Since fundholders are volunteers whom the Tory government was keen to keep happy as its main allies after the Reforms, the likelihood of overfunding — relative to health commissions — is high. Faced with a tight cash limit, fundholders might simply quit and embarrass the government. So fundholding may be achieving its improvements at a price.

But we must also beware of losing our post-Reform baby with the bathwater. There is no reason to believe that the NHS has got manifestly worse under the Reforms. In the right hands, the most radical model, fundholding, may well have made the NHS appreciably better and it has certainly been the site of the greatest rate of innovation in service models. Elsewhere and potentially in many circumstances in fundholding, there is no reason to believe that the NHS is more responsive because clinical and resource decisions are still not closely coordinated. Without population needs assessment on a very much larger scale than at present, this gap cannot be filled and the NHS must remain limited in its response to individuals. Equally, most of the time there are enough resources in the local system to enable most needs to be met fairly quickly. The NHS muddles through the uncertainties of unpredictable illness patterns and variations in professional behaviour in its time-honoured way, but perhaps with increased documentation of the compromises that result.

SHOULD THE INTERNAL MARKET SURVIVE?

The case for returning to the previous model of the NHS is at least as weak as the evidence supporting the internal market. Before the Reforms, clinical and resource decisions were even less coordinated than now. The scope for arbitrary decisions and eccentric use of resources was even greater with funding by block grant. As a result there appears to be widespread support for the principle of separating purchasing and providing. This falls in with the trend across a range of public services. If nothing else, the separation challenges the self-interest of providers in maintaining their own services regardless of cost-effectiveness. Purchasers may lack real market power in many cases but the alternatives almost always reduce it. Merging provider and purchaser organizations may offer some savings in management costs but has no obvious merit as a way of increasing the responsiveness of providers.

Based on recent policy statements, purchasers seem likely to survive as separate entities for the foreseeable future. As discussed below, separate purchasers are also the basis on which more complex models of future health service funding have been developed. No one seems prepared to go back to the jokes about the NHS being the biggest monolithic agency in Europe after the Red Army, so the prospects for turning the clock back are limited.

Fundholding is more controversial due to its perceived effects on equity, and is potentially a target for a future Labour government. Certainly the two-tier argument will always be hard to fend off because hospitals will inevitably see GP fundholder patients as representing real money and a chance for increased earnings, compared to the big block contract work of the health commissions. There is also the difficulty of creating a wide range of standards and priorities by devolving so much of the decision-making to individual practices. Equally, patients may prefer this and could, in principle, be given a voucher to opt into a fundholding practice if they wish to accept a particular pattern of care, with rules to prevent fundholders refusing the most expensive patients who cost more than an average value voucher to treat.

Locally sensitive purchasing, in its many different guises, may be an alternative model for both the main political parties. For Labour it offers a way of removing the inequality of fundholding while maintaining or improving GP influence in local health commission purchasing. For the Conservatives, locally sensitive purchasing offers a way of spreading some of the local autonomy of fundholding to those who do not wish to take it up, for example those who are reluctant to be involved directly in rationing.

So should it be more or less business as usual for the next ten or twenty years? Can the NHS look forward to an almost unprecedented period of stability? Certainly there is unlikely to be a lot of pressure for privatization of health care under either party, as radical Tory policy is no longer as popular as it was and Labour has always portrayed itself as a supporter of publicly funded health services, in spite of their move to a more market-orientated approach in a number of other areas. But at the same time as this potential outbreak of peace on most things other than fundholding, the NHS is being seen as an unsustainable model by a number of forecasters. So what is going wrong?

To address these issues, we examine below the kind of health service we might seek in the future and the ways in which we might pay for it. The discussion includes a review of some of the more wide-ranging changes that some commentators on the NHS have proposed and provides some insight into how the reformed NHS might develop further.

WHAT'S THE QUESTION?

It is claimed that on her deathbed, Gertrude Stein, the American woman of letters, was asked, 'Gertrude, what's the answer?' With her wits still sharp, she is said to have replied 'What's the question?' If we want to look for answers in the health policy field, the three key questions to be addressed by health service policy are:

- What do we want health services, public or private, to provide?
- How do we want to pay for it?
- How can we ensure that we get what we pay for at an appropriate cost and quality?

These three questions are linked, once the method of payment starts to impinge on who gets what service. They are considered below.

Clearly, at one level we want health services to provide health improvements. But we also know that these are most likely to be achieved in the long term by diet and behaviour change. I propose to leave aside the issues of health promotion and behaviour change since it seems clear that, while they have a vital role, the majority of people seem to want an illness service that will treat them when they fall ill, whether they have changed their behaviour or not. This does not mean that health promotion is not important but I am less clear that it is a role that the NHS can or should carry out.

More specifically, I think that what people in the UK want from the NHS is a commitment that they will receive appropriate and effective treatment when they are ill and that this will be provided fairly to all who need it. I anticipate that the NHS will be forced by consumer pressure to go further in this direction. Indeed, it is the logical extension of moves such as the Patient's Charter, which so far have concentrated on the service elements of health care and neglected the technical elements. Would you rather be assured of getting an appropriate treatment or of being welcomed in the outpatients department?

The British also seem keen to retain a high degree of equity in health care. Fairness is a key principle of the NHS, even though it does not always keep to it in practice. Given the limited contribution of health care to long-term health, compared to life chances, housing etc., all of which are unequally distributed, it is not clear why equity of provision of health care should matter so much. But there appears to be a general folk appeal in the notion that the duchess and the char-lady will be treated equally by the system even though one will recu-perate in a stately home and the other in a damp tower block flat. Whatever the intellectual, rather than the emotional, appeal of this model of equality in what has been seen as an increasingly unequal society in the 1990s, let us retain it for the discussion here.

To take further the policy of appropriate treatment for all, we need to define what an appropriate treatment would be for each condition. Purchasers have begun to do this but in a fragmented way. In my view this makes little sense. If we are to have a truly national health service then we need a national initiative to develop major disease pro-grammes, on the lines of those for cancer and kidney replacement therapy (Department of Health 1995, 1996). These programmes will need to set down what is and is not covered by the NHS, mandatorily for some services, perhaps with a specified local choice between other services, in a clear statement of entitlement. They should offer integrated packages of care that cut across primary, secondary and community providers and avoid incentives to overhospitalize health problems. For example, a network of providers might be funded to manage a group of chronic disease sufferers on a fixed fee per patient managed and not on the basis of cost per case. This fee could be bal-anced across a number of different treatment regimes (for example kidney transplant and hospital dialysis) to further weaken incentives to overtreat. Equally, the potential undertreatment of patients would need to be monitored by a bigger and stronger Audit Commission or similar independent watchdog.

I believe that specification of the patient's entitlement to treat-ments is a fundamental requirement from any system that, quite rightly, does not guarantee to provide and pay for every treatment that any doctor anywhere recommends for any patient who presents. In a system where the patient does not pay directly for all care, doctors have a lesser but significant responsibility to those who pay as well as those they treat. But we owe it to doctors as well as to patients to make any limits explicit. At the moment there are lots of small scale implicit and covert rationing decisions being made to the detriment of individuals, by reducing their care or spending so much on one group of patients that the care of others is reduced to an unsatisfact-ory level. I do not think that hiding inequality or showing that it is not systematic is any defence for arbitrary inequality. The British people should be mature enough to face up to the consequences of a clear statement of health service benefits which may need to exclude some treatments in order to keep the costs to what the public is prepared to pay. If we do not want to offer dialysis to those over 80 years of age who both need it and accept it, surely we owe it to them to say so and not hide behind covert and arbitrary rationing by doctors. (For an example of covert rationing, see Challah *et al.* (1984), which shows differences between individual GPs and hospital doctors in selection of patients for dialysis and transplantation.)

So how are we to fix the services in the package for each disease group? In looking at this issue, I always find it helpful to use the analysis developed by Arrow (1971), using education as an example. Arrow argues that public services can be regressive, favouring the better off, or progressive, favouring the worse off. They can also be regressive or progressive with respect to inputs or outputs. Put more simply, we can spend more per head on the education of the slower learners (input-progressive) but we might accept that in spite of this, the faster learners gained more qualifications or other outputs from their education (output-regressive). We might consider a policy of spending more and more on the slow learners until they gained as much in additional skills and qualifications as the fast learners (output equality) but this could mean spending little if anything on the fast learners. Even then, the slower learners might be less able and less well qualified overall than the fast, having gained as much but not overcome their initial deficit. To get the same final level of skills and abilities from the slow learners, we would have to spend more and more, with diminishing returns likely as expenditure increased. The gains from an extra sum spent on the slow learners might well be much smaller than would be achieved by the same spending on the fast learners. As a result, a policy of input progression seems more likely to be adopted. That is, most people are happy with some extra spending on the slower learners, so long as the fast learners do not lose too much.

Returning to health care, it is easy to see the appeal of a policy to spend more on those who are more ill, even though we might accept that the health gains are greater from services for the more healthy. For example, we might as a society be prepared to spend a lot on treating catastrophic life-threatening illnesses even when the average gain in life years is quite small. This may of course conflict with the overall efficiency of the system as judged by the total health gain. Maximization of health gains from the system is the most efficient policy, with treatments that offer a low gain in life years per pound spent on them excluded from the health service. Health economists have often proposed this policy, focusing on the Quality Adjusted Life Years (QALYs) generated by each treatment (the gain in length of life and change in the degree of disability and discomfort), and proposing that only treatments offering the greatest gains per pound of health service expenditure should be provided from a given budget. But this only makes sense if the gains to every patient are equally important.

In a relatively healthy homogeneous population, all with the same disease risks, maximizing total health gain from the budget may actually be the preferred policy. Any reduction in health gain, from spending money on less effective rather than more effective treatments falls on average on the same homogeneous group, and so it is in their collective interests to opt for the range of services that gives the maximum health gain. (To take an extreme example, a cost-effective defence policy benefits us all more or less to the same extent.) But as soon as some fall ill, the group is no longer homogeneous with regard to health gain, and the sick will be a separate interest group.

In practice, society is never homogeneous: even at birth there are clear differences in disease patterns between black and white, men and women and, over a lifetime, young and old. Fixing health services on the basis of health gain alone may mean systematically discriminating against some groups: for example, we may fail to treat breast cancer when we expand screening for testicular cancer. Developments in genetics may take this even further, with individuals labelled from birth as suffering from a potential disease or at much higher risk of developing it. Would we as a society be prepared to deny any treatment whatsoever to some of these groups, on the grounds that it is not sufficiently effective to displace other treatments (for example minor orthopaedic procedures) which offer more QALYs per pound to a different group of sufferers? Would minorities tolerate this when they had paid their contributions in taxes and been led to believe in a national service?

Faced with the different groups of sufferers from major and minor disease, there is an appealing notion of fairness in spending more on the very sick, even knowing that in most cases it will not be very effective. The effort may be deemed worth it for the minority who gain, even though their gain may be small. That is, a small gain for the most sick in our society may be deemed worth spending a lot of money to achieve. However, in practice the size of the sick group and other characteristics may be important. It is easy to see why benefactors come forward to fly a single child to the USA for specialist surgery. It is harder to see either the NHS or private benefactors agreeing to fly large groups of patients abroad for care with little prospect of improvement for the majority of them.

Overall, Arrow's approach, with a policy of input progressivity, looks appealing. We can agree as a society to spend more on the sick than the less sick without necessarily agreeing to fund every new treatment. This will be difficult for the most life-threatening diseases with the poorest prospects of recovery because it is for these diseases that relatively expensive treatments are likely to emerge, for several reasons discussed later in this chapter. But as a society we may need to face up to the fact that we either cannot afford, or choose not to pay for, the highest levels of health care of all kinds.

The approach discussed above implies that we would need to establish a national package of entitlements to treatment for each major disease area, based on reviews and consensus groups of the kind that have begun to be developed for cancer treatment, for example (Department of Health 1995). There would then need to be a review of the package every time a significant new treatment became available. For example, in 1996 evidence began to accumulate on the effectiveness of triple drug therapy for HIV/AIDS sufferers. Should the NHS fund the extra treatment? In my view, there is no alternative to an open, public debate about this and similar major cost pressures on the NHS, leading to an agreement that either we will fund the treatment and change the entitlement package (including cutting back on some services for the less sick if we choose) or we will not. Allowing the issue to be fudged by lots of individual purchaser and doctor decisions is not acceptable, particularly when both purchasers and doctors have no wider accountability to those who pay for health care: the public at large.

The outcome of the approach above would be a clear contract between the NHS (or some other care provider perhaps) and the public. Disease programmes would be specified and perhaps prioritized. For example, it might be agreed that tattoo removal and cosmetic surgery would only be done where there was clear evidence of psychiatric problems associated with them or on condition that they fitted in around more urgent work in plastic surgery, as a residual item of service. They might be dealt with only after a specified time on a waiting list. More generally, the tax cost of the package would be spelt out and, if appropriate, modified to reconcile services, needs and costs.

There is at least one danger in this approach, however, as well as some concern about its affordability. Just as a simple outcome-maximizing approach would discriminate against the sickest, so an open debate would create an opportunity for explicit discrimination against minorities. Many people may choose to discriminate against gays or smokers or those with mental illness, not least because they may feel themselves not at risk of needing such treatment. The American philosopher Rawls (1973) has argued that if only people were behind a 'veil of ignorance' and did not know where they might come in a society, they would vote for a much more equal society. But for most people, life is relatively predictable by the time they reach the age to vote and so inequality is tolerable, for the better-off majority. (If this sounds dubious, look at the way we treat those born with permanent disabilities.)

In the same way, while the majority might wish to see good health services for trauma, heart disease and cancer, since we are ignorant of our need for them even in the next week or month, many people may be willing to tolerate inequalities towards those regarded as in a separate risk group — gays, drug abusers, blacks, smokers, the opposite sex, the mentally ill, even (short-sightedly) the old. While larger and more vocal minorities may be able to take care of themselves, experience with disabled and mentally ill people suggests that the vulnerable would need protection from discrimination. My hope is that, just as with the poll tax, the sense of fairness of the British people would prevent this kind of discrimination taking place by making the decision explicit. But there are no guarantees in a democracy that the majority will not use their power against the minority.

If we agree to specify packages of care more explicitly, we still need to consider how we will specify them before answering our other two questions for the future: how will we pay for them and how will we ensure that they are efficiently delivered?

SETTING THE ENTITLEMENT PACKAGE

If the guaranteed package of health care is to be affordable, then costs must be balanced against benefits. A consensus group or citizen's jury would need to consider high cost developments and take a view on whether the gains were worth the cost. That is, given that all the most sick people would be guaranteed some treatment, as long as it had some positive effect for some patients, additional treatments would be assessed for their extra benefits and costs at the margin.

Again, the cost per QALY may not be the sole deciding criterion. For example, a big gain for a small susceptible group may justify a new treatment for a larger group, not all of whom will turn out to benefit from it. But once a baseline treatment of some kind is guaranteed there is less of a problem in using it to determine additional treatments. No one would be turned away in this model of the health service and, where treatments had some effect, more would be spent per patient on treating those in the worst health. But new treatments would be scrutinized on grounds of both cost and effectiveness. A decision to add a new treatment to the package of care programmes to which patients were entitled would be combined with the decision to fund it. Failure to do this would leave us with the same fudging of the issues as at present.

The system set out above would need an administrative structure, access to public opinion and research support. It might be expensive to set up, though electronic mail could reduce the cost of gathering views and reaching a consensus on each major treatment programme. But we might also use much of the purchasing intelligence resource currently split between 100 health commissions all trying to figure out their own local packages of care. As a percentage of what we spend on the NHS it would, in my view, be a price worth paying. At the very least it would be worth exploring through a feasibility study. But ultimately funding the whole package, under a system of clear entitlements to care, raises its own problems.

The main financial advantage of the present system of health care funding in the UK is that it is cash constrained in most areas and increasingly constrained on drug spending, the only significant item outside the direct cash limit. If more illness occurs, the system either refuses to treat it when contracts have been fulfilled or muddles through by changing the threshold for treatment. The potential financial problem for the health service is that if the cash limit is removed, and every patient entitled to a specific package of care, then costs may run away from us, bringing on the kind of funding crisis that other countries have encountered when every treatment generates a payment to providers. Indeed, even under the present system, a number of commentators have begun to predict that we will have a major spending crisis if the NHS continues to offer a nominal (but unspecified) package of comprehensive services, free of charge at the time of use. While the mechanism for payment can change some incentives and reduce the rate of cost inflation, the two key causes of rising demands and costs, the ageing of the population and the cost of changes in technology, will remain as challenges to funding.

AFFORDING THE FUTURE

As currently organized and funded, the NHS faces a potentially large change in demand due to the ageing of the population. The costs of a clearer definition of the patients' entitlements to services could increase these pressures. This section looks at the cost pressures in more detail and considers how they might be met.

Compared to a population now with 9 million people over 65 and 900,000 over 85, in 25 years time the UK will have a population of 10 million over 65 and 1.5 million over 85 (Office of Health Economics 1995). Elderly people are the greatest users of the health service. A substantially larger number of elderly people will mean greater demands on the health service, and perhaps even more demands on social services providing care and support rather than curative medicine. However, before we reach for the panic button we should remember that not every elderly person has a major chronic illness that is expensive to treat. In addition, the fitness of the next generation of elderly people, who have received much more health and risk information, may be quite different from those in the past (see for example Wilson (1991)). Indeed, it is also easy to caricature their experience. Most elderly people live independent lives and those that require institutional care may spend only the last few years of life in a nursing or residential home. (For this group, entitlement to state funding of care was redefined in the 1990s. Funding for social care only has been identified as outside the care package, except for those who cannot fund it for themselves.) Even with the growth rates projected, by 2011 there will still only be one person aged over 85 for every 25 people of working age. Compared to the current rates of one per 44, this is an appreciable increase but we will not be overwhelmed by the elderly and tax rates will not need to be doubled overnight to fund their care.

The cost of responding to the change in the population will depend not only on their access to care and their morbidity but also on the technology available to deal with it. Technical change may be costly. For example, the knowledge that cancer sufferers are a high priority group may make drug companies and commercial researchers invest large sums of money in finding a treatment, even though they can only recoup these investments from very high treatment prices. Furthermore, commercial companies are well aware of the costs of current treatments. They are therefore likely to price new treatments at a comparable price, or even higher if better outcomes result. That is, even if technology could invent and test new treatments for a low cost, the price of a patented treatment would still be on a par with current treatments because of the monopoly conferred by the patent.

In some circumstances medical technology can reduce costs, for example through the introduction of day and short-stay surgery. But we need to separate reduction in costs per case from reductions in overall expenditure. Day surgery, for example, has probably lowered the threshold at which surgery takes place, and less interventionist surgery using laparoscopes may extend surgery to more elderly individuals. The net effect, if entitlement to treatment is not clearly specified, is to expand total expenditure. Similarly, when a new treatment extends patients' lives, it also increases the cost of providing care for the other diseases of a longer life. Thus a major reduction in smoking may increase some of the costs of health and social care in the long run, not reduce them, as it will increase the number of elderly people surviving to an age where they may make the highest demands on care services.

Faced with rising numbers of elderly patients and more costly technology, a number of proposals have come forward to meet the perceived funding gap. These include hypothecated taxes, greater use of charges and a move to funding through markets and insurance rather than public finance. We consider each of these below.

INCREASING FUNDING – A HYPOTHECATED TAX?

The impact of the Thatcher years has been to change the starting point for any debate about taxes in the UK. We are now at a lower level of direct tax rates (though not necessarily of tax paid). Tax cuts are an objective of virtually all politicians and tax increases are seen as a drawback of big government. It is therefore unlikely in the next five to ten years that a government would be prepared to increase tax rates significantly, year on year, to fund rapid growth in health spending, even in the face of public opinion surveys which typically show a public willingness to pay more taxes for health care.

One popular alternative is the hypothecated or earmarked tax. By earmarking a particular share of taxes for health services, it is argued, the health service could benefit from regular growth as the economy grows (see Jones and Duncan (1995) for a detailed review). Furthermore, by showing a clear commitment to use funding for a particular purpose, the image of taxation might be changed from a general payment to the purchase of rights to key public services. Several health service groups have called for a health tax. The fact that some of these groups have a vested interest in the resources going to the NHS should not be overlooked, of course (for example British Medical Association (1994), and Ensor (1993) for the Institute of Health Service Management).

Healthcare 2000 (1995), a think-tank drawn from a wide spectrum of opinion, examined the future of funding for the NHS in its first report. It points out that the use of a hypothecated tax comes very close to that of compulsory social insurance, of the kind originally seen as funding pensions, sickness absence, unemployment and health services when the Welfare State was founded. While some differences remain, for example on ranges of income and percentages paid, the difference between a hypothecated tax and compulsory insurance is limited. Once payment has to be made and is not linked to use of services, the percentage taken from income has no service-related legitimacy and is merely a device for raising the money in an acceptable way from those able to pay.

The main objections to earmarked taxes are that they have higher administrative costs, they remove flexibility from government and they may guarantee increases in budgets whatever the pressure of demand on services. The first objection, the higher administration cost, is based on the need to collect, identify and manage a separate element within taxation. (Equally, the extra cost of this may be less than appears at first sight, for example if an agency to collect the earmarked tax is located in an area of otherwise high unemployment. This occurs currently for national insurance contributions which no longer meet all the cost of the services they were intended to fund and could be rolled into general taxation.)

The second objection to earmarking largely depends on public opinion about the merits of constraining the government. In general, the public might like to restrain politicians and link taxes and expenditure more closely. But earmarking one or two taxes seems likely to lead to earmarking of others, or calls for this, and may lead to a system closer to pricing of public services. For example, earmarking road tax for road developments, on the grounds that road users pay for the services of roads, would lead to large amounts of spending on roads. Do we as a society want this or do we merely want the convenience of taxing motorists as an easy way of raising taxes for public services?

A further complication, noted by Jones and Duncan, is that earmarking enthusiasts usually talk about what the money is to be used for and not what it will be drawn from. But the earmarkers cannot have it both ways. If taxes are to be earmarked we must specify which taxes. What will we do if these do not rise as fast as some other element of taxation? If we want to restrict government flexibility then we can hardly expect governments to be flexible when the earmarked income does not seem high enough. Equally, do we want earmarked income to rise regardless of other economic conditions? After all, our problem with the health service and an ageing population may not create financial problems at a speed which conveniently matches the growth in employment income or some other taxable economic variable.

The third concern with a hypothecated tax is that earmarking generates automatic increases in funding. Of course this could be restricted to a few popular public services such as health, education and social services – the caring end of the public sector spectrum. As noted above, models of compulsory social insurance – common in Europe – come close to this kind of system, albeit with a variety of names. But what earmarking and social funds are really for, in the eyes of those within health care, is automatic growth in funding. Growth in expenditure is constantly held up as the solution to health service problems, as much in the mid-1990s as in the period before the Reforms. The 'scandal' of inadequate services is as common and probably receives as many headlines as it ever did. A lack of adequate funds is one answer that all those in the NHS can agree upon, particularly in an environment where explicit rationing and restrictions on services are not a general part of health policy.

This is where the real difficulty lies, for economists at least, in the earmarking principle. Earmarking means giving money for a purpose, on autopilot, without ensuring that the money and the needs are well matched. It also disregards the fact that the cost of health services is not fixed but determined by market conditions. A guaranteed rising budget could be absorbed by rises in prices and wages that those providing care would come to expect.

A monopoly buyer like the NHS, in spite of fragmentation into individual purchasers and providers, can and does use its market power to keep costs down, for example through pay reviews, drug tariffs and the direct negotiation of pharmaceutical profits and prices. A substantial number of doctors and nurses currently working in the health service and the companies that sell to the NHS are not likely to withdraw, because the economic alternatives are typically worse. Medical migration to other English speaking countries is restricted by their own medical professions' control of the labour market, though movement in Europe is potentially easier for those with a European language. Viewed from the individual professional's angle, exploitation of a commitment to medicine or nursing may be unfair. But as long as the supply of willing workers can be maintained, there is no incentive for the system as a whole to feel the need to pay European or American rates for the job. From time to time, shortages develop, and nursing has had periods where recruitment suffered due to alternative careers and changing aspirations of women workers. But again we must beware of assuming there is only one way to do things and that the costs of doing so must always be met. For example, changing the job content of doctors and nurses could simultaneously release doctors from tasks which do not make effective use of their skills and increase the skill range and job satisfaction of nurses, while also reducing costs per case and creating employment opportunities for unskilled workers – Utopia!

In summary, while hypothecation offers the prospects of sustained growth in spending to care providers and suppliers such as the pharmaceutical companies, it may also lead to guaranteed income growth for suppliers and reduced pressure to achieve better value for money. The Audit Commission continues to show in its various reports that the NHS has highly variable levels of performance, and so a guarantee of rising income may not be the right way to improve the supply of effective and efficient services. Indeed, since tight cash limits have led to greater scrutiny of what is done and how it is done, a guarantee of rising income for the health service might have the opposite effect.

PATIENT CHARGES

A further method of increasing income is to introduce patient charges. This has an impact not only on how the money is raised but also how care is provided, introducing market mechanisms into the consumers' decisions about using services. Charging patients in the NHS for certain services has been part of its philosophy since 1951 when access to free false teeth and glasses could not be sustained due to the financial pressures on the then Labour government. Prescription charges have risen steadily under the Conservatives since 1979 but for the reasons discussed below, they still make a relatively limited contribution to total costs.

Charging is often put forward as a further way of raising funding, but always against a background of concern that while charges will discourage the use of health services by poorer patients, thus reducing expenditure, they may at the same time lead some patients to put off vital diagnosis or treatment (see Healthcare 2000 (1995) for a recent example). This can be avoided by a means test, preferably one that is opaque to the care providers. I believe that there are also benefits from charges through the empowerment of patients who might be less tolerant of some aspects of poor service if there was a visible element of payment, however small. But any threat to equity of access may be very unpopular.

Charges are also more likely to make a significant contribution to the costs of primary care than of hospital care. Indeed, historically the lower income groups in Britain often paid their GPs but relied on voluntary or poor law hospitals for free inpatient care. The direct costs of primary care could be recouped substantially if every user paid (for example) £5 per consultation. This would bring in around £42,000 per GP per year (based on 8,400 consultations per GP per year reported by the Office of Health Economics 1992), sufficient to pay a GP but not the support staff of the practice. But to reach this kind of contribution, we would have to charge the large number of users who are exempt from prescriptions charges: the very young, the old and the poor. Many of them may present relatively minor problems so the health damage of delayed or non-diagnosis would sometimes be small. But a risk of delay in a serious case would remain and the principle of free health care at time of use would be well and truly breached.

For hospital care, the difficulty is that individual patients incur a high cost and many would not be able to make more than a small personal contribution at the time of their treatment. For example, in Chapter 4 we noted the wide range in costs per patient in a fundholding practice (see Glennerster *et al.* (1994)). Of over 1,500 patients studied in a fundholding practice, *all* of the inpatient expenditure went on 69 individuals or 4.6 per cent of their sample. In other words, there was a less than one in 20 chance of a patient needing the inpatient services covered by fundholding. Even adding the hospital medical cases, not paid for by fundholders, would take this proportion only to 10 per cent. Similarly, if we were to look at prescribed drugs, we would find the majority of expenditure going on the minority of patients registered with a practice with chronic diseases and multiple problems, requiring complex and long-term medication.

Because of the concentration of health spending on only a small proportion of patients, the bulk of services could only carry a direct and significant charge if chronic and seriously ill patients could pay it. But our funding problem is precisely that older people, typically with lower incomes than those of working age, are most likely to experience serious and chronic illness. Even at younger ages, charges would only make a contribution if large amounts were paid by those receiving the majority of services. Charges would also probably lead the fitter and lower risk groups in the population to get insurance against potential charges, while the sickest and poorest would not be able to insure.

A more acceptable possibility might be to introduce charges for improved services (such as convenient access to care) rather than for technical services (see Healthcare 2000 (1995)). Charging for additional amenity services, such as out-of-office-hours access to GP surgeries, offers scope for raising income while only breaching the equity principle on which the NHS was founded to a limited degree. Such charges would have the merit of linking the consumer aspects of services to the fee paid and so could create incentives to offer a better service, while the technical medical service was maintained at the same level for all. But such charges would make a smaller contribution to total costs than a charge on every patient.

In summary, charges might ease the pinching of the shoe in a few places. They might also provide a mechanism for middle income groups to get service improvements such as evening GP surgeries or faster access to physiotherapy. But such charges and payments do not affect the core funding problem. If charges were to rise high enough to recoup a major part of the cost of the health service, from those able to pay, the result would probably be greater use of insurance to pay charges, shifting us effectively to a private insurance model of care. The benefits of greater use of insurance are considered in the section below.

COMPULSORY AND COMPETITIVE HEALTH INSURANCE

In a highly detailed review of health funding in Europe, Hoffmeyer and McCarthy (1995) have developed the most comprehensive statement of a future health service funding model, intended to meet cost and demand pressures. (This study was carried out by National Economic Research Associates and is usually known as the NERA proposal.) It is based on the following main principles:

• a guaranteed package of health care for everyone;
• competing health insurance agencies;
• compulsory insurance;
• income- and risk-related premiums;

- a central balancing fund, to offset income and risk-related contributions;
- a safety net for individuals who could not cope or could not find cover;
- providers selling services to insurance fund purchasers;
- no adverse selection by exclusion or unreasonable terms.

On the service side, these proposals are similar to those discussed earlier, under which the NHS would provide a stated package of care to everyone with a defined medical need. In the NERA model we would have compulsory cover, with competing health insurance funds offering us cover for services they would buy on our behalf from providers. The central funding arrangements are designed to balance risk groups so that insurers have little incentive to discriminate against higher risks. There would also be competition between insurers, an idea also proposed by Propper (1995). (Elements of the model also have a good deal in common with the pluralism of health insurance in Britain before the NHS, reviewed by Gray (1991).) Thus the proposals change the raising of the funds by introducing competing insurers who raise funds directly from their members, but with government support to remove incentives to skim off the cream of the risks.

The Hoffmeyer and McCarthy proposals have been extensively examined by Towse, Culyer and Laing (in Towse (1995)). The core of the debate is around the ability of consumers to choose between different packages. However, there are some additional dimensions which are particularly relevant to the debate on rising demands and rationing, as noted earlier. Culyer, for example, argues that the growth of medical technology and its costs are not independent of health service funding, as noted earlier.

The relatively complex funding arrangements proposed by NERA would fund a defined, and perhaps not comprehensive, package of care. Specifying a minimum package of care would of itself limit costs, if some therapies were excluded. If this is a key part of their solution through a market in health insurance, it is just as readily a partial solution to the problem of unlimited, but unspecified, demands on the NHS. Insurers require such a package to limit their financial exposure. The essence of a health insurance package is that it specifies exactly what will and will not be provided. It also demonstrates that rationing is not a simple result of public provision. Rationing of care that is provided at no, or reduced, cost is nothing more than leaving something off the package. It is central to any insurance contract and is equivalent to rationing, even if not usually given that name.

If we have a minimum package and compulsory insurance, as well as mechanisms to share the costs of high risk groups, what more do we gain from competing insurance funds? Currently consumers buy motor insurance because it is required by law and insurers offer standard packages (for example third party, fire and theft, and fully comprehensive cover) with additions at the margin for minor items. As consumers we seem able to choose readily between them. But the key for this kind of insurance is risk selection. There is no public concern to protect high risk groups. As long as insurers can compete by identifying lower risk groups and picking them out for special premiums, they may operate a sophisticated market. On the consumer side, sophistication is less clear cut. Typically it is led by price, with quality largely unknown until a claim is made. Those of us who never have a road accident may never find out how good or bad our insurance company really is. When a claim is actually made but not met to our satisfaction, we may shop around, though the quality of new suppliers is also typically unknown. Between claims we are more likely to shop around on price, with no real idea of quality. As a result, consumers may not be particularly effective buyers of motor insurance. In addition, since the government already runs vehicle licensing, it is easy to see how a monopoly insurance fund might work with substantial economies of scale. Its operations might be market tested and put out to management or insurance companies, if public sector control is seen as inherently less efficient. Nonetheless, the reductions in transaction costs from a national insurance carrier look appealing.

Returning to health care, Culyer (1995) has particularly criticized the higher transaction costs of the competing insurers foreseen by Hoffmeyer and McCarthy, and the assumptions made about the public's ability to choose. To a degree, the market might solve some of these issues for us. If patients choose largely on price and if transactions costs from multiple insurers are high, we would expect a few firms to come to dominate the market. Given the potential importance of market power, in a real market rather than the current managed market in the NHS, the tendency to big insurers would be increased, particularly if private insurers were allowed to use their market muscle but escape the political constraints which limit closely the decisions of health commissions. Private insurance firms may not face the same public scrutiny and criticism; they may be able to exercise more power, more readily, than a similarly sized health commission. But they would need considerable power to rival that already held by the

NHS in national labour and supplies markets. Britain has relatively tight controls on the pay of health care workers and systems which could be used to control drug spending (for example the PACT data on every GP's prescribing) much more closely than at present. Since the NHS has a monopoly, patient pressure for higher quality of facilities and services can be resisted or merely paid lip service. In contrast, competing private providers may feel obliged to invest more in the dimensions of their facilities which appeal most to patients, often those with least direct relationship to health improvements. Providers would want insurers to see how popular they were with patients, appealing over the heads of insurers to show patients how well staffed and equipped their facilities are. This could be countered by insurers engaging in vertical integration so that provider doctors and other clinical staff were not free to spend the insurers' money without regard to funding constraints. (This is the basis for the shift to health maintenance organizations and managed care in the USA.) But this model is moving closer and closer to local health services with a monopoly supplier of insurance and care. It sounds rather like the NHS!

Laing (1995) has defended the Hoffmeyer and McCarthy proposals while seeing them as essentially long term and, for the time being, politically contentious. In particular, he sees competing insurers as offering scope for increasing the funding of health care beyond the levels constrained by government – as many of the public might like – and increasing consumer choice. Both are undeniable consequences of the proposed changes but we need to be careful in assessing how far they deliver what is really required: improved health care or improved health.

It is difficult to see how increased funding under separate purchasing insurance agencies could avoid raising the price of key inputs as well as the quantity supplied, as noted earlier. Laing notes this problem but sees the solution in a much more imaginative view of what a future health care market might deliver. This could include insurers demonstrating not the lavish facilities and range of technologies on offer but their cost-effectiveness as purchasers who have squeezed out ineffective procedures and drugs to give a better deal to consumers. In the NHS currently, low users who adopt more watchful waiting, for example, gain nothing from the system. As a relatively low user of health services myself, I find it very frustrating when I have to join a queue at the GP's surgery or accident department behind what appear to me to be those much less sick than me (in my eyes, at least) and lots of the worried well. (As my son, doubled up with pain, remarked as we waited in the GP's surgery for his appendicitis to be confirmed, 'None of these people look ill'.) Just as car insurance offers a distinct package at a low price to non-drinking older drivers who use their car relatively rarely, so a competing insurer could offer low premiums or bonuses to those with lower utilization, for a given risk status.

The real weakness of insurance funds focused on individuals is that they would tend to blur the key issue for health care funding: health care is a lifetime issue, not a year by year problem, with the greatest demands made by the old and the sick rather than the healthy and insurable. Annual insurance contracts do not address the important redistributional issue in health care, that the sickest and oldest will never be able to pay their own costs in the current year. Those with a genetic predisposition to particular diseases may simply never be able to afford adequate insurance. While a concept of lifetime insurance is appealing, and has begun to be introduced for social care, the high premiums needed to meet the uncertainties over the cost of future treatments (and the likely public insistence on a safety net for health care) will tend to make lifetime insurance less practical in a free market. But just as we have legal restraints on individuals to ensure that they make provision for themselves, such as covering accidents on the road through motor insurance and providing for their old age through state pensions, so I have no problem with restraining people's incomes through taxation to ensure that they can have access to health care when they need it and want it – and when, due to their declining health, they may no longer be able to obtain private insurance to pay for it. I for one would be unhappy to have large numbers of sick people dying without adequate care. But I would also be unhappy to see those who think like me having to bear all the costs of care for those who did not or could not make their own provision, before they fell ill. Binding all of us together in a shared funding system makes good sense, simply because of the uncertainty of the risks to health and the costs of competing health insurers. 'One for all and all for one' may be cheaper for all, as well as meeting ethical standards by protecting the worst off.

Overall, the Hoffmeyer and McCarthy proposals appear to be a complex solution to a problem that can be solved in other ways. Introducing competing insurers who purchase care seems likely to increase the transaction costs of both raising and spending money on health care. There are few obvious advantages from the complex system of funding they propose and the costs of managing their complex system of risk adjustment may be appreciable. Since their proposals rest on compulsory insurance, tax funding may offer significant economies of scale. If the NHS wishes to explore the advantages of purchaser competition, it could do so readily by allowing health commissions to compete for registered members across current boundaries and also encourage explicit competition with fundholders. Experiments of this kind would be relatively easy to carry out and could be tested at limited cost. However, a key feature of any such experiment would be the need for the competitors to specify the package on offer to consumers. This would involve establishing clear rationing standards and guidelines of the care to be provided for any specific disorder, as discussed earlier in this chapter. It follows that rationing would to a considerable extent be a major component of any developments under the Hoffmeyer and McCarthy proposals, if only to specify the core package that all insurers would have to provide and the wider packages on which they might compete.

NEW PROBLEMS OR OLD?

Before looking at the issues raised by the delivery of a clear package of entitlement to care for the population covered by the NHS, a counterblast to the whole issue of pressure on resources from an ageing population and the need for rationing should be noted. Wordsworth *et al.* (1996) have argued that the current concern with the growth of the elderly is not different in kind from all the other pressures in the past on the NHS. In an excellent review of experience in other countries that have tried to define a core package of services explicitly, they show that most have foundered on the kind of problems reviewed elsewhere in this book, in particular that of explicitly excluding individual treatments and discriminating against individual sufferers.

The authors of this study also note that it is far from clear that increased health spending is the most effective way to improve health. There may be other methods, for example through housing and social policy, that work better. They recommend continuing to develop our evidence on what benefit is achieved at what cost.

To a degree, their point is well made. The number of elderly people will not increase overnight, and whatever methods are used to cope with their ill-health, the transition (even to higher taxation) will be a gradual one. However, I am less convinced that it is impossible to define a core of services to which patients are entitled. Indeed, the logic of Wordsworth and colleagues' call for more research on costs and benefits leads to the likely conclusion that some effective, but not very effective, treatments might not be provided if the benefits were deemed too small to justify the costs. Potentially they should have concluded that *in the absence of good quality and consistent data on costs and benefits* it is not possible to define a clear package of entitlement to services.

DELIVERING THE PACKAGE EFFICIENTLY

If we are to move to a defined package of care from the NHS, we will need to monitor its provision and its costs to ensure that we have answers to our third question – how will we ensure efficient supply of the package of care we want to have? At one level, the answer is simply better, more detailed and more vigorous monitoring. We have noted more than once in this book the problems of assessing value for money when payers and patients are not the same. Under any system of this kind, the familiar check on value for money by the customer is not built in to every transaction. As a result, competition of all kinds for contracts from purchasers cannot guarantee to provide adequate quality to patients, who in turn may feel they lack the power to challenge the poor standards they endure. After all, would you rather the Civil Aviation Authority monitored the standards of charter airlines or left them to the effects of price competition between tour operators? To resolve this difficulty we should simply start to build monitoring back in with a much greater effort than in the past.

The Audit Commission or similar body could take on this role. Indeed, the Audit Commission currently has this role in part, though it carries it out through a devolved system of auditors, which in my view leaves too much power and control in the hands of local managers. There is too much need for permission to audit certain areas and a reluctance of auditors at times to rock the boat. I would like to see much more power in the hands of auditors, or a willingness to use the powers that they have.

This audit agency would also need to take over and coordinate much of the effort in clinical audit, which is often even softer and weaker than the external audit of services. (Currently the Audit Commission remit does not cover clinical care.) In order to keep the professionals happy, clinical audit has potentially been insufficiently critical and objective. Now that it has become widely accepted, we should start to make it more effective. There is an argument for proceeding carefully with professionals but there is also an argument for eliminating poor practice more rapidly than in the past. Regular external review could be as much a part of a doctor's life as an airline pilot's, though we may have to be prepared to organize professional development more effectively to support it.

We would also need to develop contracting systems which avoid providing perverse incentives to increase the costs of treatment. This could potentially involve a different approach for different groups of patients.

For patients with chronic diseases, we might offer care programmes which provide integrated hospital, primary and community care and include payments per patient on the programme but not necessarily per patient day in hospital. That is, the providers would be required to manage the patients with limited scope for hospitalization, itself a sign that elements of chronic disease management have broken down. Networks of providers would bid for the contract to manage these patients. It is likely that the patients themselves would prefer stability of providers, given the lifelong nature of their disease. However, where a service had serious quality or cost problems, it may be feasible to re-tender while retaining the same facilities or let a new contract that would gradually take over patients, where they chose to shift, as well as treating new sufferers. But we might also have to accept that patients' preferences for stability will necessarily limit the amount of recontracting that can be undertaken and therefore the extent to which market forces can be used to control costs. Alternatives, including closer monitoring of costs and inputs might be required and elements of this detail will be needed to specify the package of care from the outset.

For emergency services, the care package might specify access to a particular range of services, which would be contracted for by purchasers as an agreed level of capacity. This might need to vary between summer and winter but there may also be scope for avoiding some elements of the pressure on hospital beds in winter through more integrated care of chronic disease patients. Such patients often end up as emergencies in hospital in winter when what is required is additional home care. Hence the need to design packages of care that cut across conventional provider boundaries.

Changing thresholds for care is a further source of cost pressure. If more patients are deemed suitable for treatment, costs will rise. This is the area where the NHS has been most successful, using the cash limit and local implicit rationing to control demands. But this is unfair on patients when the amount of disease has genuinely increased locally for some reason or when local GPs have begun to detect it more effectively. The way forward here may be to monitor referral and treatment decisions in the same way as the monitoring of prescriptions so that wide variations and rapid increases in referral and treatment can be examined. These may show that in fact we have serious problems of undertreatment for some diseases and that we have to accept the case for additional funding or change the care package. It is important not to lose sight of the fact that, without adequate monitoring of the care provided, any funding system runs the risk of paying for one package and delivering another. So while there may be cost pressures from specifying an entitlement to care, the need to monitor remains important even under cash-limited systems which do not specify clearly what patients are entitled to receive.

Paying for surgical procedures will also need to avoid both providing incentives to vary thresholds and increasing the level of treatment beyond that specified in the package of entitlements. This could be done by negotiating contracts with bands of prices to reflect marginal costs rather than average costs, or to provide incentive bonuses for additional work carried out which limit the financial risk to purchasers. But equally, if there is genuinely more of a disease than expected, the health system should either meet its costs or change the package of entitlement.

In primary care, the capitation system appears broadly appropriate for the management of minor and elements of chronic illness and the initial diagnosis of complex conditions. However, there may be scope for improving the use made of general practice by varying the number of visits for minor conditions that are included in the package of care specified for all. This could reduce the volume of consultations in general practice and potentially extend the time GPs spend in (for example) the primary care elements of integrated programmes for chronic disease management.

The debate about these issues could be long and complex. Klein (1994) notes that there is no evidence that purchasers have begun to specify such packages of care, and so a great deal of work will be needed. But he also acknowledges the scope for such work, seeing most items of care on the NHS as being driven mainly by history, not science. Public accountability for the decisions made would also be particularly important. Decisions that the UK would not adopt the latest US technology would be controversial and would need a robust defence in the face of the likely criticism. (Yet we readily accept that in other fields we will not be able to afford an American standard.)

Potentially it is more important at least to begin a debate with the relevant information on the table. Currently, additional funding is sought for all kinds of treatments and rationing is carried out in all kinds of arbitrary and covert ways. Arguably, a more open debate on rationing will become inevitable as moves to empower consumers and give them specific entitlements run up against the constraints of funding and the politicians' desire for tax cuts. The debate will also focus attention on who is to make these key decisions. Is it acceptable in a nationally funded system to have different policies locally? The strong equity principles that underpin the NHS make it more difficult to see how it could tolerate a substantial difference in the treatment of a given disease in different places. This would imply in the long run a set of national protocols and standards for every patient to follow. In this model the discretion of the individual clinician would be heavily constrained. Their work would involve diagnosis, entering of patients onto treatment programmes, monitoring of progress against treatment and changes of treatment as the condition and prognosis changed. The key difference from their current work would be that the treatment at each stage would be prescribed to quite a degree by the guidelines and not by the individual doctor. This would constrain the care professionals much more than current arrangements and no doubt they would fight this loss of discretion. But as the scientific evidence develops on outcomes and inputs, it is difficult to justify a situation in which it does not achieve maximum effect because medical practice refuses to be constrained by the evidence. Where the evidence is inconclusive, as doctors often argue, there is a case for further research, which would be helped if the alternative treatments were used systematically in different places. Saying the evidence is imperfect is not an adequate defence of the kind of breadth of clinical practice that exists at present.

An alternative to this planned rationing approach is to continue to allow resources to be allocated by implicit rather than explicit methods. As noted in Chapter 4, the continuation of GP fundholding and versions of locally sensitive purchasing come close to this model. Under total fundholding or variants of it, we would simply acknowledge the role of GPs as gatekeepers and primary care providers who could decide on the allocation of resources using their own criteria. Thus a practice might favour physiotherapy over counselling, aggressive treatment of heart disease but conservative treatment of cancer, and would be allowed to make its own decisions on these and other resource allocation issues. This model would probably be most popular at the practice level, where arbitrary decisions could be defended because they were made by doctors who knew the patients involved. The larger the purchaser and the more distant from individual patients, the greater the need for a clearer and more accountable specification of rationing decisions.

My guess is that, even with local fundholding, consumers in such a model would ultimately come to expect a reckoning with the fundholders at regular intervals to ensure that they as consumers were happy with the decisions made on their behalf. The evidence on what constitutes good or bad treatment will, therefore, come to be used by clinicians not only to practise more scientific medicine but to prove to their patients that they have done so. The approach will be reinforced by patient-held records and computerized monitoring of protocols against patients entered on each programme of care, so that all parties can see that what was promised is being delivered.

Within care programmes it need not be essential or desirable to remove all discretion from the clinicians. For example, an arbitrary age cut-off, above which a patient could not enter a kidney replacement programme, would be seen as repugnant and unfair by many people. But equally, it would be surprising to find kidney specialists as a group arguing that not a single patient should ever be denied treatment, not least because three-times-weekly dialysis is burdensome and can reduce the quality of life for a confused and frail elderly person, for example, while raising their length of life. Within agreed parameters the clinicians could be left to decide, in consultation with patients and their families, whether care was appropriate, given all the individual circumstances that a protocol or guideline could not take into account.

Overall, the move to more and more rational (and perhaps rationed) care seems inevitable. The one constraint may be the cost. If we go down this road to establish clear responses to individual diseases and patients' entitlements to them, we may find that the final cost is much greater than the current cost and that the health gains are small. Moving to a regime of carefully managed care may raise costs, even though the outcome may be greater use of more rational and consistent treatments. Equally, once we have a clear idea of who is supposed to get what, we could have a more informed debate about restricting treatments in order to stay within lower levels of funding. At present all parties obscure these issues, with those inside the health service arguing for more resources and those outside arguing that better management of the existing resources makes more sense.

However, it is easy to get carried away with the idea of this rational and rationed world, with clearly specified entitlements and treatments driven by evidence-based protocols. It will not be easy to achieve and it will certainly not be quick. But we should remember that not every patient is currently given the best, the most effective or the most expensive treatment. Practice shows a mix of all three. This is unsatisfactory, whatever the resource constraints. It is also clear that the current obscuring of rights and entitlements, as well as the lack of any specification of the resources to be provided to treat each type of case, would be the first things that a private insurance agency would begin to address. Managed care in the USA has been driven by agencies concerned to lessen the extra cost of variance in treatments and to reduce the use of resources where they have a marginal effect. By continuing to operate a publicly funded system, with weak but growing connections made between what we want and what we get, we have allowed a high level of discretion to remain with the clinical professionals. But if medicine is to be evidence based and scientifically carried out we cannot leave every care provider to have all the discretion they demand. Arguably, discretion will be constrained more and more by consumer expectations and purchaser monitoring (as it has been over the last 20 years for airline pilots, for example) due to changing technology and rising standards. Similarly, while we will always need doctors to have the discretion to decide that an individual patient should be shifted from one programme to another, sometimes at short notice and in an emergency, we will increasingly have the 'flight recorder' information needed to monitor and criticize these decisions. For doctors in turn to criticize these changes is to hark back to a golden age when the medical equivalent of 'seat of the pants' flying was seen as the way to behave. We now have the evidence and the capacity to continue to gather further information, thus making such earlier practices not only unsatisfactory but manifestly unsafe.

CONCLUSIONS

The conclusions of this chapter and, indeed, this book, are that the NHS Reforms that created the internal market have probably brought some limited improvements in health care funding and delivery, and that these improvements are difficult to demonstrate scientifically. Of itself, the internal market will not offer any 'magic bullet' solutions to the future problems of health care funding. The clear focus of one group of players on needs assessment and purchasing creates considerable scope for a move to more rational purchasing and provision of care, though greater integration of service delivery is still needed.

To fund health care, we need to raise the necessary taxes to meet the cost of the integrated care packages that we wish the NHS to provide. This model will not be achieved overnight but still appears to represent the best and most open way of addressing the challenge of health care funding. The longer we avoid facing up to difficult decisions on who should get what care, the longer we must tolerate the blurring of the issues that allows both demanding professionals and constraining politicians to assert that they are right. Pressure for a clearer statement of entitlement and rights, already started by the Patient's Charter, will lead in time to a demand for a statement of what the NHS will provide for us and how care will be managed. Medicine as science must ultimately be constrained by the weight of scientific evidence. Medicine as collectively funded care, whether private or public, must be accountable to the payers as well as to individual patients. Explicit rationing of care is also the clearest way to demonstrate, ultimately, that the NHS is underfunded, by providing the strongest link between need and resources. As such, it could provide benefits to a coalition of interests including doctors, patients and the public.

REFERENCES

Akehurst, R. and Ferguson, B. (1993) The purchasing authority. In M.F. Drummond and A. Maynard (eds) *Purchasing and Providing Cost-effective Health Care*. London: Churchill Livingstone.

Anon (1992) *Effective Health Care No. 3*. School of Public Health, University of Leeds, Centre for Health Economics, University of York and Royal College of Physicians, London.

Appleby, J., Smith, P., Ranade, W., Little, V. and Robinson, R. (1994) Monitoring managed competition. In R. Robinson and J. Le Grand (eds) *Evaluating the NHS Reforms*. London: King's Fund Institute.

Arrow, K.J. (1971) The utilitarian approach to the concept of equality in public expenditure, *Quarterly Journal of Economics*, 85(340): 409–16.

Audit Commission (1993) *Your Health, Their Business: The New Role of District Health Authorities*. London: HMSO.

Audit Commission (1996) *What the Doctor Ordered, a Study of GP Fundholders in England and Wales*. London: HMSO.

Bartlett, W. and Harrison, L. (1993) Quasi-markets and the National Health Service reforms. In J. Le Grand and W. Bartlett (eds) *Quasi-Markets and Social Policy*. London: Macmillan.

Bartlett, W. and Le Grand, J. (1994) The performance of trusts. In J. Le Grand and R. Robinson (eds) *Evaluating the NHS Reforms*. London: King's Fund Institute.

Bradlow, J. and Coulter, A. (1993) Effect of fundholding and indicative prescribing on general practitioners' prescribing costs, *British Medical Journal*, 307: 1186–9.

British Medical Association (1994) *Hypothecated Tax Funding for the NHS: A Briefing/Discussion Paper*. London: BMA Health Policy and Economic Research Unit.

Butler, E. and Pirie, M. (1988) *Health Management Units*. London: Adam Smith Institute.

Butler, J. (1992) *Patients, Policies and Politics*. Buckingham: Open University Press.

Butler, J. (1994a) Origins and early development. Chapter 1 of R. Robinson and J. Le Grand (eds) *Evaluating the NHS Reforms.* London: King's Fund Institute.

Butler, J. (1994b) *Patients, Policies and Politics – Before and After Working for Patients.* Buckingham: Open University Press.

Caines, E. (1996) *Speech to Association of MBAs.* Cambridge, 25 January.

Chadda, D. (1995) Back from the brink, *Health Service Journal,* 7 September, 14–15.

Challah, S., Wing, A.J., Bauer, R., Morris, R.W. and Schroeder, S.A. (1984) Negative selection of patients for dialysis and transplantation in the United Kingdom, *British Medical Journal,* 288: 1119–22.

Charlton, J., Patrick, D.L., Matthews, G. and West, P.A. (1981) Spending priorities in Kent: a Delphi study, *Journal of Epidemiology and Community Health,* 35(3): 212.

Clarke, R.W. and Gray, C. (1994) Options for change in the NHS consultant contract, *British Medical Journal,* 309: 528–30.

Conservative Party (1987) *Election Manifesto.* London: Conservative Central Office.

Coulter, A. (1995a) General practice fundholding: time for a cool appraisal, *British Journal of General Practice,* March: 119–20.

Coulter, A. (1995b) Evaluating general practice fundholding in the United Kingdom, *European Journal of Public Health,* 5: 223–39.

Court, C. (1996) Survey shows widespread rationing in NHS, *British Medical Journal,* 311: 1453–4.

Crump, B.J., Cubbon, J.E., Drummond, M.F., Hawkes, R., Marchment, M.D. (1991) Fundholding in general practice and financial risk, *British Medical Journal,* 302: 1582–4, 29 June.

Cullis, J. and West, P.A. (1979) *The Economics of Health: An Introduction.* Oxford: Martin Robertson.

Culyer, A.J. (1995) Chisels or screwdrivers? A critique of the NERA proposals for the reform of the NHS. In A. Towse (ed.) *Financing Health Care in the UK: A Discussion of NERA's Prototype Model to Replace the NHS.* London: Office of Health Economics.

Dawson, D. (1995) *Regulating Competition in the NHS,* Discussion Paper 131. York: Centre for Health Economics, University of York.

Department of Health (1987) *Promoting Better Health: The Government's Programme for Improving Primary Health Care* (Cmd 249, House of Commons). London: HMSO.

Department of Health (1989) *Practice Budgets for General Practitioners: Working for Patients, Working Paper 3.* London: HMSO.

Department of Health (1989a) *The Health Service – The NHS Reforms and You.* London: Department of Health.

Department of Health (1989b) *Funding and Contracts for Hospital Care: Working for Patients, Working Paper 2.* London: HMSO.

Department of Health (1989c) *Self-Governing Hospitals, Working for Patients, Working Paper 1.* London: HMSO.

Department of Health (1989d) *Funding General Practice.* London: Department of Health.

Department of Health (1994) *A Guide to the Operation of the NHS Internal Market: Local Freedoms, National Responsibilities.* London: Department of Health.

Department of Health (1995) *A Policy Framework for Commissioning Cancer Services: Report of the Expert Advisory Committee Group on Cancer* (Chair: Sir Kenneth Calman). London: Department of Health.

Department of Health (1996) *Renal Purchasing Guidelines: Good Practice.* London: Department of Health.

Department of Health and Social Security (1980) *Health Services: Structures and Management, HC(80)8.* London: DHSS.

Department of Health and Social Security (1983a) *Competitive Tendering in the Provision of Domestic, Catering and Laundry Services, HC(83)18.* London: DHSS.

Department of Health and Social Security (1983b) *Report of the NHS Management Enquiry (The Griffiths Report), DA(83)38 I.* London: DHSS.

Department of Health and Social Security (1984) *Health Service Management: Implementation of the NHS Management Inquiry Report, HC(811)13.* London: DHSS.

Dixon, J. (1994) Can there be fair funding for fundholding practices? *British Medical Journal,* 308: 772–5.

Dixon, J. and Glennerster, H. (1995) What do we know about fund-holding in general practice? *British Medical Journal,* 311: 727–30.

Dixon, J., Dinwoodie, M., Hodson, D., Dodd, S., Poltorak, T., Garrett, C., Rice, P., Doncaster, I. and Williams, M. (1994) Distribution of NHS funds between fundholding and non-fundholding practices, *British Medical Journal,* 309: 30–4.

Edwards, B. (1993) *The National Health Service: A Manager's Tale 1946–1992.* London: Nuffield Provincial Hospitals Trust.

Ensor, T. (1993) *Future Health Care Options: Funding Health Care,* Discussion paper. London: Institute for Health Services Management.

Enthoven, A. (1985) *Reflections on the Management of the National Health Service.* London: Nuffield Provincial Hospitals Trust.

Glennerster, G., Matsaganis, M., Owens, P. and Hancock, S. (1994) *Implementing GP Fundholding: Wild Card or Winning Hand?* Buckingham: Open University Press.

Goldsmith, M. and Willetts, D. (1988) *Managed Health Care: A New System for a Better Health Service,* Health Review Paper 1. London: Centre for Policy Studies, 1988.

Graffey, J.P. and Williams, J. (1994) Purchasing for all: an alternative to fundholding, *British Medical Journal,* 308: 391–4.

Gray, A. (1991) A mixed economy of health care: Britain's health service sector in the inter-war period. In A. McGuire, P. Fenn and K. Mayhew (eds) *Providing Health Care: The Economics of Alternative Systems of Funding and Delivery.* Oxford: Oxford University Press.

Hackett, G.I., Bundred, P., Hutton, J.L., O'Brien, J. and Stanley, I.M. (1993) Management of joint and soft tissue injuries in three general practices: value of on-site physiotherapy, *British Journal of General Practice*, 43: 61–4.

Ham, C. (1986) *Managing Health Services*. Bristol: School of Advanced Urban Studies.

Ham, C. (1994a) *Management and Competition in the New NHS*. London: National Association of Health Authorities, Radcliffe Medical Press.

Ham, C. (1994b) Managing the market, *Health Service Journal*, 1 September, 18–20.

Ham, C. (1996) Contestability: a middle path for health care, *British Medical Journal*, 312: 70–1.

Ham, C., Robinson, R.V.F. and Benzeval, M. (1990) *Health Check: Health Care Reforms in an International Context*. London: King's Fund Institute.

Harrison, S., Hunter, D.J., Marnoch, G. and Pollitt, C. (1992) *Just Managing: Power and Culture in the National Health Service*. Basingstoke and London: Macmillan.

Healthcare 2000 (1995) *UK Health and Healthcare Services: Challenges and Policy Options*. London: Healthcare 2000.

Hoffenberg, R., Todd, I.P. and Pinker, G. (1987) Crisis in the National Health Service, *British Medical Journal*, 295: 1505.

Hoffmeyer, U.K. and McCarthy, T.R. (1995) *Financing Health Care*. Amsterdam: Kluwer Academic Publishers.

Howie, J.G.R., Heaney, D.J. and Maxwell, M. (1995) *General Practice Fund-Holding: Shadow Project – An Evaluation*. Edinburgh: Department of General Practice, University of Edinburgh.

Hunter, D.J. and Harrison, S. (1993) *Effective Purchasing for Health Care: Proposals for the First Five Years*. Leeds: Nuffield Institute for Health.

Institute for Public Policy Research (1996) *Cambridge and Huntingdon Citizens' Jury*, Report. London: IPPR.

James, J. (1994) *Transforming the NHS: The View from Inside*. Bath Social Policy Papers No. 18, University of Bath.

Jones, A. and Duncan, A. (1995) *Hypothecated Health Taxes*. London: Office of Health Economics.

Kelly, J. (1995) *The Independent*, 25 March.

Klein, R. (1994) Can we restrict the health care menu? *Health Policy*, 27: 103–12.

Laing, W. (1995) The case for the NERA proposals for the reform of the NHS. In A. Towse (ed.) *Financing Health Care in the UK: A Discussion of NERA's Prototype Model to Replace the NHS*. London: Office of Health Economics.

Lawson, N. (1992) *The View from No. 11*. London: Bantam Press.

Lee, M.L. (1971) A conspicuous production theory of hospital behaviour, *Southern Economic Journal*, 38(1): 48–58.

Le Grand, J. and Bartlett, W. (1993a) *Quasi-Markets and Social Policy*. London: Macmillan.

Le Grand, J. and Bartlett, W. (1993b) Quasi-markets and social policy: the way forward? In J. Le Grand and W. Bartlett (eds) *Quasi-Markets and Social Policy*. London: Macmillan.

Lerner, C. and Claxton, K. (1994) *Modelling the Behaviour of General Practitioners: A Theoretical Foundation for Studies of Fundholding.* York: Centre for Health Economics, Discussion Paper 116, University of York.

Levitt, R., Wall, A. and Appleby, J. (1995) *The Reorganised National Health Service* (fifth edition). London: Chapman and Hall.

Lowy, A., Brazier, J., Thomas, K., Jones, N. and Williams, B.T. (1993) Minor surgery by general practitioners under the 1990 contract: effects on hospital workload, *British Medical Journal*, 307: 685.

McGuire, A. (1985) The theory of the hospital: a review of the models, *Social Science and Medicine*, 20(11): 1177–84.

MacKerrell, D.K.D. (1993) Contract pricing: a management opportunity. In I. Tilley (ed.) *Managing the Internal Market*. London: Paul Chapman Publishing.

Maxwell, M., Heaney, D., Howie, J.G.R. and Noble, S. (1993) General practice fundholding: observations on prescribing patterns and costs using the defined daily dose method, *British Medical Journal*, 307: 1190–4, 6 November.

Maynard, A. (1986) Performance incentives in general practice. In G. Teeling-Smith (ed.) *Health, Education and General Practice*. London: Office of Health Economics.

National Association of Health Authorities and Trusts (1992) *Project Paper 7: Implementing the Reforms: Second National Survey of District General Managers*. Birmingham: NAHAT.

National Audit Office (1987) *Competitive Tendering for Support Services in the National Health Service*. London: HMSO.

National Audit Office (1994) *General Practitioner Fundholding in England, HC 51 Session 1994–95*, 9 December.

National Audit Office (1995) *Contracting for Acute Health Care in England, Report by the Comptroller and Auditor General, HC 261 Session 1994–95*. London: HMSO.

Nettel, J. (1993) The purchaser/provider split as seen by a major provider: the case of King's healthcare. In I. Tilley (ed.) *Managing the Internal Market*. London: Paul Chapman Publishing.

NHS Management Executive (1993) *Purchasing for Health: A Framework for Action*. Leeds: NHSME.

NHS Trust Federation (1995) *Analysing Changes in Emergency Medical Admissions*. London: King's Fund and NHS Trust Federation.

Office of Health Economics (1992) *Compendium of Health Statistics*. London: OHE.

Office of Health Economics (1995) *Compendium of Health Statistics* (9th edition). London: OHE.

Packwood, T., Keen, J. and Buxton, M. (1991) *Hospitals in Transition: The Resource Management Experiment*. Buckingham: Open University Press.

Propper, C. (1994) *Market Structure and Prices: The Responses of NHS Hospitals to Costs and Competition* (mimeo). Bristol: Department of Economics, University of Bristol.

Propper, C. (1995) Agency and incentives in the NHS internal market, *Social Science and Administration*, 40(12): 1683–90.

Rawls, J. (1973) *A Theory of Justice*. Oxford: Oxford University Press.

Redmayne, S. (1996) *Small Steps, Big Goals: Purchasing Policies in the NHS*, Research Paper 21. Birmingham: National Association of Health Authorities and Trusts.

Redmayne, S., Klein, R. and Day, P. (1992) *Patterns of Priorities*. Birmingham: National Association of Health Authorities.

Redmayne, S., Klein, R. and Day, P. (1993) *Sharing out Resources*. Birmingham: National Association of Health Authorities.

Roland, M.O., Bartholemew, J., Morrell, D.C., McDermott, A. and Paul, E. (1990) Understanding hospital referral rates: a user's guide, *British Medical Journal*, 301: 98–102.

Secretaries of State for Health, Wales, Northern Ireland and Scotland (1989) *Working for Patients: The Health Service – Caring for the 1990s*. London: HMSO.

Shiell, A. (1991) *Self Governing Trusts: An Agenda for Evaluation*, Discussion Paper 78, Centre for Health Economics, University of York.

Small, N. (1989) *Politics and Planning in the National Health Service*. Buckingham: Open University Press.

Surender, R., Bradlow, J., Coulter, A., Doll, H. and Brown, S.S. (1995) Prospective study of trends in referral patterns in fundholding and non-fundholding practices in the Oxford region, *British Medical Journal*, 311: 1205–8.

Tennant, A., Fear, J., Pickering, A., Hillman, M., Cutts, A. and Chamberlain, M.A. (1995) Prevalence of knee problems in the population aged 55 years and over: identifying the need for knee arthroplasty, *British Medical Journal*, 310: 1291–3.

Thatcher, M. (1990) *The Downing Street Years*. London: HarperCollins.

Towse, A. (ed.) (1995) *Financing Health Care in the UK: A Discussion of NERA's Prototype Model to Replace the NHS*. London: Office of Health Economics.

Treasury Committee of the House of Commons (1996) *Sixth Report: The Private Finance Initiative*, Session 1995–96, House of Commons Paper No. 146.

Vanstraelen, M. and Cottrell, D. (1994) Child and adolescent mental health services: purchasers' knowledge and plans, *British Medical Journal*, 309: 249–61.

Whynes, D.K. and Reed, G. (1994) Fundholders' referral patterns and perceptions of service quality in hospital provision of elective general surgery, *British Journal of General Practice*, 44: 557–60.

Wilson, G. (1991) Models of ageing and their relation to policy formation and service provision, *Policy and Politics*, 19(1): 37–47.

Wilson, R.P.H., Walley, T. and Buchan, I. (1995) Alterations in prescribing by general practitioner fundholders: an observational study, *British Medical Journal*, 311: 1347–50.

Wordsworth, S., Donaldson, C. and Scott, A. (1996) *Can we Afford the NHS?* London: Institute of Public Policy Research.

INDEX

EVALUATING THE NATIONAL HEALTH SERVICE

Martin A. Powell

This is a fresh and innovative study of the National Health Service. Drawing on his unusually wide research experience relating to British health care from the 1930s to the present, Martin Powell avoids the well-worn path by concentrating on the problematic area of evaluation. He demonstrates that balanced assessment of the NHS has been impeded by political correctness and rhetoric to such an extent that it is extremely difficult to arrive at objectively firm conclusions about the record of health service past or present.

In this ambitious, astute and indeed audacious study, Dr Powell penetrates the fog of obfuscation, and outlines a conceptual approach likely to yield more certain conclusions in the future.

Charles Webster, official historian of the NHS

- To what extent has the National Health Service achieved its objectives?
- How well does the performance of the National Health Service compare with health care before the NHS and with other countries?
- What impact have the recent reforms had on the National Health Service?

This book provides the first single, comprehensive evaluation of the National Health Service. It draws on original research to examine health care before the NHS, and health care in other countries in order to locate the service in its wider context. In eight, well-structured chapters it traces the changing policies of the NHS, analyses its successes and failures, examines the current situation in the service, and attempts to predict its future direction.

Evaluating the National Health Service is intended for textbook use by students of social policy, health policy and politics. It is also directly relevant to a wide variety of health care professionals both in training and in practice.

Contents
Series editor's introduction: Chris Ham — Introduction — Health care before the NHS — The settlement of 1948 — The NHS 1948–1996 — Temporal evaluation — Intrinsic evaluation — Extrinsic evaluation — Conclusion — References — Index.

240pp   0 335 19530 X (Paperback)   0 335 19531 8 (Hardback)

MANAGING MEDICINES
PUBLIC POLICY AND THERAPEUTIC DRUGS

Peter Davis

- What are the principal features of the system responsible for the production, regulation, distribution and funding of therapeutic drugs?
- What are the major problem areas and issues of policy concern that have arisen in the pharmaceutical sector and how have the participants – particularly the State – responded to such controversies?

Medicines, and the policy issues they raise, are the subject of this book. Therapeutic drugs are widely used – some on a routine basis, others in a highly selective and specialized fashion. Although we take the availability of such potent agents for granted, there stands behind them a complex and sophisticated system of scientific innovation, industrial production, State audit and professional distribution. Major issues of price, innovation, safety, professional practice and consumer autonomy arise. Pharmaceuticals account for about ten per cent of health care costs, they are produced by a flagship industrial sector, they are jealously guarded by key professional groups, they raise formidable questions of quality and safety, and they are watched over by a vigilant and vociferous consumer movement. *Managing Medicines* seeks to disentangle these issues and come up with concrete suggestions as to how we might move forward in an area of public policy that is hotly disputed. It will be of interest to health professionals and policy makers as well as students of public health, nursing studies, social policy and social work.

Contents
Series editor's introduction – Introduction – Therapeutic drugs: the social and policy context – The rules of the game – Medicines and culture – The health care system and the practice of medicine – Drugs and money – Science, consumers and the law – Future directions – Glossary – References – Index.

192pp   0 335 19292 0 (Paperback)   0 335 19447 8 (Hardback)

MANAGING SCARCITY
PRIORITY SETTING AND RATIONING IN THE NATIONAL HEALTH SERVICE

Rudolf Klein, Patricia Day and Sharon Redmayne

The 'rationing' of health care has become one of the most emotive issues of the 1990s in the UK, causing much public confusion and political controversy. This book provides a comprehensive and critical introduction to this debate. It does so by examining the processes which determine who gets what in the way of treatment, the decision makers involved at different levels in the NHS and the criteria used in making such decisions. In particular it analyses the relationship between decisions about spending priorities (taken by politicians and managers) and decisions about rationing care for individual patients (taken by doctors), between explicit and implicit rationing. As well as drawing on research-based evidence about what is happening in Britain today, *Managing Scarcity* also looks at the experience of the NHS since 1948 and puts the case of health care in the wider context of publicly funded services and programmes which have to allocate limited resources according to non-market criteria.

Managing Scarcity is recommended reading for students and researchers of health policy, as well as health professionals and policy makers at all levels in the NHS.

Contents

176pp   0 335 19446 X (Paperback)   0 335 19447 8 (Hardback)